Julian Davidson
May 14, 1951

U. Store
375
3

D1285833

KATHERINE MANSFIELD

Published on the Sophie Hart Fund
of Wellesley College

KATHERINE MANSFIELD, 1914
*From a miniature in the possession
of Mrs. Mackintosh Bell*

KATHERINE MANSFIELD

A CRITICAL STUDY

BY SYLVIA BERKMAN

PUBLISHED FOR WELLESLEY COLLEGE BY
YALE UNIVERSITY PRESS · NEW HAVEN · 1951

London · Geoffrey Cumberlege · Oxford University Press

Copyright, 1951, by Yale University Press. Printed in the United States of America. All rights reserved. This book may not be reproduced, in whole or in part, in any form (except by reviewers for the public press), without written permission from the publishers.

TO MY SISTER

CONTENTS

List of Illustrations   *viii*

Introduction   *1*

ONE *Kathleen Beauchamp*   *11*

TWO *Et Ego in Bohemia*   *33*

THREE *"Prelude"*   *69*

FOUR *The Soul's Desperate Choice*   *103*

FIVE *Katherine Mansfield*   *149*

Notes   *205*

Appendix   *227*

Selected Bibliography   *231*

Index   *237*

ILLUSTRATIONS·

Katherine Mansfield, *1914*   Frontispiece

Vera, Kathleen, and Charlotte Beauchamp, 1904
                                        Facing page 22

Katherine Mansfield, 1913   Facing page 58

Annie Burnell Dyer Beauchamp   Facing page 90

Katherine Mansfield, 1921   Facing page 140

INTRODUCTION

IN DECEMBER, 1920, when the first issue of *Bliss* was published, Katherine Mansfield had been a practicing writer for over a decade, but except to a small circle of friends and literary associates her name as a creative artist was unknown. Two years later, in January, 1923, she was dead, with only one book, *The Garden Party*, added to the two volumes already published in her lifetime. In that period of two years she had come into a recognition which focused widespread notice upon her death. Almost immediately began the growth of the legend attaching to her name—the legend of the beautiful, unearthly figure which moved mysterious and aloof, finding the world too brutal for its abiding place. Less than two weeks after her death, in a commemorative essay in the London *Nation*, she was described as "a pale star sacramental to what was unknown . . . half phantom, likely to go out, to depart." Before long, as his wife's literary executor, Middleton Murry set himself to the launching of Miss Mansfield's posthumous works. In June, 1923, *The Doves' Nest* appeared, prefaced by an introduction which includes a number of the most intimate passages of the later *Journal*. The following month, in the second issue of his new magazine, the *Adelphi*, Mr. Murry published further extracts from Miss Mansfield's journal. From thence on, for nearly two years, the *Adelphi* devoted a large number of its pages to Miss Mansfield's poetry and prose, particularly the journal excerpts. In America, also, a comparable group of journal passages appeared in the *Yale Review* in issues for October, 1923, and January, 1924. In November, 1923, Mr. Murry brought out Miss Mansfield's *Poems*, and in August, 1924, the early and the later discarded stories as *Something Childish* (*The Little Girl* in the American edition). By this time the legend was firmly grounded: *Something Childish* attracted far more attention in the press than had *Bliss* or even *The Garden Party*. In all, between 1923 and 1930 eight volumes of Miss Mansfield's writings were issued. For the most part these books received an acclaim that at its highest is best called tender and at its lowest can only be termed maudlin. The mass of the reviews—of *The Doves' Nest*, *Poems*, *Something Childish*, the reissue of *In a German Pension*, the *Journal*, the *Letters*, *The Aloe*, *Novels and Novelists*— forms an interesting record of Miss Mansfield's reputation in its first stage. The *Journal* and the *Letters*, in particular, evoked a wash of sentiment that inundated the periodicals of England, America, and France.

The Mansfield legend is based upon a real element of truth, idealized, emphasized, and isolated. It centers in the motif of the secret, the pure, even the holy. Partly as a result of her illness, in her later years Miss Mansfield had withdrawn into her own world of preoccupation. The injustice of the legend erected on the basis of this retreat is that it sets its subject above and apart from the human.

She is no longer a woman but an enigmatic deity, half saint, half elf.

It is not surprising that the legend took quick root and flourished. The story from which it sprang is moving: its subject had been beautiful, she had been gifted, she had suffered and died young. By the late twenties the devotional attitude, with its peculiar blend of worship and indulgent love, reached the proportions of a cult. Perhaps the most restrained expression of this cultism is found in the story by Conrad Aiken, "Your Obituary, Well Written," which appeared in his volume *Costumes by Eros* in 1928.

Very naturally in these years, since the *Journal* and the *Letters* made public a body of intimate material, the chief emphasis in the many essays and reviews was upon Miss Mansfield herself—the extreme sensitivity, the ardor, the high courage of her temper, likened most often to that of Keats. Yet a few voices were raised also in dissent. Mr. Murry had already aroused an occasional anticultist by his indiscriminate publication of Miss Mansfield's work. Both he and Miss Mansfield were subjected to attack as the successive volumes appeared, he on the charge of exploitation of his wife's personality, she on the charge of her shortcomings as a woman and a writer thus revealed. By far the most vitriolic onslaught was Aldous Huxley's satiric portrait of Burlap and his dead wife in *Point Counter Point*.

Now that a quarter of a century has passed the extravagance of both the cultists and the anticultists is of merely historical interest. The publication of Miss Mansfield's letters and journals, though premature, to my mind has been justified. Without the knowledge of her being and experience contained in these volumes full understanding of her artistic accomplishment would always be incomplete. As for the inferior stories which were hurried into publication, they also are of value to the serious student of Miss Mansfield's development.

With the waning of the legend, in the early thirties, a corresponding shift of emphasis took place in the critical evaluation of Miss Mansfield's work. During the twenties, with few exceptions, reviews consisted chiefly of hyperbolic praise. But even during that period a quieter growth in Miss Mansfield's reputation was under way, based upon an honest attempt to interpret and estimate her work, without prejudice and without emotionalism. At first this criticism took the form of a general study of her art, appearing as a magazine essay or a chapter of a book on modern literature. Though for the most part this criticism is superficial, its prime concern is with Miss Mansfield's accomplishment. She is being judged here for what she did, not for what she was. Among the earliest and most detached of these considerations is Edith Sitwell's essay, "Three Women Writers," in the London *Vogue* for October, 1924, in which she defines Miss Mansfield's stories as "exquisite, flawless, narrow, sweet, poignant." In the following ten years over a score of these essays appeared, a few, rather to one's surprise, by university professors, who relate Miss Mansfield's art to that of almost any figure in literature, "the *Mimes* of Herondas, or the Letters of Alciphron," for example. As the decade of the thirties unfolded Miss Mansfield's reputation was thus in its second stage, with the twilight of the cultists at hand, general critical appreciation in the ascendant, and more formal objective appraisal coming into view. In succeeding years the third stage of her reputation was reached. Criticism now operates almost exclusively upon her work.

This shift in critical attitude is best exemplified by David Daiches' chapters in *New Literary Values* (1936) and *The Novel and the Modern World* (1939), which are concerned solely with Miss Mansfield's technique and its relationship to contemporary literature.

Biography to the present remains fragmentary and largely repetitious. *The Life of Katherine Mansfield* (1933), by Ruth Elvish Mantz and Mr. Murry, closes with the year 1912. (More accurately the French translation of this volume, of 1935, is entitled *La Jeunesse de Katherine Mansfield*.) Miss Mantz has collected a great deal of interesting material in the *Life*, and she has enjoyed the immense advantage of being the first in a rich field. It is perhaps because her material was so abundant that the book sags under its own weight. Greater discrimination would have sharpened the outline of the narrative. This book remains the only generally available source of information on Katherine Mansfield's early years; and since its appearance it has formed the basis of every biographical account of her childhood and early youth. The only "full" biography yet written, *La Vocation de Katherine Mansfield* (1946) by Odette Lenoël, concentrates on her spiritual evolution, utilizing some of the source materials which I have drawn upon independently.

In New Zealand appreciation of this most famous of its daughters has been of slow growth. Only recently has a sense of pride in Miss Mansfield's accomplishment begun to emerge. At the time of her death a few scattered pieces by former schoolmates or acquaintances added something to the material relating to Miss Mansfield's youth. Thereafter a few essays and reviews appeared intermittently. Undoubtedly the memorials to his daughter established by Sir Harold Beauchamp did much to awaken interest. In the tenth anniversary year of Katherine Mansfield's death a tablet in her honor was unveiled at the Karori Primary School, where forty years earlier the children of "The Doll's House" had forgathered. In the same year Sir Harold commissioned the establishment of a memorial to his daughter at 47 Fitzherbert Terrace, Wellington, the former Beauchamp residence from which Kathleen Beauchamp left for London in 1908. To the Alexander Turnbull Library in Wellington he later donated a sum of money for the purchase of first editions of his daughter's works, launching thus the present fine collection. An additional quickening force no doubt was the visit of Miss Mantz in pursuit of biographical materials and the subsequent publication of the *Life*.

A decade after her death Miss Mansfield began to receive in New Zealand something of the attention she had already attracted in England, America, and France. Sir Harold's memorials and the *Life*, indeed, evoked considerable comment in the press. In 1936 appeared the first "home" critical study, by Professor Arthur Sewell, of Auckland University, a volume which stimulated the late Mr. G. N. Morris, of Auckland, to embark upon his excellent collection of Mansfieldiana. That Miss Mansfield's "precious island" is at length claiming her for its own is evident in the titles of the articles of the last dozen years—"Lest We Forget Our Greatest Woman Writer," "Wellington's Genius," "New Zealand Now is Proud of Katherine Mansfield"—and in the Mansfield studies issued by the Beltane Book Bureau since 1944.

Miss Mansfield's reputation has not been limited to the English-speaking world. Her writings have been translated into at least nine languages, including Danish, Czechoslovakian, Japanese, and Chinese. In Germany she has received learned recognition chiefly by scholars whose work makes up in weight for what it may lack in range. She has never touched the German heart with the strong personal appeal she has exerted in France. There she has been embraced with a rapture unrivaled in any other country, even in England and America during the early legend days. The difference between the French attitude and that of the cultists of the twenties is one of emotional fiber rather than intensity. The cultists saw Miss Mansfield as an exquisite martyr-saint; the French perceive in her an enchanting spirit—mystic, poet, child—which strove courageously to come to terms with life, yet failed. It is Katherine Mansfield's extreme femininity which delights the French, her capacity for joy which wins their love, her chastening through pain which stirs their pity. The French charge their considerations with lyrical compassion; but when they judge, they judge calmly, sanely, and wisely. Stripped of rhapsody, their accounts generally present incisive, lucid treatment, though it is always the woman and the artist on whom they concentrate.

Even before the translation of Miss Mansfield's work into French in the decade of the thirties, her talents were celebrated by Louis Gillet, one of her earliest and most active admirers, in the *Revue des deux mondes*. From the time of her death she has continued to fascinate the French mind. It is significant of the deep personal regard of the French that the tenth anniversary of her death received far more attention in their press than across the Channel, and that they have surpassed her compatriots in honoring her memory. In March, 1939, a marble memorial plaque was set in the wall of the Villa Isola Bella, in which she had once lived among them, at Mentone, and in the same year, in June, a commemorative tablet was installed at Le Prieuré, at Avon, where she died, at the ceremonies that gave her name to a path, a rock, and a woodland crossroads in the Forest of Fontainebleau.

It seems fitting now to look back over time, to view again Miss Mansfield's life and work and trace their interacting relationship, for this integration of the two has not before been undertaken. She was the writer of little things, of a mood or a moment, to be sure; but if the selecting hand is gifted the implications of the large are always present in the small, and at her best she deals with the enduring substance of human experience. That Katherine Mansfield, who left a few books of short stories, her journals and her *Letters,* is today still read and still discussed, translated and anthologized, is proof of her artistic vitality.

Throughout the course of my work I have been greatly assisted by many persons whom I have called upon for help. My first acknowledgment is to Mrs. Mackintosh Bell, Katherine Mansfield's eldest sister, of Ottawa, Ontario, who has made accessible to me photographs, letters, her scrapbook of Mansfield clippings, and her father's privately circulated *Reminiscences and Recollections.* I am almost equally indebted to the late Mr. G. N. Morris, of Auckland, New Zealand, who put the resources of his collection of Mansfieldiana at my disposal, in so far as typescripts and the mails allowed, and drew my attention to many bibliographical items which otherwise could not have been known to me. Mrs. Frieda Lawrence and the Honorable Dorothy Brett have been very kind in giving me their impressions of Katherine Mansfield as they

knew her in womanhood, and Mrs. Howard Ambrose, of
Hamilton, Ontario, her impressions of Kathleen Beauchamp the schoolgirl. Professor Harry T. Levin and the
late Professor Theodore Spencer of Harvard University
have helped me with valuable suggestions made at an early
stage of my manuscript. Mr. J. Middleton Murry has
very kindly supplied me with the photograph of 1921,
of which he holds the copyright, and Mrs. Cecil Pickthall, Katherine Mansfield's elder sister, with that of 1913.
To many libraries and institutions I owe thanks for
courteous assistance: particularly to the staff of the Wide-
ner Library, Harvard University, to the officials of
Queen's College, London, of the General Assembly
Library, Wellington, and of the Public Library, Mu-
seums, and National Gallery of Victoria, Melbourne.
To Wellesley College I am indebted for a research grant
which has assisted me in the preparation of my work.
Permission is gratefully acknowledged to Alfred A.
Knopf, Inc., for reprinting excerpts from the various
books they have published by Katherine Mansfield as follows: *Journal of Katherine Mansfield*, 1927; *The Letters
of Katherine Mansfield*, 1929; *The Scrapbook of Katherine Mansfield*, 1940; *Bliss and Other Stories*, 1921; *The
Garden Party and Other Stories*, 1922; *The Doves' Nest
and Other Stories*, 1923; *The Little Girl and Other Stories*,
1924; *In a German Pension*, 1926. (*The Short Stories of
Katherine Mansfield*, 1937, includes all the stories published in the five previously cited volumes, which are no
longer available separately in print.)

This study was already in page proof when my way
crossed that of Mr. Antony Alpers, of New Zealand, who
is currently writing an extended biography of Katherine
Mansfield. Mr. Alpers has very generously let me read a

draft of his manuscript. His careful research throws light on a number of obscure portions of Miss Mansfield's life, particularly the period between 1908 and 1912. My own account has not been invalidated by this fuller knowledge, however. It therefore stands intact, except for the revision of a few factual details.

CHAPTER ONE

Kathleen Beauchamp

LIKE JAMES JOYCE, Katherine Mansfield rejected the society into which she was born; like Joyce, she never recovered from this act of violence. But her youthful rejection of provincial Wellington stemmed from a cruder emotion than Joyce's rejection of provincial Dublin. She had not Joyce's highly trained, dialectical mind; she was not impelled to break away, through will and reason, from the unbreakable hold of the Catholic Church. Her act in leaving Wellington was an act of instinctive assertion, the first of her many efforts to find her spiritual home. Joyce's early revulsion came harder and bit deeper. He never forgave Dublin for driving Stephen Dedalus abroad. Katherine Mansfield was of more yielding composition. In time she came to look upon New Zealand as a lost paradise, transmuting her childhood memories into the nostalgic beauty of her finest work.

Between 1903 and 1906, when she was a student in London, Katherine Mansfield contributed five stories to the school literary journal, the *Queen's College Magazine*.[1] Four of these stories deal with children and relate to her own childhood. Immature though they are, they contain surprising freshness, humor, and vitality. A sunny light plays through these juvenile pieces. Even thus early Miss Mansfield could capture the free dimensions in which children exist. Time is limitless, the realm of the imagination unbounded; the world is spacious and clothed in living green.

The fifth story, "Die Einsame," written when Katherine Mansfield was fifteen, stands apart. In a somewhat conscious style it tells of a lonely spirit, an innominate "she," alien and solitary in her house on the land, drawn, in an agony of exile, to the sea, frightened by the descent of night after a day of unfulfilled expectancy outdoors.

She feared the silence and the darkness and the forest. Could she reach her cottage before the sun went down? She sprang to her feet and sped swiftly along. Her hands became torn with the brambles. Often she fell, but ever struggled to her feet again. . . . No! it was hopeless. The sun had gone. Darkness had come. "I am afraid," she cried aloud.

But when she turns to the sea and the waves receive her, she is again terrified.

"I must go back," she cried, sobbing, "back to the land. I shall be drowned. Help me, God!" She started hurriedly, and her foot struck a sharp hidden rock. . . .

Then a great wave came, and there was silence.

It would be extreme to state without reservation that in these five juvenile pieces lies the basic substance of Katherine Mansfield's later philosophy. Nevertheless, the relationship between the ideas in this early work and her subsequent attitude toward life is remarkably close. Insistently, in her letters and her journals, one finds two dominating themes: that of childhood as Eden, a fusion of Wordsworth's vision and Traherne's, and that of the anguish of the "lonely one," unfulfilled, expectant, torn by the brambles of the world, falling often, hovering in desperation between advance and retreat, between land and sea. Repeatedly in her hours of despair Miss Mansfield uses the image of herself as a child, a vulnerable, helpless little creature mortally stricken by the brutality of the world, longing for companions who would deal with her, as she dealt with them, in candor and affection. Equally, in her hours of bliss she perceives herself as a child, brimming over with spontaneous love, faith, and joy. Broadly speaking, her entire work is based on these two aspects of the Wordsworthian concept that we must all become as little children to know the kingdom of heaven on earth: a rapturous embrace of the world through childlike love and an agonized revulsion from a world in which she could not feel at home. Always she sought to find the gateway to Eden; always she fell back from an impenetrable wall. That so many of her stories embody disillusionment and frustrations is the issue of this protracted and vain search.

This search, in the latter years of her life, quickened almost to frenzy by the threat of death, led to an increasing withdrawal from the world, not only through the physical isolation imposed by her illness but through a heightened sense of spiritual loneliness. For solace she turned to dreams and the past. At the very end of her life, it is true, she was groping toward a surer foundation on which to base existence; but the direction she took was misguided, and she died when the effort was scarcely begun. Her entire life, from adolescence to her death at the age of thirty-four, was spent in constant seeking, and turning empty away.

Katherine Mansfield, born Kathleen Mansfield Beauchamp, came of colonial pioneering stock. Her great-grandfather, John Beauchamp,[2] from whom the New Zealand branch of the family dates its immediate history, seems to have been a variant on the traditional Beauchamp pattern. For generations the Beauchamps had been established in London as reliable gold- and silversmiths.[3] In John Beauchamp's hands the family business fell into decay. He was fond of poetry—he himself wrote occasional verses; his tastes were those of a country gentleman. By his marriage to the sister-in-law of C. R. Leslie the painter, he gave to the Beauchamp family a cultural heritage—a connection, not altogether tenuous, with such figures as John Constable, Washington Irving, Sir Walter Scott, Wordsworth, and Coleridge.[4]

By the middle of the nineteenth century, when John Beauchamp's children were coming of age, the colonization of Australia was well under way. Henry Herron Beauchamp was the first of the sons to emigrate. (His daughter Marie Annette, later Gräfin von Arnim, and subsequently the Countess Russell, early became famous as the author of *Elizabeth and Her German Garden*.) Gradually, most of the remaining Beauchamp brothers made their way overseas. Arthur Beauchamp,[5] Katherine Mansfield's grandfather, arrived in 1848, at the age of twenty-one, a young man of assured self-confidence, with his father's gift for easy rhyme. The new land, he soon found, offered little beyond a rough, precarious existence. As gold prospector or storekeeper he shifted from one spot to another, now in the lawless mining communities, now in the growing towns. In 1861, with his wife and his three-year-old son Harold, he established himself in New Zealand as general merchant and auctioneer. Through the next half century he ranged from one New Zealand settlement to another, never attaining more than an ordinary living, and that at times with difficulty. In the private language of the Beauchamps, he was a true "pa man"—lively, vigorous, voluble, with a marked streak of eccentric imagination.

Harold Beauchamp [6] inherited his father's energy and independence, and he exceeded him in ambition. No doubt the rootless life of his childhood bred in part his drive toward tangible security. Very early he determined to become a man of influence in New Zealand. Through the shifting fortunes of the island's growth he clung tenaciously to this purpose. His mind was logical, shrewd, able, yet also with a touch of the original "pa" quality. Leaving school at the age of fourteen, he acted first as his father's assistant, later as clerk in a Wellington mercantile house, W. M. Bannatyne and Company. In a short time the firm recognized his unusual ability for business and finance. In January, 1889, at the age of thirty he was taken into partnership. His subsequent career was increasingly active, expansive, and successful. By his fiftieth year he had become identified with some dozen of the leading commercial and financial projects of Wellington, as company chairman, director, or board member. From 1898 to 1936 he served as a director of the Bank of New Zealand, acting for nearly fifteen years as chairman of the board. In 1923 he was knighted in recognition of distinguished public services, particularly in connection with matters of finance. Yet his life held also its inner conflict. To the world his concentration of purpose may have made him appear dictatorial, brusque, and aggressive. To his children he was a figure of authority, entering the nursery at times to talk genial nonsense but established in omnipotence. But a finer spirit was recognized by his daughter when she became a woman, a vulnerability and division in the face of life that could be healed only by the understanding of those he loved. Miss Mansfield's sympathy for her father, in her adult years, was very deep.[7] She too had descended into those "absolute *pits* of depression and loneliness" [8] which she saw marking his path.

In the group of New Zealand stories based upon her childhood recollections Miss Mansfield has depicted her father in the character of Stanley Burnell. One must allow for the fact that the creative mind of the artist both consciously and unconsciously selects and heightens detail. The process is not one of falsification but rather of particular stress. In the portrait of Stanley Burnell, energetic, impatient, authoritative, baffled by subtlety, desperately in need of affection, somehow pathetic because somehow lost, Harold Beauchamp perhaps achieved his deepest success.

On February 18, 1884, Harold Beauchamp married Annie Burnell Dyer, daughter of Joseph Dyer, a pioneer in Australia and later first resident secretary in New Zealand of an Australian insurance company. She was just twenty years old.[9] Annie Beauchamp was a slight, finely made woman, with beautiful dark eyes, strongly defined arched eyebrows, and abundant chestnut hair; sensitive, fastidious, aristocratic, with a quality of distant loveliness about her—"something between a star and a flower," [10] her daughter later described her. She bore six children; [11] for many years she suffered from chronic heart trouble.

Yet in spite of physical depletion he lived with courage, strength, and gaiety, though necessarily somewhat detached from the common routine of the home. In the group of family stories, Linda Burnell, imbued with mystery, is drawn from Katherine Mansfield's mother, seen with new insight by the daughter after the experience of her own later years. We can recognize Linda, somewhat older, in a letter Miss Mansfield wrote to a friend shortly after her mother's death on August 8, 1918:

She was the most precious, lovely little being, even so far away, you know, and writing me such long, long letters about the garden and the house and her conversations in bed with Father, and of how she loved sudden, unexpected cups of tea "out of the air, brought by faithful ravens in aprons"— and letters beginning "Darling child, it is the most exquisite day" . . .

Ever since I heard of her death my memories of her come flying back into my heart—and there are moments when it's unbearable to receive them.[12]

By 1894 five Beauchamp daughters had been born, of whom one died in infancy, and at last a Beauchamp son. Kathleen, the third child, was born on October 14, 1888, at 11 Tinakori Road, Wellington. Happily for his children, on Mr. Beauchamp's marriage his wife's widowed mother, Margaret Mansfield Dyer, had joined the family, with her youngest daughter Belle. As Beryl Fairfield, Belle Dyer figures in the New Zealand stories, with some admixture of Miss Mansfield's own youthful temperament. But beyond all others in these stories, it is the grandmother who is most lovingly portrayed. It was the grandmother who founded the children's life upon the bedrock of security. Quietly and surely she infused into the home that spirit of love, order, and control upon which children depend and from which they draw their own strength. Her life had been long; she had borne nine children. Like all lives, hers had held its measure of sadness; but it flowed now in ways of satisfaction and serenity. Unhurried, patient, she watched over her daughters, she served her son-in-law, she devoted a wise and tranquil spirit to the care of her grandchildren. Between Kathleen and her grandmother the bond was particularly close. In her the child found the haven of love and sympathy she was to require throughout her life.

Until Kathleen's sixth year the Beauchamps lived at 11 Tinakori Road, the house in "Prelude" where Lottie and Kezia were left that lonely afternoon, to be picked up later by the storeman, because there was not an "inch of room" in the buggy carrying the others to their new residence. Kathleen's second home was in the country, at Karori, a little village a half-hour's drive from Wellington. Here there were grassy banks to roll down, countless flowers to pick, orchards and paddocks to explore. The air from sea and mountains was fresh. Here was the house of "Prelude" with its long pillared verandah, fronting the curved drive that embraced the grass plot with the aloe tree. Pat Sheehan, the gardener-coachman, cared for the grounds and drove Mr. Beauchamp in and out from Wellington. Kathleen—"Kass," the family called her—loved to trail after him as he worked about the gardens, watching him shake clean the fresh-pulled carrots or sniffing the speckled bean flowers in the vegetable beds. Her lifelong passion for flowers, all growing things, was rooted deep in the very early years of her life.

Not far from the Beauchamps' big house, about a mile down the Karori road, lived the Waters family. Mrs. Waters ("Doady" of "The Aloe") was Mrs. Beauchamp's sister, a beautiful woman like all the Dyers, who lived half her life in a darkened room suffering from headache. Her husband, Frederick Waters, thin, kindly, charming, was somehow out of stride with ordinary life, like Jonathan Trout in "At the Bay." Unlike Harold Beauchamp, he felt no compulsion to conquer the world by material means. He loved to frolic with the children, the little Beauchamps and his own two boys. These are the five— Vera, Charlotte, and Kathleen, Barrie [13] and Eric Waters —who made up the ghostly company of "precious children" who sat with Katherine Mansfield years later, in Switzerland, when she was writing "At the Bay." [14]

To Karori, also, belonged the family of MacKelveys, five children, the insignificant father, and the hard-working mother, the village washerwoman. These down-at-the-heel MacKelvey children were familiar to Kathleen not only as the riffraff of Karori but as her fellows at school. Two of the brood, Lil, the eldest, and Our Else, the little white owl, have been reborn, to haunt the heart. Out of the memory of the village school with its social differentiations, primitive and cruel, as such distinctions always are among children, flowered the beautiful "Doll's House" after a score of years.

Kathleen Beauchamp of Karori was a round-faced little girl with dark hair and intent dark eyes behind the glasses which constant reading had necessitated. She was plump, given to daydreams, good at arithmetic, poor at spelling, enraptured by reading and "poetry learning." Like Kezia of the New Zealand stories, she was quick in sympathy for the unfortunate. When the teacher of the school rebuked a lad for sleeping at his desk, Kathleen spoke up to explain that he was forced to rise at three o'clock each morning to help with the family milk delivery, and the boy escaped a caning.[15]

As the third daughter among five children, Kathleen

held an undistinguished position in the family. Even as a child in the midst of abundant life she was troubled by that sense of being alien which drove her, as a woman, to turn inward upon herself. She was slow, her family thought impatiently at times; she flared up in temper; she had her secret places of retreat. It was perhaps at this age that she so impressed a fellow passenger on a brief sea voyage that he remembered her clearly even after many years. She went about the boat, most often alone, alert, observant, quiet, seeming to absorb and ponder with an intensity unusual in a child.[16] She was busy. She was gathering the myriad impressions which were to be recaptured in the pages of her finest work.

In 1898 the Beauchamp family moved back to Wellington, to 75 Tinakori Road, a short distance from their earlier residence. The house was large, set far back from the street, facing a terraced garden which sloped to a nasturtium-covered wall. Tinakori Road was not a fashionable part of town, though some good old houses, like the Beauchamps', still remained, tucked away, half hidden in their gardens, amidst the shabby dwellings of the poor. This is the setting, apparently, of "The Garden Party," and this the garden with the old pear tree near the violet bed where Kathleen and her brother Leslie found quantities of tiny pears scattered over the lawn after a South Pacific storm. The little brother, six years younger than Kathleen, had become her loved companion as she roamed outdoors.

On the return to the larger social sphere of Wellington, Kathleen entered the Wellington Girls' High School, which she attended, with her two elder sisters, for the fol-

lowing three years. Here she had the gratification of seeing her first "stories" in print, in issues of the school
magazine for 1898 and 1899,[17] two pleasant little narratives very well handled for a child of ten. Here she found
a friend of her own age [18] to share the secret world of
fantasy she always loved to invent. During the long vaca-
tions the family moved out to Day's Bay, where Mr. Beauchamp had bought a summer place, a sequestered, almost
private retreat. Time at the Bay was in suspension. The
tranquil hours slipped by, while the Beauchamp and the
Waters children played along the shore, busy with their
colored stones and shells, knowing the terrors and the
wonders of their own enchanted sphere.

When Kathleen was twelve the Beauchamp children
were sent to Miss Swainson's school at Fitzherbert Terrace, as befitted the son and daughters of a man of growing importance. To the sharp eyes of the headmistress
Kathleen appeared careless and unruly. She differed from
her gentle, dainty-mannered sisters. She was now on the
verge of adolescence, undergoing the common rebellion
and rage of the strong individual still young enough to
suffer the imposition of adult power. She was becoming
critical and assertive; her sense of her "difference" from
her associates sharpened. At home she felt hampered and
misunderstood. She was irritable; she quarreled violently
with her sisters. She resented the orthodoxies of her substantial bourgeois life. But the period was not wholly one
of contention. It was Kathleen who began and edited the
first school magazine. She found romantic pleasure, also,
in her friendship with a half-caste Maori girl a few years
her senior, a glowing beauty reputed to be a princess,
whom Kathleen adored, perhaps the more ardently because her family disapproved of the friendship; or she

could dissolve into tears under the mild blandishments of her sentimental music master. And already she was dreaming of farewell.

When the three elder Beauchamp girls were sent to London to complete their education, early in 1903,[19] Kathleen was still a child; but she was a child who felt within herself the gathering forces of an intensely individual nature. At Queen's College she was free to indulge— even to exploit—her individuality. Though she was never widely popular [20] she made congenial friends, in particular among them Ida Constance Baker, with whom she sustained a close if difficult relationship throughout her life. She attended the theater and concerts. With Ida Baker she roamed the London streets. She went to the London Academy of Music for 'cello lessons, continuing the study of this instrument she had begun in Wellington. She was involved in her first love affair. In the school magazine, of which for a time she was an editor, she saw her first real stories in print.[21] The poetry she was writing attracted the attention of one of her professors, a young literary dilettante who fed her voracious spirit on Walter Pater, Oscar Wilde, Arthur Symons, Paul Verlaine. She discovered her destiny: she was an artist—perhaps a musician, perhaps a writer. She discovered, through Oscar Wilde, that only the young have the capacity to live. Her reading notes for 1905–07 are studded with the brittle epigrams of *Dorian Gray*.

At the age of seventeen, during her last term at Queen's College, Kathleen began a novel, *Juliet*,[22] a slightly veiled diary recording her fluctuations of restless mood. Since only excerpts from this work have been published, its lit-

VERA, KATHLEEN, AND CHARLOTTE
BEAUCHAMP, 1904
From a photograph in the possession of Mrs. Howard Ambrose

erary merit cannot fairly be judged. The style of the excerpts, however, is worth noting. Already Kathleen possessed a good command of words, though her expression
is likely to become diffuse through reliance on large general statement and an absence of imagery. But occasionally
the prose sharpens with a satiric flash: "Does the glory of
England rest upon old customs? She rather fancied it did
—when to start overcoats and when to stop fires—have
boiled eggs for Sunday supper and cold lunches." [23] For
the most part, however, the style is mannered, with a conscious use of diction reflected from Oscar Wilde. Juliet
wraps herself in "a fierce white reserve"; she is "dominated by her moods which swept through her and in number were legion." " 'I have four passions,' she wrote in an
old diary—'Nature, people, mystery, and the fourth no
man can number.' " [24] From the available excerpts *Juliet*
seems thus immature and derivative work. Apart from biographical interest, its value appears to lie chiefly in its
early display of the stylistic mannerisms which were to
mark Kathleen's writing for the next few years and in the
first gleams of the satiric sense which, still later, was to
dominate her work.

Queen's College, sheltered and gracious, gave but little
formal education to Katherine Mansfield. She had never
at any time a scholarly habit of mind. She thought deeply;
she had flashes of profound insight. She possessed whimsical imagination, perceptive critical judgment, a delightful sense of humor. But she rebelled against any rigidity
of method; she fought always the necessity of imposed
discipline. "I lived in the girls, the professor, the big, lovely
building, the leaping fires in winter and the abundant
flowers in summer," she wrote in 1916. "The views out
of the windows, all the pattern that was—weaving." [25]

During her three years at London she was educated, rather, more fully into the imperious demands of her own nature. She was an artist; as an artist she would wrest from life her heritage. She would live deeply, richly, in conscious exploration of experience. She would live in the world; she must live in London. When the time came she sailed home with her sisters, but in her heart was buried the determination to return, and to return with speed.

Wellington, on Kathleen's arrival in December, 1906, seemed unendurable. By now Mr. Beauchamp had attained a position of wealth and prominence. The family,[26] established in the big new house at 47 Fitzherbert Terrace, was involved in consequent social activity which seemed trivial and unworthy to the disciple of Oscar Wilde. During the Queen's College years her mind had developed rapidly to the false sophistication bred by "advanced" reading with no true moral or literary perspective. Her intellectual horizon expanded, very naturally with an attendant expansion of intellectual arrogance.

I am ashamed of young New Zealand, but what is to be done [she wrote to her sister Vera shortly after her arrival home]. All the firm fat framework of their brains must be demolished before they can begin to learn. They want a purifying influence—a mad wave of pre-Raphaelitism, of super-aestheticism, should intoxicate the country. They must go to excess in the direction of culture, become almost decadent in their tendencies for a year or two and then find balance and proportion. We want two or three persons gathered together to discuss line and form and atmosphere and sit at the street corners, in the shops, in the houses, at the Teas. People who would quote William Morris and Catulle Mendès, George

Meredith and Maurice Maeterlinck, Ruskin and Rodenbach, Le Gallienne and Symons, D'Annunzio and Shaw, Granville Barker and Sebastian Melmouth, Whitman, Tolstoi, Carpenter, Lamb, Hazlitt, Hawthorne, and the Brontës. These people have not learned their alphabet yet.[27]

Exiled in the wilderness, Kathleen turned to music for assuagement. During this winter of recoil and rebellion she continued her study of the 'cello, becoming an able performer. To play a Bach concerto could draw her from herself to the center of exultation. Her teacher, upon whom she drew gratefully for spiritual relief, was the father of Arnold Trowell, the Wellington boy 'cellist already established as a European virtuoso. Kathleen had met Arnold shortly before leaving for Queen's College, forming a romantic friendship which had continued by correspondence while she was in London and he a student at the Brussels Conservatoire. In 1906, when Arnold Trowell came to London for a series of recitals, they had met again. During the three years of their separation he had grown into an idealized figure in Kathleen's mind, about which she centered her impetuous emotions. The renewed encounter was both delight and shock, as very often when the ideal resolves itself to reality. Much of the turbulence of this experience is written into the pages of *Juliet*. Now, condemned to Wellington, she fed on her relationship with Arnold, enlarging and exalting its proportions, crossing the seas to join him through the touch of his own instrument.

Her music, her letters from London, her work—these furnished the real substance of Kathleen's life. She spent hours behind her locked doors, writing or in moody reverie. Part of her effort was given to poetry—she had written verses intermittently from childhood on; but with increasing consciousness at this time she was moving toward her true field of expression. She had felt at Queen's College an unfocused ambition to become famous, as a musician or a writer. Now, through the voluminous pages of her letters and notebooks, she had reached a fixed purpose: she would write, she must write. Always she had been the observer, as a child, as a schoolgirl scratching down a description of a neighbor at a concert, as a young woman unburdening her heart for its relief. Now she began to write with deliberate care. In this way she shaped the little sketches she called "vignettes," of which a few examples have survived.[28]

Mrs. Beauchamp, who had herself a gift of charming expression, was in sympathy with her daughter's ambition. Mr. Beauchamp was more skeptical, inclined to oppose anything tainted with unconventionality. These youthful fancies would pass, he was certain, and Kathleen would settle down. Yet it was indirectly through his means that the first stories for which Kathleen received payment were published. He had spoken of his daughter's work to a journalist friend, who suggested that a few manuscripts be sent out.[29] The Melbourne *Native Companion* at once accepted three. "Vignettes" by "K. Mansfield" [30] was published in October, 1907; "Silhouettes" appeared in November and "In a Café" in December of the same year. Eagerly Kathleen awaited "her" issues, hurrying out to buy a copy of the magazine at the Lambton Quay, standing under a lamppost with her brother Leslie to ruffle through the pages, to see if her story were actually in print. In July, 1908, a fourth piece, "Study: The Death of a Rose," was printed in the *Triad*, a New Zealand magazine.

The chief fact revealed by this early material is that

Kathleen was following the Symbolist tradition, imbibed at Queen's College largely in denatured form by way of the English representatives, though she knew something too of the continental Symbolists. Except for "In a Café" no one of the pieces contains a thread of plot. They are impressionistic explorations of mood, prose lyrics stressing musical rhythm and color harmony, fusing subjective emotion with natural scene. For the most part the musical tone is well sustained; mood, color, and moment are satisfactorily combined—most often, melancholy with the greyness of evening. (Verlaine's echo sounds in the line: "And the grey thoughts fall upon my soul like the grey rain upon the world, but I cannot draw the curtains and shut them out.") With Symbolist intershifting of the senses, the darkness "mutters," the 'cello case is "wrapt in profound thought." There are, of course, many crudities in this early work. At times the muted Pater-Symons cadence is displaced by the rhinestone phraseology of Oscar Wilde—for example, in "Silhouettes": "I want the night to come, and kiss me with her hot mouth, and lead me through an amethyst twilight to the place of the white gardenia" [31]—or in the entire execution of "The Death of a Rose," which deals solely with exquisite floral decay. Derived from Wilde also are the sophisticated aphorisms of "In a Café" ("Misunderstanding keepeth Love alive"); from Shaw the "Ten Deadly Conventions" scornfully invoked. This last story indicates, however, a desire to work in more solid materials, to deal with character and plot. Though the technical handling is uncertain, the narrative moves swiftly to a climax, and beneath the ornate expression a moment of poignant emotion is caught—a young girl's shock of disillusion in a first love affair, a reflection of her own experience with Arnold Trowell.

Overwritten, immature, these early stories nevertheless contain many of the elements that pervade Miss Mansfield's later work: the sense of loneliness first perceived in "Die Einsame," an awareness of the painful incongruity of human happenings, a keen response to the delicate forces in the world of natural beauty. And here and there, even in this derivative work, her native talent for the vivid phrase asserts itself: she mentions a field of blue cabbages in the moonlight shimmering "like a cold sea," little people seen from a tower walking in the streets "like flies in the folds of some gigantic tablecloth." The intrinsic merit of the work, of course, is not great; yet beneath the falsity of expression throbs a current of passionate feeling—the longing of the fledgling for its own powerful and buoyant flight. It is not surprising that her immersion in her own sensibility—the source of all her later accomplishment—led her first to the literary tradition which would best express her youthful turbulence.

At the time her first stories were being published Kathleen Beauchamp was a scant nineteen. She had a look of maturity far beyond her years; it gratified her to be taken for a woman of twenty-eight. In Wellington she was known as ultramodern—the manuscripts she showed her friends aroused their consternation. "Life," she wrote in "In a Café," "to a girl who had read Nietzsche, Eugene Sue, Baudelaire, D'Annunzio, Georges Barres, Catulle Mendes, Sudermann, Ibsen, Tolstoi, was, in her opinion, no longer complex, but a trifle obvious." [32] She delighted in her worldliness.

She was not worldly. She was very young, with a force of raw emotion thinly veiled by her pose of sophistication. Her heart was sick with despair. Wellington with its provincial crudities and mean decorum was killing her, she felt. When the Trowells left New Zealand for permanent residence in England she felt the closing in of death. She was a castaway, lost in the stormy seas of her own longing; she would perish. And her great cry was to live.

From Marie Bashkirtseff, whose *Journal* she was reading in the fall of 1907, she undoubtedly absorbed much of the tone which marks her notebook records of this period:

Here in my room I feel as though I was in London—in London. To write the word makes me feel that I could burst into tears. Isn't it terrible to love anything so much? I do not care at all for men, but *London*—it is Life. . . . I am longing to consort with my superiors. What is it with me? Am I absolutely nobody, but merely inordinately vain? I do not know. . . . But I am fearfully unhappy. That is all. I am so unhappy that I wish I was dead—yet I should be mad to die when I have not yet lived *at all*.[33]

Very probably Kathleen's ambition, as well as her introspective tendency, was strongly influenced by the outpourings of that girl artist of other years, the wealthy Russian who could draw upon the rich life of the continent—Paris, Rome, Venice—who could move in fashionable circles as an accomplished coquette, and who renounced her birthright for the austere hermitage of art. Like Marie Bashkirtseff, Kathleen Beauchamp had a driving passion for fame. Temperamentally, indeed, the two are closely akin, though Kathleen's nature was less stormy, her mind less intellectual. Both were self-centered, unremittingly introspective, torn between the violence of self-arrogation and the violence of despair. Many of Kathleen's journal records of this time bear Marie Bashkirtseff's unmistakable quality: one finds the passages of self-apostrophe, in the same agonized terms; the adjurations to take courage, to act, to fulfill destiny; the strange fiercely tender love of the ego which is writing for the ego which is suffering. The later development of the two is also curiously similar. After the actual apprenticeship to art was begun the vision clears; the youthful arrogance falls away. Accomplishment rather than worldly fame dominates as purpose; the spirit abases itself before the discipline of art, with the frantic prayer for time, a little time, as the half-hours strike for each, and the branch that might have grown full straight is hewn.

Very naturally, in this season of rebellion, Kathleen's life at home was tempestuous. To her family she must have seemed more than ever difficult as she shuddered away from a degrading consultation on the butcher's order or abruptly ordered her sisters to leave her room. In November, 1907, her father, who was seriously disturbed and puzzled, arranged for her inclusion as a member of a party making a caravan trip through the New Zealand country, where the Maori natives lived in their *pahs* scarcely touched by civilization. The trip, for the six weeks it lasted, was beneficial. The natives, gracious, friendly, picturesque, stirred Kathleen's imagination; the wild luxuriance of nature soothed the fever of unrest. Kathleen observed and absorbed the countryside with the intense identification which was her peculiar gift. She wrote constantly, in the jolting van, at night in the rough camp of a Maori settlement, noting the look of light and water, of leaf, of flower, of a native woman and her child, of the hideous cracked sulphur baths at Rotorua.

The expedition gave her momentary peace. Each day brought healthy physical exhaustion, a sense of freedom, of unity with nature, a release into self-unity. Inevitably the return to Wellington brought reaction. Here was no scope for her gifts, in this raw new land which could offer no fire to meet her own fire. Through late winter and the spring she suffered. Then suffering hardened to determination. She summoned all her courage and faced her father. At last he acceded to her demands. He had no wish to thwart his daughter's life. She was free to go to London. On July 9, 1908, she left New Zealand, never to return.

CHAPTER TWO

Et Ego in Bohemia

KATHLEEN BEAUCHAMP—Katherine Mansfield—arrived in London with the gifts of her own talent and an allowance from her father of £100 a year. The former was to await fruition for a dozen years; the latter provided a modest living. Once established at Warwick Crescent, Paddington, at Beauchamp Lodge (the coincidence of the name with her own was accidental), she hastened to renew her friendship with the Trowell family, who had settled in the bohemian community of St. John's Wood. In the days that followed she saw her friends frequently; for some weeks she stayed with them as their guest. With Arnold Trowell she had come to a pleasant comradeship; but the need of expending her emotion was still imperious. She turned to his brother Garnet. The motivation of this step was in part a hunger for experience as an enrichment of life and, through life, of art, the principle she had seized upon, as a young girl, in Oscar Wilde. "But it hasn't ALL been experience," she later wrote, in an hour of judgment of her past. "There is waste, destruction, too." [1] There was waste, destruction, now. The issue of this alliance was suffering and bitterness. With abrupt determination, on March 2, 1909, at the Paddington Register Office, she married Mr. George Bowden, a musician some ten years her senior whom she had met in the artistic circles of St. John's Wood. It was her morbid fancy to dress for her wedding entirely in black. Ida Baker was her single attendant. She had looked to find in marriage security and freedom for artistic development—an illusion born of disillusion. Within a short time she left her husband.[2] It is, conjecturally, at this period that she became an "extra" in a traveling opera company.

The news of her marriage, followed soon by the cabled announcement of her separation from her husband, brought her mother to London. She found her daughter with child, and admittedly not by her husband. The mother was appalled; the daughter, far from being contrite, was defiant. There was no sympathy between the two women at this time. The matter must be concealed, above all, must be kept from seeping back to Wellington. Hurriedly the daughter was dispatched to the Bavarian village of Woerishofen. Only one fragment of her notebook of that period has by chance survived, for Katherine Mansfield cared to preserve no record of her life between 1909 and 1914. "It is at last over, this wearisome day," the entry, of June, 1909,[3] begins. She was sick with a bad chill, sick at heart as well. She thought longingly of her grandmother as a haven of comfort and love—the only "adorable thing" she could imagine. The coming of her baby she awaited eagerly: she would have this rock on which to build, this fortress against loneliness. Her child was born prematurely, dead.

Woerishofen, where living was healthful, retired, and

cheap, was a favored resort of a varied group of continental writers and journalists, shabby, poor, but inde-
pendent. In their conversations the artistic world expanded to embrace all Europe. They planned literary
journals; they talked of translating Miss Mansfield's stories. Association with these men reawakened her own
creative zest. She began to write the sketches of German life later collected and published as *In a German
Pension*.

As her health returned her native independence be-
stirred itself. A poem of January, 1910, commemorating
the Polish poet Stanislaw Wyspiański, reveals the rallying
of her energy. In full, free cadence the young voice speaks
proudly:

I, a woman, with the taint of the pioneer in my blood,
Full of a youthful strength that wars with itself and is lawless,
I sing your praises, magnificent warrior. . . .[4]

This poem is further valuable as an indication of Miss
Mansfield's changing attitude toward New Zealand. With
distance and a little time she was coming to perceive her
country with more sympathy, as a land in the making,
"piecing together this and that, finding the pattern, solv-
ing the problem." Against the long, ghost-ridden history
of Europe, she could see its life as elemental—simple,
fresh, and vigorous, though crude and clumsy, as young
things often are.

By February, 1910,[5] restored to health, Katherine Mansfield was back in London. In the same month the first of
her Bavarian sketches, "The-Child-Who-Was-Tired,"
was published in the *New Age*. A. R. Orage, the editor,
was generous in his encouragement of the new talent he
had recognized.[6] Through his introduction Miss Mansfield made further entrance into the world of artists and

writers. Orage himself became her valued friend. But she had no real sense of happiness. The immediate past was painful; her present life was insecure; even her health was uncertain. She was living here and there, in the spring of 1910 in Rottingdean, above a grocer's shop, convalescent after an operation; in the following autumn and winter at 131 Cheyne Walk, in a studio lent by an artist acquaintance. She was rootless, unstable and unsatisfied.

This period in Katherine Mansfield's life is largely veiled; but through an odd circumstance her own voice speaks out briefly from the silence covering those days. In an autobiographical work [7] published many years later by an intimate friend of this time a few of her letters and journal notes have been preserved. From these fragments one can sense the nervous agitation of her life. She was living at a pitch of high excitement, still exploring—or exploiting—Passion, intensifying every emotion by fevered analysis. Not yet had she come to recognize her own basic needs. She could have no peace without security; she could have no security without a reduction of existence to its most genuine elements. Experience had not yet taught her the value of simplicity; she clung to the decadent belief that the artist must be the exotic. Her rooms at Cheyne Walk were fantastically arrayed in the perverse taste of the *fin de siècle*, with lamplight arranged to shine through flowers and candles stuck into a skull. This setting, representing more than an eccentric fancy, was symbolic. It was the pattern to which she consciously attempted to shape her life. The same deliberate "arrangement" of effect appears in the few published letters:

The windows are wide open and the river so beautiful that I shall stay here watching it for one thousand years. . . .

And there is not one star in the sky. The sky is like a shell—
I have red and white tulips growing in the centre of the
praying mat. The red ones look as though they have fed on
brackish blood. But I like the white ones best. They are
dying—each petal ever so faintly distorted—and yet such
dainty grace. I wish you were here.[8]

With spring, 1911, Miss Mansfield took a flat at 69
Clovelly Mansions, Gray's Inn Road, looking upon the
roof tops of London. The smaller of her front rooms,
which she called "the Buddha room," contained nothing
but an image of Buddha and two couches draped in black.
Here she was living when her entire family came to London for the coronation of George V in June. This was the
last time Katherine Mansfield saw her mother.[9]

To the Beauchamps their errant daughter must have
seemed more than ever alien. She had wandered far from
Wellington, to seek the life she had conceived as essential
to her needs; yet her feeling of estrangement from human-
kind grew increasingly acute—that curious agony which,
filling the mouth with ashes, quickens the external world
to unbearable loveliness. More sharply than in her prose
pieces, this sense of loneliness appears in the poems she
was also writing at this time. Like many aspiring writers,
in her earliest attempts Miss Mansfield hovered between
the mediums of prose and poetry.[10] In large measure
her mind possessed the qualities of poetic apprehension.
But she never applied herself systematically to the mastery
of verse technique, and when she began her serious work
she turned by instinct to a prose form—a form which,
within brief compass, would allow room for the play of
her talents for dialogue, characterization, and dramatic
scene, as well as for lyric expression. In the years between
1909 and 1912, however, she practiced the writing of
poetry more consistently than at any other time of her

life. Of these subjective pieces, largely in unrhymed verse, a number relate fragmentary childhood happenings; the remainder reflect an emotional mood, most frequently a mystic adoration of earth or sea or sky, often at the same time crying for sanctuary. As poetry the value of this work is small. Until Miss Mansfield found a vehicle generally receptive to all her offerings in Mr. Murry's magazine *Rhythm*,[11] very little of her verse appeared in print.[12] The real value of the poems lies in their corroborative evidence of her sense of loss and homelessness, revealed through her preoccupation with the experiences of her childhood and her escape through mysticism from the brutal pressures of daily life. She had fought her way to freedom, at the age of nineteen. She had insisted on her right to individual development. In the first struggle she had triumphed; yet every triumph contains also its element of loss. She had lost first protection, the solid if despised security that comes with moving in a predictable, familiar world. She had lost next—though she would not admit the knowledge—the assurance that life must accede to her demands on her own terms. She was again engulfed, again a castaway.

More important as relating to the evolution of her art is the varied group of stories written between 1909 and 1912. In December, 1911, the collected Bavarian sketches had been published by Stephen Swift as *In a German Pension*. Reviews spoke of the author's "acute insight," her "unquenchable humor," her "realistic skill." The book soon went into a third edition. Only three years after her arrival from Wellington Miss Mansfield seemed thus to have won considerable success. In addition, she had completed a number of other stories, some of which had appeared in print.

This body of work, examination reveals, presents many irregularities. Already Miss Mansfield could write with controlled force; but the control is intermittent, and the force is achieved through varying means. She had not yet evolved the technical method that would serve her gifts best, nor had she yet arrived at any clearly defined attitude toward her material. Consciously and unconsciously she experimented.

A few of the stories require only a glance. "How Pearl Button was Kidnapped," written in 1910,[13] depicts in symbolic semifable the repressive confinement of city life. There is an air of artificiality about the story in the sleight of hand with realism and parable. What charm it has springs from the investment in fresh and exact detail. "A Fairy Story," published in December, 1910, in an esoteric little magazine, the *Open Window*, is in the manner of the earlier Wellington productions, though the execution is far less juvenile.[14] The prose is now deliberate and polished, recalling Wilde's *Happy Prince*, with a liberal admixture of Shavian epigram. This is, one may remark, the last example of preciosity in Miss Mansfield's writings. Two later pieces, "Tales of a Courtyard" and "Spring in a Dream," feebly imitative Russian stories published in *Rhythm* in the autumn of 1912,[15] may be dismissed as wholly negligible. "The House," which appeared in the November 28, 1912, issue of *Hearth and Home*, is also very faulty, though here the underlying personal utterance of a fatalistic deep mistrust of happiness makes the story of great biographical interest.

More fruitful for examination is "Mary," published in the *Idler* in March, 1910, a simple, straightforward narrative about two little "Beetham" girls at school, told in the first person by "Kass." "New Dresses," of the same year,[16] and "The Little Girl," of 1912,[17] both tales of infantile crime and punishment, again are drawn from childhood recollections. "Mary" runs along freely and poignantly, more autobiographical sketch than short story; but in "New Dresses" the material is more firmly shaped. Though the execution is uncertain—the focus wavering, the substance overample—character in action emerges with real force. Here in 1910 we look upon Stanley Burnell, the grandmother, Isabel, and Kezia of the later New Zealand stories, struck off in rough but unmistakable form. The charm and tenderness of the later stories are absent, to be sure. Katherine Mansfield was still too close to the past, in which she had suffered through misunderstanding, to deal with it without the expression of grievance. Her attitude toward her parents, distinctly hostile here, had yet to soften. But from the first the grandmother and the children are consistently perceived. The little scene in "New Dresses" following Helen's concealment of her iniquity might well be taken from "Prelude" or "At the Bay":

Henry visited their bedroom the last thing. She heard him come creaking into their room and hid under the bedclothes. But Rose betrayed her.

"Helen's not asleep," piped Rose.

Henry sat by the bedside pulling his moustache.

"If it were not Sunday, Helen, I would whip you. As it is, and I must be at the office early to-morrow, I shall give you a sound smacking after tea in the evening. . . . Do you hear me?"

She grunted.

"You love your father and mother, don't you?"

No answer.

Rose gave Helen a dig with her foot.

"Well," said Henry, sighing deeply, "I suppose you love Jesus?"

"Rose has scratched my leg with her toe-nail," answered Helen.[18]

"The Little Girl," based on a slight but moving incident, concerns itself wholly with Father and Kezia—"Kass," she is still called in the original version of the story. Miss Mansfield's ability to recapture the living heart of childhood experience has been highly praised, perhaps more lavishly than any other quality in her work. This ability she unquestionably possessed; but it is worth remarking that, with one or two minor exceptions, the children she has created are embodiments of the children in her own family, and that the elder members of this circle are drawn with equal strength. Whenever she sought her material in the experience of her childhood she struck a hidden source of power, an authenticity of knowledge—of the secret depths of character, of delicate, conflicting interrelationships—that vibrate in overtone throughout the narrative.

But Miss Mansfield was examining the present as well as looking backward. In the series of sketches begun in Bavaria, for the most part it is the precocious satirist who holds the pen. German conduct is seen as a disgusting concentration on the physical processes; German character as pompous, chauvinistic, sycophantic, and sentimental; German happiness as domestic comfort and substantial means. The author sits apart and observes, noting down an acute, mordant description: the little Baron dining solitary and remote because his stomach "requires a great deal of food"; [19] Frau Fischer, who formerly could have found happiness anywhere "with a clean sheet and a good cup of coffee" [20] but who now unfortunately suffers from nerves; the Herr Professor, trombone player and exuberant eater of cherries, making love to a morbid Viennese *artiste*, his "tigress with a flower in the hair." [21] No touch of subtlety shades the presentation. In sharp outline we are curtly given characteristic type and scene.

These sketches present an immediate, uncomplicated situation; character is drawn with forcible quick strokes through excellent dialogue and compressed minor action, in a manner similar to Dorothy Parker's later pungent satirical sketches. But unlike Mrs. Parker, who maintains strict impersonality, Miss Mansfield focuses squarely upon the scene as it is observed by a first-person narrator. Indeed, the major flaw in the technique is the part this figure plays. The writer intrudes with lavish comments. The reader is constantly distracted by the supercilious British voice condemning the gross stupidity of German burgher life, which is already sufficiently condemned by the very harshness of the presentation.

More pleasing, though less clever, are the two *New Age* sketches of 1911 which *In a German Pension* omits, "The Journey to Bruges" and "A Truthful Adventure," [22] in which the narrator herself is the chief object of the satire —mildly humorous here: the romantic young woman who finds the suffrage question and New Zealand compatriots abroad even in the seclusion of medieval Bruges. These two pieces are chiefly of interest as early examples of a form of writing Miss Mansfield practiced throughout her life: the arrangement of immediate experience into lively narrative. She had drawn on the same source in the Wellington days as well, but the "vignettes" of that period represent a conscious exploitation of mood. Now she presents a casual adventure so ordered as to make a specific point—a quality of character caught in momentary revelation, or the disparity between the apparent and the real concealed within a trifling event. The *Letters* and the journals contain scores of these narratives, often very amusing, always vivid and economical, with unerring choice of detail and sprightly dialogue. They served the purpose, one may judge, of a kind of whetstone, sharpening the edge of an observation already keen.

Of the stories collected in *In a German Pension* a few require more extended notice than the others warrant: "The-Child-Who-Was-Tired," "At Lehmann's," "Frau Brechenmacher Attends a Wedding," and "A Birthday."

"The-Child-Who-Was-Tired," the first of the stories to appear in the *New Age*, was published on February 24, 1910, shortly after Miss Mansfield's return from Bavaria. The remarkable correspondence of this story to Chekhov's "Sleepyhead" has already been examined by Miss Elisabeth Schneider,[23] who attributes the parallelism of plot and detail to the phenomenon of unconscious remembrance. It is probable, rather, that Miss Mansfield consciously adapted the story; she was later to catch many of her ideas from Chekhov's work. What is of interest at present is Miss Mansfield's selection of this material. The child, an abused maid of all work, focuses her exhausted mind on the incessant crying of a baby as the obstacle keeping her from sleep. She smothers the baby; at last she sleeps. This is not the voice of satire speaking; it is the voice of despair, and perhaps guilt.

"Frau Brechenmacher Attends a Wedding," the most memorable of all the stories in the volume, stems from emotional violence—a savage pity expressed in terms of a harshness that drives the narrator to underline every revolting detail. A German *hausfrau*, submerged in the physical aspects of domesticity, attends a local wedding. It is not a marriage of love. The bride's sordid history is repeated. There is abundant eating and drinking; the air grows stale and hot. Stumbling home, Frau Brechenmacher reflects on her own marriage, dully questioning the purpose of life. Her husband, jovial with beer, reminds her of her ignorance on their wedding night. "Well she remembered." [24] The material is presented with complete objectivity; yet beneath the words beats a pulse of anger at the stupid subjugation of Frau Brechenmacher's life; and pity is manifest in that Frau Brechenmacher, unlike the other German characters, is created as one sensitive enough to suffer but who must yet endure.

"At Lehmann's" likewise springs from a controlled fury that woman is physically at the mercy of man, with heavy emphasis placed on the ugly details of childbirth. "A Birthday," again a story of childbirth, presents the scene in obverse, through the egocentric vision of the man. The treatment here is doubly pointed, for not only is the woman depicted as the helpless instrument of the man; the man himself, as the figure through whose consciousness the story is told, is self-exposed in all his unshakable conceit.

These naturalistic stories, with their violent revulsion against the male, I believe embody Miss Mansfield's fierce protest at the suffering her recent experiences had forced her to bear. Katherine Mansfield was a proud woman; along with an extremely sensitive nature she possessed a core of hard strength and a determined will to dominate. Immediately upon her first major assertion of individuality she had been caught up and dominated by life. She was helpless and humiliated. Her furious resentment still burns through the lines of this early work.

Technically these stories are handled with varied degrees of success. "The-Child-Who-Was-Tired" is the least satisfactory. The emphasis on sordid detail, the generality of the names (The-Child-Who-Was-Tired, the Man, the Frau), the broad strokes of character delineation, produce what might be termed a naturalistic parable—not quite one thing or the other. "At Lehmann's" and "Frau Brechenmacher" are far superior, in the technique of the lighter Bavarian sketches, with strong, direct presentation, rapid movement, and excellent use of dialogue. "A Birthday," technically considered, is the most interesting. Here in 1911 we find the author fumbling with the method she was later to concentrate upon: a transference of dramatic action to *within* the character. In a very early story, "The Tiredness of Rosabel" (which one wishes she had written in 1918 instead of 1908),[25] Miss Mansfield first brushed against this method. In this story she was handling three levels of time: the present, the immediate past as Rosabel reviews it, and the future as Rosabel envisions it in dreams. Especially skillful is the interfusing of the detail of one time level with that of another, accomplishing in an extremely minor way what was later to be accomplished on a grand scale in *Ulysses*. In "New Dresses" also at times the characters slip into interior monologue, though by and large an external vantage point of observation is maintained. "A Birthday" concentrates more steadily on inner experience. The treatment, to be sure, is clumsy. The author depends upon quotation marks, interspersed phrases such as "he heard himself whispering" and "he reflected" to depict inner consciousness; but now and again, by its own impulsion, the story falls into vivid representation of inner action; and the reader is impressed, as in no other story in the book, with the depth and veracity of the character portrayal.[26] A year or so later in "The Little Girl" this technique is under firmer control, though the slightness of this story perhaps makes comparison unfair.

As in all her work of this period, in "A Birthday" Miss Mansfield overexplains and overemphasizes. The grandmother, worn out by a bedside vigil, is reporting to her son-in-law:

"Anna has been in pain all night. She wouldn't have you disturbed before because she said you looked so run down yesterday. You told her you had caught a cold and been very worried."

Straightway Andreas felt that he was being accused.[27]

A few years later Miss Mansfield would have deflected the impact, conveying Andreas' response through a revealing bit of action or dialogue.

In "The Swing of the Pendulum," one of the two stories in *In a German Pension* wholly unlike the rest, Miss Mansfield again utilizes the interior monologue. (The other story, "A Blaze," a lurid depiction of a siren and her prey, need not detain us.) [28] "The Swing of the Pendulum," concerned with sex in a more urbane society than the provincial bourgeoisie, probes the shift in mood of a young girl's passion: her revulsion from her sensitive lover because of the ugly poverty they must endure, then the ardent reversal, after a coarse experience with a strange man. Here the technique has strengthened to a considerable degree: the transitions from exterior to interior scene are more skillful; nuances of emotion are made concrete by correlation with external detail. Imagery, too, for the first time is growing individualized. Viola, the central figure, has been angered by a moody note from her lover:

Staring at the letter she began braiding her hair—a dull feeling of rage crept through her—she seemed to be braiding it into her brain, and binding it, tightly, above her head. . . . Of course that had been a mistake all along. What had? Oh, Casimir's frightful seriousness. If she had been happy when they first met she never would have looked at him—but they had been like two patients in the same hospital ward—each finding comfort in the sickness of the other . . .[29]

Still another turn of Miss Mansfield's active mind is revealed in "A Marriage of Passion" and "At the Club," both uncollected items published in the *New Age* on March 7, 1912. "A Marriage of Passion," containing the minor action of "Bliss" and "Marriage à la Mode" without any plot, satirizes the aesthetic posturings of a group of dilettantes at a dinner party. In similar vein, "At the Club" attacks a desultory gathering of idle English folk. The latter piece is sketched too rapidly to be more than momentarily diverting; but "A Marriage of Passion" has some excellent passages, in spite of the heavy-handed presentation—compressed description and action are hurled at the reader in heavy blocks. It is interesting to see that here, two years or so after the first Bavarian sketches, Miss Mansfield has learned to suppress personal intrusion completely, to let character and situation speak for themselves. Portions of this story, in the dialogue especially, equal the handling in "Bliss":

. . . a maid announced "Mr. Carrington Faber." He was tall and lean, with a habit of caressing his chin as though to make certain he had one. Greetings over— "Do you know," he cried, "the shadow cast by the tree to the left of the street-lamp upon the blind of your kitchen window?" They did not know. "It's quite wonderful. Japanese, you know, with a touch of Sime and just a suggestion of Aubrey Beardsley in the tassel. I've been watching it for ages. In fact, I knocked off a little thing to it," he shrugged and smiled; "borrowed a pencil from a policeman and wrote it on my cuff—had nothing else with me." He dreamed over to an electric light and shot out his tablets. "Oh, yes, it's here right enough." "Do read it," said Mrs. De Voted. "Fancy! the kitchen window!" [30]

With "Sunday Lunch" [31] as fuller evidence, it is apparent that Bohemia, even as Wellington, offered no grain in the corn.

The remaining stories, "The Woman at the Store" and "Ole Underwood," both published in *Rhythm*,[32] are best considered in conjunction with "Millie," which appeared in the successor of *Rhythm*, the *Blue Review*, in June, 1913. All three deal with crime and insanity in the rough sections of New Zealand, calling to mind William Faulkner's later explorations of the diseased passions of the South. "The Woman at the Store," a remarkable achievement, contains the most carefully wrought plot Miss Mansfield ever utilized. A woman, taken from the busy life of a coastal public house to the unsettled bush country, neglected by her roving husband, is driven in her hatred to kill her husband and conceal the crime. In terse, controlled prose, the narrative moves steadily to a climax; the atmosphere of heat, dust, and loneliness, breeding evil, is relentlessly sustained; character depiction is strong and firm. The narrative is given with scrupulous objectivity. The scene is set, the figures move and speak, the plot unfolds, without a word of comment. "Ole Underwood," the slightest of the three stories, deals also with murder. Here the reader is taken within the obsessed mind of the central figure, the derelict sailor released after twenty years' imprisonment for killing his wife. "Millie," again a story of murder and morbid psychology, employs the technique noted in "A Birthday"—in part impersonal narration, in part interior monologue, skillfully combined.

As examination of this early work has shown, Miss Mansfield was immersed in the two chief literary currents of her time, caught up first by one, then by the other. Under immediate "influences," as well as her own experience, she abandoned the Symbolist preciosities of her first manner, turning chiefly to naturalism, which she was shortly to abandon as well. At this stage one finds as broad characteristics of her work that she has a keen eye for excellent detail, perceived sharply and often satirically; that she has admirable command of lively dialogue, always made to serve a functional end; that she can present dramatic scene with concentrated force, though she is better at catching an emotionally charged moment than at constructing substantial plot—qualities which are all incorporated in her later work. Further, one sees that she is moving, unsurely but steadily, toward the vehicle of expression she was later to perfect—the fluid combination of inner and outer "view." Notably, she had not yet discovered an important element in her later technique: the value of economy achieved through implication. In all these stories she presents her material too abundantly, illuminated by a strong, unshaded light. The broad themes which emerge from a study of this work are not many: escape from the oppressions of reality (but there never is escape); the sensitive apprehensions of the child, leading often to shock; the falseness and stupidity of contemporary social herds; the painful nature of all sexual relationships. Played with various modulations and variously combined, these four general ideas were to furnish the thematic substance of her entire body of work.

In December, 1911, at the home of W. L. George, the novelist, Miss Mansfield had been introduced to John Middleton Murry. The two young people were not unknown to each other. Already, with Mr. George acting as intermediary, Miss Mansfield had contributed "The Woman at the Store" to *Rhythm*, the literary magazine Murry had founded at Oxford; and *In a German Pension* had confirmed the young man's admiration of the promising new writer. From Mr. George's account she was formidably clever and aloof; but at their actual encounter he found her rather subtle than cynical, a stimulating conversationalist, very charming in her dove-grey evening dress and gauzy scarf.

Soon the initial attraction between the two strengthened to friendship. Murry, mentally precocious, emotionally immature, torn daily by excessive introspection, drew gratefully on Katherine Mansfield's interest; and she responded generously. For however often, however honestly, she might consecrate her life to art, a second primary urge would assert its claim: she must rest secure in the knowledge of a constant source of human sympathy. She required a stronghold of affection that would stabilize her life and yet leave her free for individual development —perhaps an impossible demand. Less consciously than she sought the fulfillment of ambition, but no less persistently, she sought the satisfaction of her emotional needs. Early she assumed the role of command which was to mark her part in this new relationship, for though she might draw heavily upon Murry for complete understanding, in the crucial hours of their life together hers was always the deciding voice. Encouraged by her support, Murry gave up his life at Oxford, which he believed he had outgrown, to enter the field of literary journalism. To

Miss Mansfield coercion of self was a mark of cowardice. She applauded his decision as the active display of moral strength.

It was necessary now that Murry find cheap and comfortable living quarters. To his surprise, Miss Mansfield solved the problem: she offered him a room in her Clovelly Mansions flat. On April 11, 1912, he became her lodger.

For some weeks the two went separate though friendly ways. The immediate attraction between them had been very strong, as Miss Mansfield had recognized earlier than Murry. Inevitably, on closer contact, intimacy followed. They began to meet, late at night, after the day's work, to talk, chiefly of themselves. Each had suffered recent unhappy experiences. Each found this unexpected harbor of affection at once miraculous and wholly natural. Each quickened in the other a sense of genuine being, of entity stripped free of artifice, which made them strong against the world.

Through Murry's introduction Miss Mansfield was taken into the bohemian literary circle which frequented Dan Rider's bookshop, in a court off St. Martin's Lane. Here Frank Harris sat as the presiding master, surrounded by an admiring group of younger writers—Lovat Fraser, Haldane Macfall, Holbrook Jackson, Hugh Kingsmill, and others.[33] It was Miss Mansfield's dominance over Murry, rather than her sustenance of him, which apparently impressed acquaintances of that period. She seemed a "formidable partner for Murry," with her "smoldering restlessness" and hostile glance, one associate has remarked.[34] Perhaps the satirical perception which was to utilize the experience of these days in "Bliss" and "Marriage à la Mode" worked not altogether silently.

They could not marry, for Miss Mansfield's husband

did not pursue the divorce proceedings to which at first all three seemed to assent. Not until six years later, in 1918, could they become legally man and wife. Both regretted the practical difficulties incurred by their irregular union. Both were grieved by the antagonism of Murry's conventional parents and the displeasure of Miss Mansfield's family. But they had no hesitation of mind.

Their life together was destined to be hard, scored by poverty in its early years, constant moving and removing, protracted separations, misunderstanding at times, at times alienation. From the very start misfortunes beset them. They were both impractical, both utterly ignorant of the common, realistic elements of daily life. They were both young, Katherine Mansfield twenty-three, Murry a year younger. Each, in his own way, was nervously defensive against the suspected evils of the world. Joining hands, they struck out into the wilderness with greater confidence, whatever might impend.

In August, 1912, the Murrys leased an attractive cottage at Runcton, near Chichester, for three years. Before the house stretched the salt marshes; behind lay pasture fields. A magnolia tree stood at the door. Here guests came to stay with them—Rupert Brooke, Edward March, Frederick Goodyear, Murry's Oxford associate, who had early become Miss Mansfield's devoted friend. By November the entr'acte was over. They were forced to leave the house; their furniture, bought on installment payment, was removed; their own few personal belongings were lost. Murry's magazine *Rhythm*, which he had continued to edit after leaving Oxford, had drawn them heavily into debt. Earlier in the year, in June, Stephen Swift, Miss

Mansfield's publisher, had taken over the financial sponsorship of *Rhythm*, allowing the Murrys a salary of £10 a month as editors. By autumn Stephen Swift had gone into bankruptcy. Their assured income disappeared, along with all royalties from *In a German Pension*. Through a series of business complications they found themselves facing a printers' bill for £400. They were stunned; yet they clung stubbornly to the conviction that *Rhythm* must continue to appear. It symbolized their faith as young artists; it represented the expanding future of the arts. Miss Mansfield's entire allowance from her father was turned over to meet the payment by installments. By now the magazine had attained a distinguished if narrow following. Help was given at this crisis, financially and through literary contributions, notably by H. G. Wells, Lord Dunsany, Ford Madox Hueffer, and Frank Swinnerton. Martin Secker agreed to act as publisher. A little office flat was taken at 57 Chancery Lane. But the blood transfusion sustained life for only a year. After July, 1913, *Rhythm*, which had become the *Blue Review* for its last three numbers, ceased to exist.[35]

Through *Rhythm* the Murrys had come into contact with most of the *avant-garde* writers and artists of their period. Among these the acquaintance with Henri Gaudier-Brzeska, the talented, little-known young sculptor admired by Ezra Pound, flared to sudden and intense friendship, which soon terminated in sudden and intense enmity. Sophie Brzeska, the unhappy middle-aged companion of Gaudier who lived with him as his sister, was bitterly hurt by Miss Mansfield's rejection of her attempts at intimacy. Miss Brzeska had experienced a life of repeated frustration. She had been on the brink of suicide when she met Henri Gaudier in Paris, in the spring of

1910.[36] The subsequent association she formed with the young artist furnished a centralizing point for her warped faculties. She undertook the practical management of Gaudier's life. More than once she drew upon her meager savings for their common support. At Gaudier's death, at the age of twenty-three in the battle of Neuville St. Vaast (June 5, 1915), she went insane.[37]

In Katherine Mansfield Miss Brzeska felt that she had at last found a sympathetic friend to whom she could open "the deepest abysses of her mortified soul." [38] At their first meeting she plunged into a lengthy and impassioned recital of her intimate life with Gaudier. Miss Mansfield shuddered and withdrew into frigid reserve. She would give abundantly to those she recognized as "her" people; but she could not bear assault. Though she found Gaudier attractive, after that evening she shrank from Miss Brzeska in distaste. On that rock the friendship crashed.

With Gilbert Cannan, one of the prominent if not enduring writers of the period, and his wife Mary a pleasanter relationship developed. When the Cannans took a house at Cholesbury, Buckinghamshire, at their suggestion the Murrys engaged a cottage near by for the summer of 1913. The rent was low; London was readily accessible. Early in the summer Miss Mansfield removed completely to the cottage, while Murry stayed at the Chancery Lane flat through the week, occupied with his work for the *Westminster Gazette* and the *Blue Review*. Her two dominating concerns were her work and her financial worries. But in spite of debts and budgets there were hours of merriment at Cholesbury, with the Cannans and the Murrys' Irish barrister friend Gordon Campbell. It was here that the opening handful of Miss Mansfield's published letters were written, and it was here that she wrote the sketches she called "epilogues" for the *Blue Review*.[39]

Through *Rhythm*, also, the Murrys had met the D. H. Lawrences. Many pens, recriminatory and defensive, have stirred the troubled waters of the Lawrence-Murry relationship. That vortex of emotion does not concern us here. The friendship in its early years was comparatively uninvolved, and Katherine Mansfield's part in it throughout was relatively simple. She was herself too genuinely gifted to walk among the group of Lawrence's disciples. She admired Lawrence as a writer; she felt closely akin to him as an artist; she liked him, warmly and sincerely, as a friend. After the friendship had waned, with the redispositions of time, she always remembered Lawrence with fondness. A decade later she wrote his name, with that of Chekhov and a few others, in the list of the enduring affections of her life.

In June, 1913, Lawrence and Frieda Weekley came to England after their first winter together in Italy. Lawrence had already contributed an article [40] to *Rhythm* and a short story [41] to the *Blue Review*, and was interested in the magazine and its editors. Soon after his arrival he and Frieda called at the office flat in Chancery Lane.

Spontaneous, direct, the Lawrences met life with primitive grace and, inevitably at times, primitive violence. What they liked or disliked they knew immediately. At once a cordial friendship with the Murrys sprang up. On her part Miss Mansfield always responded with delight to authenticity of being, whether she found it in an aged serving-woman or a fellow artist; and Murry from the start was fascinated by Lawrence.

With the issue of July, 1913, the *Blue Review* came to an end, since financially it was a total failure. The Chancery Lane flat was given up; new rooms were taken at

Barons Court. Yet though Murry was by now well established as a book reviewer for both the *Daily Mail* and
the *Westminster Gazette* and was earning a comfortable
salary, both he and Miss Mansfield were restless. When
the Lawrences returned to Italy at the end of the summer
they begged the Murrys to join them at Lerici. But
Murry's work confined him to London; he refused to
migrate, to become dependent on Miss Mansfield's allowance, in spite of Lawrence's vigorous condemnation of his
attitude.[42]

With the departure of the Lawrences, however, something of their free, roaming spirit seized the Murrys; they
too longed for new lands and new adventure. Italy was
impossible; but Paris was only across the Channel. Early
in the winter of 1913 they left, on the strength of a vague
job for Murry as reviewer of French books for the *Times
Literary Supplement*. At great expense they had their
furniture and personal goods transported and, blithely
confident, took a flat at 31 Rue de Tournon, in a rather
shabby building with an uneven stone-paved courtyard,
close to the Place de l'Odéon and the Luxembourg Gardens. Solid London with its blur of fog-filled days was left
behind. Here was color, delicate and fine in the wintry
sunlight; here was constant stimulation—quick steps,
quick voices, brilliant eyes; a glimpse of Proust; the ever-
shifting drama of the streets. During an earlier stay at
Paris, in the winter of 1910, Murry had formed an acquaintance with the young Parisian writer Francis Carco,
who had later served on the staff of *Rhythm* as French
correspondent. Like the Murrys, Carco was not yet se-
curely established in his profession, but he maintained a
slight foothold in literary circles, and, above all, he knew
Paris. Together the three friends would sally forth, *en*

camarades, to explore the little music halls and cafés of the Montagne Sainte Geneviève or the Place d'Italie, returning sometimes only with the dawn.[43]

But Paris proved cold, with the icy winds of indifference as well as the blasts of winter. Murry's projected engagement with the *Times* came to nothing. The small capital the Murrys possessed dwindled alarmingly. Within three months they were reduced to living on Miss Mansfield's allowance, abandoning the monthly payments still due the printers of *Rhythm*. When Murry was offered the post of art critic on the *Westminster Gazette*, both he and Miss Mansfield were ready to retreat. Even so, Miss Mansfield was not vanquished. "Depend upon us—" she wrote to Murry during his trip to London to settle arrangements, "we're quite strong enough now to find a way out of our difficulties and we *will* and be happy, too, and do our work." [44] But to herself she admitted her bitter disappointment: "It is as though God opened his hand and let you dance on it a little, and then shut it up tight—so tight that you could not even cry." [45]

The books and furniture the Murrys had conveyed to Paris were sold for a pittance, since they could not afford reshipment to England. By March, 1914, veritably destitute, they were in London again.

For Katherine Mansfield the return to London meant a new plunge into wretchedness. After a short stay at Beaufort Street, Chelsea, where their back windows overlooked a cemetery and a timber yard, the Murrys found a dismal flat at Edith Grove, off Fulham Road. In the ugly little rooms both were intensely unhappy— Murry because of the journalistic hack work to which he

was bound, Miss Mansfield because her creative powers
seemed extinct. At the beginning of the Paris sojourn, in
December, she had written her long story, "Something
Childish But Very Natural." Now she could not write.
Her old fluency had vanished; ideas, captured with great
effort, dissolved under her hands. Always her ability to
write was closely linked with the physical circumstances
in which she lived. Without privacy, without beauty to
touch and gaze upon and feel—in the design of rooms and
of furniture, in flowers, in color and light—she sickened.
All her senses were now affronted daily, by the dirty stair-
case, the sordid common water closet, the dank smell of
soiled clothing and stale vegetable water permeating the
halls. She was burdened with anxious despair, brooding
constantly on "*Paris* and *money*." The little work she
managed to accomplish she destroyed in disgust.

Social diversion brought no relief. In revulsion she perceived the life of her circle as false, pretentious, trivial; the
"sham Meredith" atmosphere aroused her scorn. Unconsciously, in this troubled interval, she was turning to the
past for escape. "Dreamed about New Zealand. Very delightful," she noted on March 19.[46] The smell of fresh
wood and straw from a packing warehouse summoned
up Wellington; the sound of sparrows "cheeping like
chickens" outdoors in the rain carried her back to the
idyllic Karori days.

At this time Miss Mansfield was a young woman of
twenty-five; yet her conception of the artist was still
juvenile. The artist, in her eyes, was a superior being, detached and aristocratic, who comprehends and therefore
rejects the ugly world of the mob. In an essay written
jointly with Murry a year before and published in

KATHERINE MANSFIELD, 1913
From a photograph in the possession of Mrs. Cecil Pickthall

Rhythm, she had formulated her attitude. The artists are viewed as free adventurers, sailing the open seas.

[They] see the land that it is barren and miserable, and they sail onwards. Then the little people are frightened, and cry out to them in rage, and abuse them. Their voices are drowned in the mighty swishing of the green waves. But clean and true rings back their answer, the singing of the sailors, the joyful laughter of serene delight.[47]

From the time of her return to Wellington in 1907 Miss Mansfield had built her life on this conception of the artist. That the conception was mistaken does not alter the fact that her faith in the artist, and in herself as an artist, was profoundly sincere. The neutral virtues of patience and moderation were never hers; acceptance and endurance were to be achieved only after long suffering, and even then less as practice than as theory. It is not surprising that under the early schooling of her life—the repeated, crass instruction that the world makes no concessions to its sensitive children, especially when they are penniless—she grew arrogant and defiant.

In June, 1914, the Lawrences returned to London from Italy. To them, as trusted friends, Miss Mansfield could speak without restraint. In vivid terms, to Murry's chagrin, she disclosed her loathing of the ugly Chelsea rooms. Her outburst bettered the situation. Even at the cost of higher rent they decided they must move. Soon they found a pleasant house in Arthur Street, Chelsea, with an upstairs-window view into a leafy tree.

They saw the Lawrences often during the summer months of 1914. Hours were spent in involved discussions, probing the new ideas of Freudian psychology which, in part, Lawrence had embodied independently in *Sons and Lovers*. Such discussions, which sooner or later swung to personal analysis, revealed, dimly ahead, the separate roads the Lawrences and the Murrys were destined to walk. They had no true identity of conviction. "By pretending a bit," Lawrence wrote in his last letter to Murry, in 1929, "we had some jolly times, in the past. But we all had to pretend a bit—and we could none of us keep it up." [48] Undoubtedly those summer days before the war held the seeds of the emotional and intellectual ambivalence, in Lawrence and Murry, which was later to destroy their relationship. Nevertheless the affection between the two families at that time was a genuine and vital element in their lives—the "pretence" perhaps assumed larger proportions after the cleavage of later years.

By the end of August, overnight it seemed, London was mobilizing for war. The air was charged with ominous unrest. A young Oxford friend of the Murrys came in to say good-by before reporting for duty the next day. Already the regiments were filing through the streets. To the Murrys the war at first was an immense and ghastly spectacle which shocked and frightened them. Their instinct was to close their eyes. The intense personal tragedy of war, through which its heaviest meaning is revealed, had not yet shaken Miss Mansfield's heart. As they had previously planned, the Murrys left for a short holiday at Cornwall, where, secluded from the feverish atmosphere of London, they continued until autumn in Arcadian tranquillity.

Money was once more a serious problem, for with the war literary journalism and art criticism had scant place in the press. In October, therefore, after a short stay in London, they decided to take for the winter an ugly cot-

tage at the Lee, Missenden, Buckinghamshire. The Lawrences were near by, at Chesham, near Cholesbury where
the Cannans lived, about an hour's walk away through
the woods and fields. Through the Lawrences the Murrys
met for the first time S. S. Koteliansky, the Polish transla-
tor of Russian classics, who became Miss Mansfield's sympathetic friend. Gordon Campbell, too, was often with
them.

At first Miss Mansfield was at peace, as she was repeatedly at the beginning of any new phase of experience. But
with the closing in of winter the torment of depression
again gripped her heart. An increasing hostility to Murry,
born of pain and loneliness, was undermining her last
refuge in life; for Murry in his emotional instability had
turned to Gordon Campbell for strength against his own
weakness and self-distrust. By the end of the year she was
ready to break away. "I see you and G. discussing the
extraordinary *time* it lasted," [49] she noted with secret
bitterness.

The Lawrences, friends though they were, were rather
a source of additional strain than of comfort; the long
discussions they habitually provoked heightened the general unhealthy atmosphere of acute self-consciousness.
Moreover, the Lawrences themselves were frequently engaged in unconcealed and uncontrolled quarrels, in which,
now and again, the Murrys were forced to mediate.
Lawrence, too, at this time was a diseased man, poisoned
by the war. Sick at heart, he formed a plan of escape from
the horrors of civilization: he and his wife, the Murrys,
and Koteliansky would get away to an island, to establish
the nucleus of a new world. Night after night the group
discussed this island retreat. They even gave their Utopia
a name, taken from one of Koteliansky's Hebrew chants,

"Rananim." But actual life was pressing too hard upon Miss Mansfield for escape by fantasy. Her secret comments on Lawrence's plan were antagonistic.[50] One day, not without malice, she presented Lawrence with a mass of complex information about suitable islands, and Lawrence let the subject drop.[51]

As December waned the division between the Murrys grew sharper. The new year, with the bright promise it always brought her, inspired Miss Mansfield with resolution and hope. She saw the old year pass, to the ringing of bells. She determined to write, to make money. "All will be well," she told herself. But the days were dismal; snow shrouded the earth; the cottage was cold. Lack of money and inability to write—the familiar torments—consumed her mind.

Again the devastating misery of her last year at Wellington descended. Again she experienced the cycle of wretchedness, despair, and finally revolt. Again she longed for the brilliant life of cities. Again the shore across the water seemed the threshold of escape. This time she fixed her eyes on France; and this time, instead of a vague longing for "her" people she distinguished a single deliverer, Francis Carco. His letters to Murry had seemed to her to reveal a spirit very like her own: he shared her love for the poetic and the marvelous, the humorous, the absurd. They had entered into correspondence. When her brother Leslie arrived in England to begin a period of military training, Miss Mansfield's problem of immediate funds was solved. By the third of February she had made her decision. On February 19 she joined Francis Carco at Gray, in northeastern France.

Spiritually and emotionally, by 1915 Katherine Mansfield had not yet come of age. Misery, anger, and willful

self-assertion had impelled her to set out on this escapade.
The events of her seven years in London had given her
a more genuine sophistication than the spurious armor she
had assumed in her last years at Wellington. But she had
not yet passed through sophistication to wisdom; she had
not yet learned that the way to conquer reality is to meet
it face to face.

The trip to Gray contained an abundance of adventure,
for Gray was in the zone of the army encampments along
the frontier and was forbidden territory to women. "An
Indiscreet Journey," [52] the expansion of Miss Mansfield's
Journal record of her experience,[53] depicts the hazards of
that trip to join "the little corporal." But once the journey
was accomplished, the sojourn at Gray proved unexciting.
Through the day Miss Mansfield kept closely to her rooms.
Carco's military duties kept him fully engaged, except
for a hurried meal at noon which he shared with *la re-
cluse* at her lodgings. Only in the evening could they
meet at greater leisure. After three days, bored perhaps
with this semi-imprisonment, Miss Mansfield left for Paris.
Within another week, at the end of February, she returned
to London, to Murry, since she had nowhere else to go.

Brief as it was, this "indiscreet journey" was not without later issue. It was from her fuller knowledge of
Francis Carco that Miss Mansfield drew many of the distinguishing qualities of Raoul Duquette in *"Je ne parle
pas français."* [54] The portrait is cruel, but it is no more
cruel than the picture of Miss Mansfield which Carco
presented in his novel, *Les Innocents*, in 1916. The physical description of his subject is unmistakable—the "petite
femme menue" with her short dark hair and "immenses
yeux noirs." The running lilt of her expression, too, is
closely followed, even in the French. "Winnie's" quick,

lively accounts of a concierge or a cinema hero, the flying bits of description in her letters, are recognizably Katherine Mansfield's as, indeed, they actually are, for Carco incorporated them bodily from letters she had written to him.[55] What poetic communion had existed between the two young writers had evidently dissipated rapidly. Winnie of *Les Innocents* is presented as an insatiate monster, avidly feeding on human material for the book upon which her entire energy and emotions are fixed. Looking back after twenty years, M. Carco has drawn Miss Mansfield with a gentler hand. She possessed "une douceur, une ingénuité de petite fille," he states, "très pure, très reservée," [56] along with a vibrant sensitivity, an eagerness to explore the heart of all experience. Only characteristic details of manner and appearance, only the traits of innocence and delicacy in Winnie, were taken from Miss Mansfield.[57] Indeed, as a character, Winnie of the novel is perplexing. Through intimate detail she emerges, in spite of the brutal heart assigned her, a figure of provocative charm.

On her return to Rose Tree Cottage Miss Mansfield was ill, crippled with arthritis, still rebellious and miserable. "My God, what poverty!" she wrote to Koteliansky on March 8. "So I write about hot weather and happy love and broad bands of sunlight and cafés—all the things that make life to me." [58] Rose Tree Cottage, despite its lyric name, was damp, cold, and depressing. In the middle of March, on her partial recovery, Miss Mansfield left for a short stay with the Lawrences at Greatham, West Sussex, where they had moved to a cottage lent them by Viola Meynell. Under happy circumstances, as always, her spirit revived. At Greatham there were daffodils and primroses in flower; the marshes were filled with gulls; the downs stretched free and lovely to the sea. In the open country she felt her heart cleansed of its bitterness; she was carried back to harmony with Murry.

Nevertheless Miss Mansfield was determined to go to Paris again, this time for the regeneration of creative power which she believed she drew only from the rich Parisian world. After her long period of sterility she had felt the quickening of life. She had written "The Little Governess" [59] and had "much better" work in mind. "I *cannot* write my book living in these two rooms," she wrote to Koteliansky on March 17. "It is impossible—and if I do not write this book I shall die. So I am going away tomorrow to finish it." [60]

In Paris, settled in Carco's apartment at the Quai aux Fleurs, on the sheltered side of the Ile de la Cité, she felt the desired reawakening. From her window she could look leftward to the charming lesser isle, Saint Louis, and the arches of its graceful bridge, or rightward across the river to the isolated shaft of the Tour Saint Jacques rising above its encircling group of trees. Sitting in a café, smoking, sipping her hot black coffee, watching the snowflakes fall outside, she knew that she was ready, waiting in a strange silence—"the same silence that comes one minute before the curtain rises." [61] Freely and happily, she began to write the novel she had planned. She read; above all, she observed—the life of the streets, of the Luxembourg Gardens, of the Paris cafés. Suddenly she felt cured of her sickness; she was eager for England again. Impetuously, at the end of March she returned.

Still occupied with her novel,[62] which evidently pleased her, Miss Mansfield crossed once more to Paris in May.

Again the value of the sojourn lay in the quickening of all her senses through the vigorous life in which she was immersed. This was spring in Paris, warm and flower-filled, children at play in the gardens under the shadow of Notre Dame, lovers idling in the evening light along the quais, stirring loneliness and longing. By the end of May, with characteristic shift of mood, revulsion once more set in; detachment turned to depression. She returned to England, to spend a few weeks in the rooms Murry had prepared at Elgin Crescent. In July they took a charming house at 5 Acacia Road, St. John's Wood, with a patch of lawn and a slender pear tree in the garden. Here their friends came often, Koteliansky, and the Lawrences, who were now living at Hampstead. With Lawrence the Murrys planned to launch a new little magazine, the *Signature*. Lawrence, clinging to his earlier belief, was convinced that the only possible hope for society lay in the formation of a new and honest world by a nuclear group of kindred spirits—Rananim in London, or anywhere else available. The organ of this group was to be the *Signature*, in which Lawrence was to set forth this philosophy; [63] Murry was to present his ideas on freedom for the individual; Katherine Mansfield, furnishing jam for the pill, as she later put it, was to contribute stories and sketches.

Throughout September Lawrence was busy soliciting subscriptions among his friends, anxious as much to secure their faith in his enterprise as their subscription money.[64] By late September the first issue was in preparation. Two rooms were taken at 12 Fisher Street, Red Lion Square, to serve as headquarters for discussion meetings, but in this extension of the plan the Murrys had little interest. The scant subscription funds, however, allowed for the publication of only three issues of the *Signature*, in extremely cheap form, on October 4, October 18, and November 1, 1915. The three issues contained only a long essay by Lawrence and one by Murry, both running through the three numbers and both incomplete, and Miss Mansfield's stories "Autumns: I, II" [65] (later called individually "The Apple-Tree" and "The Wind Blows") and "The Little Governess." [66] With this venture Miss Mansfield was never so closely identified as she had been with *Rhythm;* and by the time the *Signature* was suspended she was too much preoccupied with grief to lament the passing of a magazine.

To the house at Acacia Road Miss Mansfield's young brother Leslie came often after completing the six months of military training which qualified him as a bombing officer. Before crossing to France, in September, 1915, he stayed with the Murrys for a week. Together the brother and sister walked in the garden, recalling the days of their New Zealand childhood. Time took on a dual dimension: they lived in past and present simultaneously. The pear tree at Acacia Road, with its hard fruits falling in the dusk, brought before them the old pear tree at Fitzherbert Terrace; again they saw the little pears, pricked mysteriously at times with the mark of tiny teeth, scattered in the grass under the violet leaves. They believed now they had shared days of flawless happiness in that uncorrupted world on the shores of the South Pacific. They would go back, they planned, after the war was over; together they would go back.

Leslie Beauchamp was killed at Ploegsteert Wood on October 7, 1915, by the premature explosion of a bomb in his hand. He was buried across the French border, a little north of Armentières.

The shock to Katherine Mansfield was overwhelming.

At first she was stunned, as from a physical blow; later withdrawn, remote and sorrowing. She dwelt in heart with her dead brother, apart from the living. The house at Acacia Road must be given up. It was ghostly with memories.

CHAPTER THREE

"Prelude"

A MONTH AFTER Leslie Beauchamp's death, in the middle of November, the Murrys set out for the south of
France. The presence of her brother was beside Miss
Mansfield. "All this is like a long uneasy ripple—nothing
else—and below—in the still pool there is my little
brother," [1] she wrote to Koteliansky during their stop at
Marseilles. Cassis, where the Murrys decided to settle, met
them with a raging mistral; the very leaves on the trees
looked desolate. Miss Mansfield remained submerged in
grief. At the end of three weeks, finding their life intolerable, Murry returned to London, to lose himself in his
work. Miss Mansfield stayed on in France, at Bandol, a
little winter resort on a beautiful Mediterranean Bay.
Gradually a new purpose took form in her heart. A duty
lay before her, impelling her to sustain existence. She must
write, for her brother, of their shared and lovely past.

The slow force gathered, struggling against the sweep
of despair. Lawrence her friend wrote his encouragement,
with sensitive understanding of her inner sickness:

Do not be sad. It is one life which is passing away from us, one "I" is dying; but there is another coming into being, which is the happy, creative you. I knew you would have to die with your brother; you also, go down into death and be extinguished. But for us there is a rising from the grave, there is a resurrection, and a clean life to begin from the start, new, and happy. Don't be afraid, don't doubt it, it is so.[2]

Bandol itself offered assuagement, with its long stretch of beach and its fields of flowers—jonquils, daffodils, violets, and white roses. The solitary walks along the sea wrought their quiet process of regeneration. The sense of acutely detailed vision which France always aroused in Miss Mansfield began its active play. With delight she began to observe her little world—the sea, the sky, the fishing vessels, the olive trees on the hills, the picturesque old men and women of the countryside. Life at Bandol was simple, unaffected, and honest. She drew it in deeply; it revived her, like the strong salt air of the sea. By the middle of December the form of her new work had begun to assume shape in her mind. She was looking homeward; and she looked back now with loving tenderness.

Bandol had become "as fair as New Zealand" [3] to her. When at the end of the month Murry decided to join her for the winter, her tranquil joy flowered to delight. She found for them a little house, called the Villa Pauline, sunny and "very private," with an almond tree outside the window of the dining room. The last bright December days sped by, filled with light and color. The key to the villa was hers; all the saucepans hung in place; the modest provisions were ordered; the rooms were filled with flowers. For the present she could not write, she could not read; she could only make ready and wait.

Life at the Villa Pauline was an interlude of happiness.

Murry was busy with a book on Dostoevski, commissioned by Martin Secker to clear the debt incurred by the publication of *Rhythm* and the *Blue Review*. By half past eight each morning both were at their writing desks. For the first time in her life Miss Mansfield lived under the circumstances vital to her for creative stimulus: she had harmonious companionship, modest security, simplicity and charm of living. With steadily increasing confidence she began to grope her way toward the first of her long stories based upon her childhood, drawing near the source of a new limpidity of expression. The form and nature of her earlier stories she rejected: "No novels, no problem stories, nothing that is not simple, open." [4] She would write of her native island, the beloved people and places she and her brother had known. "But all must be told with a sense of mystery, a radiance, an afterglow, because you, my little sun of it, are set," [5] she resolved.

In February, 1916, she began "The Aloe." With her brother she walked again, she saw again, the memorable past. The big white-pillared house rose before her, washed with sunlight or shadowed under the moon; people moved within—the grandmother, the father, the beautiful mother, the three little girls. As Lawrence had foretold, she knew resurrection.

Not that the loss of our darling one is any less real to me [she wrote to her father on March 6]. It never can be, and I feel that it has changed the course of my life *for ever*, but I do feel very strongly that I fail in my duty to his memory if I do not bear his loss bravely, and I could not bear to fail him.[6]

Since early January the Lawrences had been living in Cornwall, in a cottage lent them by the Beresfords. More desperately than ever the wish to assemble a little community of kindred minds consumed Lawrence's heart. His letters to the Murrys throughout their stay at the Villa Pauline voiced his anxious longing for them to join him.[7] As the winter drew to an end his appeals became importunate. He was sick, in body and in spirit. His book *The Rainbow* had recently been suppressed. The war dragged on, torturing his heart. He felt alien, choked by the rank corruption of the world; he needed his friends, and to preserve faith in his friends.

By March he and Mrs. Lawrence had found a two-room cottage at Higher Tregerthen, a little Cornwall village near the moors and sea. Close by was a second and larger cottage with a tower. "I call it already Katherine's house, Katherine's tower," he wrote affectionately. ". . . You must come, and we will live there a long, long time, very cheaply."[8] It was impossible to refuse his call. Reluctantly the Murrys agreed to leave the villa where, for three months, they had been completely happy. By early April they had joined the Lawrences, arriving in a cart, perched high on all their goods.

But Miss Mansfield was out of sympathy with the venture. She had always distrusted Lawrence's Rananim. Only a few weeks after their arrival she was writing to Koteliansky of her loneliness and discontent:

I am very much alone here. It is not a really nice place. It is so full of huge stones, but now that I am writing I do not care, for the time. It is so very temporary. It may all be over next month; in fact, it will be. I don't belong to anybody here. In fact, I have no being, but I am making preparations for changing everything.[9]

Again Murry was swinging away from her, this time toward Lawrence, in an ambiguous relationship charged with tension and conflict. Moreover, Lawrence and his wife still quarreled violently. Soon Miss Mansfield was engulfed by her old oppressive despair. She determined that they must leave. Toward the end of May the Murrys removed to the south side of Cornwall, giving as their excuse the harshness of the northern shore. They parted from the Lawrences in outward amity; but Lawrence was deeply wounded at the failure of his experiment.[10]

At Mylor, near Falmouth, the Murrys found an attractive cottage which they engaged for the summer. There were flowering bushes in the front garden, vegetable greens in back. The cottage was equipped with a devoted serving maid and a kitten. Less than this at times to Katherine Mansfield could mean happiness. But in Cornwall she was restless. She was not writing, at least not to her satisfaction; no work of this period has been preserved. As often as her funds allowed she traveled to London, seeking distraction. For the first time, during this summer, she stayed with Lady Ottoline Morrell, Lawrence's literary patroness. It was at Garsington Manor, Lady Ottoline's country house near Oxford, that she first met Dorothy Brett. Both Lady Ottoline and Miss Brett became her intimate friends.

By the summer of 1916 Murry was soundly established as reviewer of French books for the *Times Literary Supplement*. His work and the extensive reading for which he at last had time absorbed him happily. No doubt part of Miss Mansfield's restlessness arose from her sense of isolation, for though like all hypersensitive persons she cherished her inmost self apart, she did not enjoy neglect. Further, during the winter preceding she had undergone a devastating shock. She was forced to grapple at first hand with the knowledge of reasonless destruction, of violent and irremediable loss. For strength she turned to the fixed dimensions of the past. She wrote "The Aloe." In her work she found tranquillity, and a kind of exaltation. Then the work was done. The present closed upon her—difficulties with Murry, creative exhaustion, a world that could not be controlled and ordered into harmony and beauty. Against the buffets of this world the past offered no permanent shelter. It could not protect her from loneliness and fear.

When in September Murry was called to service in the Department of Military Intelligence, she returned with him to London, where they took rooms at 3 Gower Street. For months now she had been unproductive. She thought, she planned; but she could not write. London, envisioned in her girlhood as the vital heart of stimulus, proved recurrently the environment which paralyzed her gifts. And now the city, with all the world, was locked fast in the clutch of war. One after another of the Murrys' friends were reported killed—the talented young Oxford men Miss Mansfield had met in the first years of her association with Murry, among them their beloved Frederick Goodyear. The face of life was disintegrating before her very eyes, revealing skull and grinning molars. Not one of the persons to whom she was attached came back from the war.

By now the war obsessed Murry. Consumed by his military duties and his journalistic work, burdened with an intense, unvarying depression, he proved an exacerbating companion.[11] Early in 1917 Miss Mansfield took a studio for herself at 141a Church Street, Chelsea, while Murry engaged rooms a short distance away at Redcliffe Road. They continued to meet each day, but for the time they found life more supportable apart.

Miss Mansfield accepted, and no doubt controlled, the situation with a temperateness somewhat touched with melancholy. Church Street, with its low, irregular houses, some with colored doorways, was picturesque; the studio offered seclusion, the front door opening on an enclosed courtyard, the back door into a little garden with a fig tree. In the relative peace she had established her mind was stirring to activity again, recalling New Zealand, Bavaria, Paris. She began to write. During the spring of 1917 she returned to the *New Age*,[12] contributing in the following few months a series of pieces, all more or less trifling except for "Mr. Reginald Peacock's Day," "A Dill Pickle," and "The Common Round" (later reshaped and published in *Art and Letters* as "Pictures"). In addition, during the summer she refashioned "The Aloe," molding it to the firmer and more subtle prose of "Prelude." The Hogarth Press, recently established by Leonard and Virginia Woolf, had arranged to bring out the story as one of its first ventures. By the middle of August the revised copy was in the typist's hands. In spite of illness, for the heavy summer rains brought on Miss Mansfield's rheumatic pain "plus ghastly depression *plus* fury," [13] in spite of her longing for escape from London to the sea, Miss Mansfield was bleakly satisfied with the main outline of her life, if not with its details. "It is the only life I care about—" she wrote to Lady Ottoline Morrell, "to write, to go out occasionally and 'lose myself' looking and hearing and then to come back and write again. At any rate that's the life I've chosen." [14]

Lady Ottoline's friendship was a source of great pleasure to Miss Mansfield. Garsington Manor with its lovely gardens appeased her constant longing for the world of nature, and in Lady Ottoline herself she found a sympathetic mind. During this summer, also, for the first time she visited Mrs. Woolf at Asheham. The two women, both hypersensitive to the nuances of each moment, both dedicated to their art, both gifted with intense appreciation of the significance of minute detail, shared a unique apprehension of life.

It was good to have time to talk to you [Miss Mansfield wrote to Mrs. Woolf after her return from Asheham]; we have got the same job, Virginia, and it is really very curious and thrilling that we should both, quite apart from each other, be after so very nearly the same thing. We are, you know; there's no denying it.[15]

Katherine Mansfield did not reveal her secret thoughts to many associates. Frequently she was considered cold, reserved, even supercilious. Particularly, she held silence about her work. But to Lady Ottoline, to Dorothy Brett, to Virginia Woolf she could speak with confidence and candor. The experience was salutary. Her conception of the artist grew more integrated, more sinewy in fiber, as it emerged from the vapors of romantic fancy to the clear atmosphere of considered thought. Her attitude toward technique, corroborated by attentive reading of Chekhov, gained increased clarity. The artist, the real artist, she always venerated as the highest expression human nature could achieve. But after her years among the dilettantes her demands grew stringently exacting. She had come to recognize beneath the surface glitter the malice, the ostentation, the conceit, the sawdust brain and sawdust heart of the poseurs. She required now of the artist the strength to explore his own vision of truth, alone if necessary, and craft, the control of craft. To the discipline of her own craft she now turned.

Between 1913 and 1915 Miss Mansfield had written very little with which she was satisfied. The journals contain a scattering of fragmentary pieces, one or two fairly long and provocative, but only a half-dozen completed stories exist from this period of unrest. These, except for a refinement in technique, are chiefly in the manner of her earlier work. Like the personal sketches of 1911, the "epilogues" of 1913 [16] shape a minor personal experience to convey a specific theme—again, as in the earlier pieces, the contradiction of the apparent by the real. The execution is more controlled than formerly. Characterization, brushed in with quick, light strokes, is sharper; and the imagery is beginning to resemble that of Miss Mansfield's later work, striking off a vivid impression in a brief simile or metaphor: "Her round red face shone like freshly washed china" [17] or "one little rug escaped and flopped down to the avenue below, like a fish." [18] The narrator is still too conscious of being whimsical and witty, but these little sketches contain real vivacity and charm.

The one substantial story from this time is "Something Childish But Very Natural," written during the Paris stay with Murry late in 1913. This story of very young love— Lucy Desborough and Richard Feverel meeting not on the shores of the still-vexed Bermoothes but in a London commuters' train—is essentially simple. The theme is the shy withdrawal of a sensitive girl before the physical manifestation of love, until, of its own accord, her resistance melts, but only because she has at last been swept out of herself—later recoil follows. The story could be told with poignance of lovers of no other age than this boy and girl, she "over sixteen," he "nearly eighteen." Throughout, their extreme youth is stressed, but unobtrusively. By now Miss Mansfield was drawing closer to a mastery of implication. Henry and Edna themselves impress their immaturity upon us.

The story is really Henry's. It opens and closes with him, and focuses throughout upon his figure. We come to realize Edna as much through Henry's consciousness as through her direct participation in dramatic scene. Again the technique is that of mixed dramatic action and interior monologue, the latter still scrupulously embraced by quotation marks but very flexible and spontaneous. Henry's train of thought is perhaps a little feminine, recognizably close to his creator's; but his emotion is conveyed with delicacy and strength.

Miss Mansfield's treatment of the material is very slow and ample. She was not yet employing implication for the purpose of economy. She had merely become more subtle in method. Background and scene are copiously established at the start of the narrative, and the idyllic though flawed relationship is developed at length. The end, however, is given in a sentence or two. "The garden became full of shadows—they span a web of darkness over the cottage and the trees and Henry and the telegram. But Henry did not move." [19] Here for the first time Miss Mansfield employs the kind of ending she uses almost without exception in her later work—a cutting short of scene at a climactic moment. But later she was to begin *in medias res* as well.

"An Indiscreet Journey," the sketch based on Miss Mansfield's trip to Gray in 1915, is chiefly of interest for the opportunity it offers to glimpse the author's hand at work. The sketch is really unfinished, reading more like the first chapter of a novel, somewhat cryptic to one who is not familiar with the circumstances from which it is drawn. The *Journal* gives merely a condensed narration of the end of the trip and the meeting with the "little corporal," vividly described, enlivened by a few touches of dialogue. In the second version the material is considerably expanded, both by the addition of several scenes and by the introduction of details of color, movement, and sound, which quicken the whole expression to heightened vivacity. Thus in the *Journal* account Miss Mansfield writes: "Two women, their arms folded, leaned against the counter." [20] In the sketch the picture is intensified: "On the counter, beautiful with coloured bottles, a woman leans." [21] Perhaps the most interesting changes concern condensation of the imagery—for example, the phrase "eyes . . . like two grey stones" has been changed to "pebble eyes," the "long curly ash" of a cigarette to "long creamy ash." Each one of the changes—and there are many—is designed to achieve a more concentrated vividness.

Of the three *Signature* stories of 1915,[22] two are based on New Zealand material. "The Apple-Tree" recounts a childhood incident in a narrative that moves swiftly and lightly, packed with sharp detail—windfalls "marked with a bird's beak" in the coarse orchard grass, the "polished" leaves of the apple tree, the beautiful flesh of the apple looking as though it had been "dipped in wine." In this piece character is only touched upon, yet the figure of the father emerges with vigorous clarity—the unmistakable lineaments of the later Stanley Burnell. "The Wind Blows" is more a virtuoso piece, carrying in its staccato expression the emotional turmoil of an adolescent girl. The rough wind blows through the story, pushing, whirling, tearing, and the girl's rebellious spirit beats equally. Here mood and external scene are admirably identified.

The remaining *Signature* story, the longest of the three, is "The Little Governess," that tale of innocence abroad in Munich. The author's attitude here has shifted from that of the early German stories with their fierce antagonism against the male, for although the little governess is set upon by a philandering old gentleman, we are given to see clearly that her own ignorance and unworldliness largely bring about her discomfiture. Like "Something Childish" this story builds up the situation slowly, through a thoroughly developed beginning and frequent full descriptive passages. Again the technique is the admixture of interior monologue and dramatic action, fluently merged, consistently presenting the material through the apprehension of the little governess.

"The Little Governess" is the last of Miss Mansfield's stories to be executed in an ample, leisurely style. In writing "The Aloe" she had discovered her particular gift for oblique revelation through detached, apparently casual incident. Thereafter her technique remained fixed. For years she had been seeking her artistic way along diverse paths. The process of this search was slow and indirect. We have seen that she essayed, with varying success, aestheticism, naturalism, realism, turning repeatedly for her material to her own early experience. By the end of 1917 she had come to discard many of her first propensities, particularly the intrusive witty comment she had affected at the start of her career. She had also evolved the method of character presentation she was to utilize exclusively—revelation through the channel of inner consciousness combined with significant dramatic action. This is not to say that Miss Mansfield invented the method. The great writers have always been more concerned with inner than with outer being, though their means of presentation may seem clumsy after the development of the "stream of consciousness" device. But device is always and only device, and in Chekhov or Tolstoi, to take two of Miss Mansfield's favorite authors, we can find so authentic a transcription of inner experience as to make many more recent investigations seem juvenile. Also, Miss Mansfield dwelt in the climate of her age, with its preoccupation with the inner man, and she imbibed its atmosphere, though in large part she rejected its fruits. It is not necessary here to trace her philosophical and literary attachments. At present we are following the evolution of her technique in a narrower sense.

In this sense Miss Mansfield's work of 1917 has particular interest, for it incorporates the final step in the process. Part of this work, a number of pieces she contributed to the *New Age* between May and October of that year, is inconsequential except for its embodiment of her experimentations in a semidramatic form. In "The Festival of the Coronation," a trifling jest on a current event published in the *New Age* in 1911, she had first made use of the dramatic dialogue, that is, the presentation of two characters entirely by means of their speech, with several shifts of scene within very short scope. Four years later she appeared in the *New Age* [23] with an equally trifling piece, "Stay-laces," executed in similar form, though here the role of one of the speakers is reduced to significant interrogation and exclamation marks. The lesser *New Age* pieces of 1917 vary the method of dramatic presentation. "Two Tuppenny Ones, Please," exposing the idle interests of idle women, far more effectively utilizes the method of "Stay-laces"; "Late at Night" presents the inner ruminations of an unwanted, introspective spinster; "The Black Cap" facetiously depicts a love-triangle debacle in an armchair playlet of many changing scenes; "In Confidence" and "A Pic-nic," satiric attacks on the vanity of women, are both technically erratic pieces made up of elements of the short story and the play. All these productions are merely ephemera, of significance only because they reveal, running alongside Miss Mansfield's more highly finished work, her continuing inclination toward a dramatic form. With her acute sense for characterizing speech Miss Mansfield was well equipped to reveal character through dialogue, but with her inability to create complex and sustained situation she was not equipped to write plays. Moreover, her interest was shifting progressively to the exploration of interior action. The relationship between the dramatic monologue and what might be termed the "stream of being" technique is very close. Browning's figures—Fra Lippo Lippi, Andrea del Sarto, the Duke of Ferrara—inform us of what they are, in essence, through the total implication of the words they say; the interior monologue, so to speak, is given at one remove. By these experimentations, which required similar high condensation and selectivity, Miss Mansfield gained firmer control over the presentation of inner experience.

Of the four *New Age* stories later included in *Bliss*,[24] "Pictures" appears in a first version under the title "The Common Round." Here the material is given in a mongrel dramatic form which utilizes dialogue, interior monologue, frequent shifts of scene, and many incidental characters. The presentation is naked, flat, and crude. When a year and a half later Miss Mansfield expanded the material to a rounded story, she wove the original substance almost unaltered into a fabric of interconnective narrative. The story now moves fluidly and swiftly, with sharp and moving effect. By a comparison of the two versions one can see how much Miss Mansfield's technique depends upon the interlinking of emotion with external concrete detail. Miss Moss of the story is a stout, middle-aged contralto out of a job, facing eviction and a sordid future. Before dressing for the day she sits on her bed, in her ripped nightgown, staring at her "fat white legs with their great knots of greeny-blue veins." [25] By the addition of this detail, and of others similar, the ugliness of the central theme, only roughly indicated in the first version, is made to pervade the whole.

These several experiments no doubt contributed to Miss Mansfield's skill when, in the summer of 1917, she revised "The Aloe" to "Prelude." In writing this story, a year and a half before, she had carefully examined her artistic purpose and the best means of its expression. ". . . the form that I would choose has changed utterly," she noted. "I feel no longer concerned with the same appearance of things. . . . Oh, I want for one moment to make our undiscovered country leap into the eyes of the Old World. It must be mysterious, as though floating. It must take the breath." [26]

Describing the story to Dorothy Brett, in a letter of October, 1917, she stated her intention more fully:

"What form is it?" you ask. Ah, Brett, it's so difficult to say. As far as I know, it's more or less my own invention. . . . You know, if the truth were known I have a perfect passion for the island where I was born. Well, in the early morning there I always remember feeling that this little island has dipped back into the dark blue sea during the night only to rise again at gleam of day, all hung with bright spangles and glittering drops. . . . I tried to catch that moment—with something of its sparkle and its flavour. And just as on those mornings white milky mists rise and uncover some beauty, then smother it again and then again disclose it, I tried to lift that mist from my people and let them be seen and then to hide them again.[27]

This "sparkle" and "flavour," the "bright spangles and glittering drops," Miss Mansfield has conveyed by catching up into the narrative a mood of vernal brightness, freshness, buoyancy, or the ethereal hush of evening calm. Flowers of delicate or brilliant color, streams, skies, bushes, trees, and orchard grass form the vivid outdoor setting, changeful under the play of changing light. Particularly in the extended description of early dawn does the little island seem to rise again from the sea. This setting, interfused throughout the story in descriptive passages, constitutes an inherent element of the piece; it cannot be detached, as poetic decoration, without complete structural unraveling. The creek on the fringe of the paddocks, described in precise, evocative detail, is the stream where among the congregated ducks swims Pat's destined victim; in the first paddock stands the old stump which Pat uses as a chopping block when he beheads the duck. Kezia, eluding her eldest sister's domination, explores the wild tangled garden with its rich profusion of flowers, fulfilling the demands of her own individuality. The grandmother, looking at the aloe, sees it as part of the natural world, of genuine interest because it appears on the verge of blooming, while Linda, beside her in the moonlight, perceives it as a symbol of herself.

Within and of this setting, not against it, the figures are revealed. The "mists rise and uncover" now Linda and Stanley Burnell, now Stanley and the young Aunt Beryl, now Kezia and her sisters, now Linda and her mother, following the fluid course of interacting relationships, simultaneously establishing character and theme through an apparently casual interlinking of episodes. Actually the line of movement is not casual at all. The events recounted, in themselves unspectacular, make up the interwoven texture of the life of the Burnell family during the week after their removal to their new country place, given through a series of representative dramatic scenes. Within an episode, or at times as a link between two sections, a blending of one dramatic scene into another often takes place, not in the "dream play" sense of fantastic confluence but by a deft shift of the spotlight focus from one character to another who has just entered the scene in a minor role. In Proustian recurrence a number of thematic notes in this way are played. Thus the sixth scene opens with the grandmother in the kitchen, reminded by the grapevine at the window of an incident in the far past. Presently joined by Beryl, she goes about her work in her deliberate fashion, ignoring Beryl's irritable impatience, serving Linda when she comes in for a late breakfast, suggesting to Linda at length that she give some attention to her children, especially Kezia. At this, within the same episode, the focus swings over to Kezia—the real if intermittent heroine—as she pursues her solitary exploration of the grounds, and the scene culminates in her meeting with Linda before the aloe tree, in a passage which first touches on the central image of the story.

By this device of shifting illumination the filaments of many relationships are interwoven, revealing character in its hidden depths as well as its exterior display. We see Stanley pitching his wet towel on Linda's clothes, giving himself a "good scratch on his shoulders and back before turning in," [28] paring his nails with a penknife, reveling in his "real feeling for food," and we can sympathize with

Linda as her delicate organism is jarred. Later we see Linda shrinking in fear and hatred from his physical importunities, turning to the constant serenity of her mother for her real support, lightly dismissing any obligation to her children, and we can sympathize also with Stanley in his underlife of bewilderment and self-distrust. We catch a glimpse of Beryl flirting with Stanley for lack of other game, out of sheer self-enchantment attacking an impervious wall, and can better understand her caustic spitefulness toward him at other times, her jealousy of Linda, especially since Stanley does not include a sister-in-law in his household without the exhibition of lordliness. Through the various scenes the children flit as minor actors, emerging memorably now and again to a full scene of their own, living the dual life of children, part in the unpredictable world of the adults, part in the secret world of their own reality. Steady and unperturbed the grandmother comes and goes, accepting her lot as ministrant to all with the calm dignity of those who have grown also wise in growing old. Even Pat the handy man and the maidservant Alice are illuminated at moments, for they also act, think, feel, contributing to the family life their own unique influence.

Within this narrative texture Miss Mansfield has enmeshed her unifying theme: that the emotional intercrossings of a group of intimates are extraordinarily complex, even though outwardly their life seems to pursue an even way; that this complexity has at its heart the ultimate loneliness one must endure within—perhaps particularly within—his most intense relationships; that in the recognition of this mortal quality—of the salt, inevitable taste at the core of the rich fruit—lies the sharpest meaning the human mind can apprehend.

However conscious her intention as she shaped "The Aloe," however vigorously many of the scenes sprang to life, Miss Mansfield was too much involved in her material emotionally to guide the course of her story with complete success. To write of the past was to talk again with her brother, as they had talked in the garden at Acacia Road, while the moonlight glittered on the ivy. All that she looked back upon glowed with bright significance. It was easy and delightful to wander through the ways and byways of recollection. That she did so even more extensively than appears in "The Aloe" is shown by her journal writings of this period.[29]

Structurally, as we have seen, "Prelude" is built upon the unit of the episode, each one included centering in some member of the Burnell family. To be technically successful the narrative must not digress into irrelevancies. In no episode in the final version does the focal interest depart from one or another member of the family group; but in the earlier draft several deviations from the central figures appear. Thus in "The Aloe" we find a long humorous-satiric account of Mrs. Samuel Josephs, fat and asthmatic, and her obstreperous children, who live next to the Burnells' former city residence;[30] a detailed description (in the copious vein of Dickens) of the general store where Lottie and Kezia stopped with the storeman Fred on their way to the new house;[31] "Burnell courting Linda,"[32] as Miss Mansfield put it in her brief notes for "The Aloe," which runs off into a depiction of Linda's father, then shifts to a social given by the Liberal Ladies' Political League, which Stanley and Linda attend;[33] an extended view of Linda's sister, Mrs. Trout, a related but not intrinsic member of the group,[34] another of Beryl Fairfield's earlier relationship with her school friend Nan Fry.[35]

Those readers who have come to love the Burnell family
through the several New Zealand stories delight in these
little windows opening for a moment on a fuller scene.
Linda as a young girl, high-spirited, capricious, already a
little aloof; young Stanley Burnell, as determined in matters of love as he is later in matters of business; Linda's
father, Doady Trout—all these figures are cherished. But
the force and swiftness of the story are impeded by the
circuitous account.

" 'The Aloe' is right. 'The Aloe' is lovely. It simply
fascinates me," [36] Miss Mansfield wrote in her journal
shortly after beginning the story. But when she came to
the revision of her work after a year and a half the critical,
not the emotional, force was dominant. She must hold her
story to its basic unit; and however much of the past history of her figures she might or might not be able to suggest—and she managed to suggest a considerable amount
—she must keep her group within the limits of the single
week she had chosen to represent. Each one of the digres-
sive episodes was excised.

In Miss Mansfield's depiction of her family in "The
Aloe," consciously or unconsciously she seemed to wish
to preserve intact her close intimacy with her characters
by relating even their names to those of their originals.
Burnell itself was the middle name of her mother, and
Harold Beauchamp's mother before her marriage was
Mary Elizabeth Stanley. Surely it is not by accident that
these two names are conjoined in Stanley Burnell. The
name of the grandmother, Mrs. Fairfield, is no more than
Beauchamp "Englished," and "Aunt Beryl" is not very
far removed from "Aunt Belle," Mrs. Beauchamp's
younger sister. Charlotte, Miss Mansfield's older sister, re-
tains her own name in the diminutive Lottie; Pat Sheehan,

the Beauchamps' gardener-coachman, his Christian name as Pat the handy man; and "Kezia" is as close as one could come to "Kass." Later, in "The Doll's House," the little MacKelveys, the village washerwoman's children who attended the Karori Primary School, were to appear as the Kelveys, merely shorn of their initial syllable.

Out of this intimate communion most of the figures in "The Aloe" sprang from the first to integrated life; only negligible changes in their delineation appear in "Prelude." But the Linda Burnell of the second version has undergone distinct alteration. The Linda of "The Aloe" has more vitality than the Linda of "Prelude." She is in more immediate connection with her daily world. In both speech and action she is a shade more ordinary than the later Linda—a beautiful young woman, a semi-invalid, with a mocking wit, a vividly fanciful imagination, a divided emotional response to marriage. By skillful emphases and excisions this Linda has been developed to a figure of mystery and elusive charm.

It is probably a safe conjecture that the earlier Linda reflects more accurately than the later the original from which she was drawn, Miss Mansfield's mother. No other member of the family has been comparably changed. Further, the other figures resemble very closely the corresponding characters in Miss Mansfield's earliest stories based upon her childhood experience. But the mother is greatly altered since her first appearance. There is no resemblance between Linda, exquisite and languid, and the querulous Mrs. Carstairs of "New Dresses." Rather, Mrs. Carstairs is of the blood of Mrs. Wilberforce, in Miss Mansfield's juvenile novel *Juliet:* "The mother was a slight, pale little woman. She had been delicate and ailing before her marriage and she could never forget it." [37] In "The

"Aloe" Miss Mansfield's evocation of her mother sprang from a heart charged with compassion and love. She emphasized Linda's personal beauty; she transferred to Linda her own characteristic whimsicalities; she gave to Linda her own vivacious wit. Then in "Prelude" she consciously heightened Linda's original quality of detachment, to transfer her to the borders of another world.

The later Linda has no part in commonplace existence. She has been denuded of every earlier expression of liveliness. In "Prelude" Linda does not explore the kitchen the first morning to find something to eat; she is not impressed by the "grandeur" of a pantry and a larder; she does not playfully tease her sister; far from jesting about the servant girl, she has no connection whatever with practical affairs.[38] Even a mocking concern with the welfare of her children is more than she is allowed—in "Prelude" the grandmother assumes the few expressions of interest Linda shows in "The Aloe." In this suppression of Linda's warmth no example better illustrates Miss Mansfield's vigilance than the parallel passages in which Kezia asks her mother if the aloe tree ever blooms. " 'Yes, my child,' said her Mother, and she smiled down at Kezia, half shutting her eyes, 'once every hundred years,' " [39] the first version reads; and the second version: " 'Yes, Kezia,' and Linda smiled down at her, and half shut her eyes. 'Once every hundred years.' " [40] By this very simple alteration the desired effect has been wrought. The words "child" and "mother" with their ancient reverberations of tenderness are replaced by the impersonal proper names, so that voice merely speaks to voice, and we are given the sense that although Linda is smiling down at Kezia, she is actually smiling at the unspoken thoughts within herself.

In the second version, also, Linda's speech has been

ANNIE BURNELL DYER BEAUCHAMP
*From a photograph in the possession
of Mrs. Mackintosh Bell*

modified to a characteristic semiformality which increases
the distance between her and the other members of her
world. She now speaks more briefly. She has dropped her
childish and facetious mannerisms. No longer does she cry
robustly on Stanley's arrival home, "Hullo, you old
boy!" [41] She merely says, with languid recognition,
"Hullo! Are you home again?" [42] In speech as in action
the pattern is deliberately shaped: detachment, sometimes
infused with subtle irony, pervades all she says.

Moreover, Linda's original quality of secret hate has
been distinctly sharpened. Waking on their first morning
at the new house, she catches sight of her cape and hat
lying across a chair. "Perhaps I'm going away again to-
day," she thinks in "The Aloe," "and for a moment she
saw herself driving away from them all in a little buggy—
driving away from every one of them, and waving." [43]
In "Prelude" the passage reads: "Looking at [the cape
and hat] she wished that she was going away from this
house, too. And she saw herself driving away from them
all in a little buggy, driving away from everybody and
not even waving." [44] Here the fanciful thought of the
first version has been hardened to concrete desire, embittered also by the closing change from light insouciance
to the cold finality of the figure who turns her face from
home and will not once look back.

Through unflagging attention, even in minute details,
Miss Mansfield thus strengthened and integrated Linda's
original endowment of exterior detachment and interior
absorption, shaping the provocative figure of "Prelude."
With Beryl Fairfield, however, she seems to have had
some difficulty in presenting a successfully integrated
character. The outer personality—the pretty, self-
dramatizing young woman who strikes picturesque atti-

tudes and retreats from the banality of the present into romantic dreams—she depicted with swift confidence; but she wished to penetrate farther, to reach Beryl's hidden self—the self that is too often distorted or extinguished by the pressures of common life. Such a self emerges in Linda through her continued introspective musings and her sensitive devotion to her mother; such a self Linda could perceive in Stanley—rarely, it is true, but clearly—so that the reader perceives it too. But with Beryl Miss Mansfield has less satisfactorily achieved this dual presentation. In "The Aloe" she groped a way toward her subject, leading Beryl through the mazes of rather crude self-analysis. One long passage of this kind is nothing more than the author's attempt to clarify her own sense of Beryl's character. In "Prelude" it is entirely omitted; but even at the moment of its writing Miss Mansfield realized that she was searching her own mind for an understanding of Beryl rather than presenting Beryl from the fullness of knowledge, for at this point the manuscript of "The Aloe" is interrupted by the note:

What is it that I'm getting at? It is really Beryl's *Sosie*. The fact that for a long time now, she hasn't been even able to control her second self: it's her second self who now controls her. There was a kind of radiant being who wasn't either spiteful or malicious, of whom she'd had a glimpse—whose very voice was different to hers—who was grave—who never would have dreamed of doing the things that she did. Had she banished this being, or had it really got simply tired and left her? I want to get at all this *through* her, just as I got at Linda *through* Linda. To suddenly merge her into herself.[45]

Miss Mansfield's trouble, I believe, arose not so much because Beryl was complex as because she probably "made up" more of Beryl Fairfield than of any other character in her story. With Beryl, from the first, her conception, if not undefined, was at least uncertain. She knew what she meant Beryl to be, but she must create her from the mind rather than the heart, as she had created the grandmother, the father, and the three children. Linda Burnell, as we have seen, was to undergo marked alteration, but she was reshaped largely through the process of strengthened emphasis upon a few original qualities. With Beryl Miss Mansfield was called upon to graft conscious purpose upon recollection. This fact, to my mind, explains the difficulty with which she was created, and the occasional falseness in certain of her acts in both "Prelude" and "At the Bay."

The remaining figures in "The Aloe" stand essentially unchanged in "Prelude." Even so, there are evidences of the care with which Miss Mansfield scrutinized even relatively trifling detail. Every deviation from consistent character portrayal has been pruned away. In the short story Miss Mansfield could not go into high complexities of character. She was dealing, all in all, with a large group. To bring her people alive she must emphasize a few distinctive qualities in each. By means of the shifting relationships in which she presents her figures she has included a remarkable amount of variation; but the characters themselves, individual as they are, act and react from a constancy of nature which is based upon the bedrock of a few dominating traits.

By natural endowment Miss Mansfield possessed a lively gift for characterizing speech. Even so, in her revision of "The Aloe" she carefully reviewed the dialogue, striving for succinctness and higher dramatic force without loss of flexibility. We have already noted that she removed all traces of the ordinary or the vivacious from

Linda Burnell's speech, to heighten her aura of detached indifference. Equally, with the other figures she sharpened the individual cachet with which the talk of each is stamped, distinctively, though unobtrusively. It is not by eccentricity of speech that the characters are marked but by the quality of the emotion or the thought behind their words. Linda's speech, even when inconsequential, carries an undertone of mockery, as though from the remote world in which she really lived all things of earth appeared in a half-ludicrous light. The grandmother speaks thoughtfully of practical matters, with the leisure and assurance of one beyond life's emotional tide. Beryl, varying with the variation of her moods, effervesces in an overflow of feeling with everything she says. Stanley is earnest, direct, plain, somewhat excitable, more than a little complacent, at times touching in his inarticulateness.

Particularly delightful is the dialogue of the children. Miss Mansfield uses the nursery patois with a very sparing hand; she had no need of phonetic transcription to give the illusion of childish speech. She could so readily enter the sphere of her children's thought that she needed only to set them in action and of their own accord they seem to speak. But again, although the source of her power was innate knowledge, its perfecting was the result of critical scrutiny.

At times the changes made in the revision of "The Aloe" are very small, yet they always add significantly to the designed effect. Early in the story we have come to know that Kezia is a child beset by nightmare bogies. In "The Aloe" when the grandmother puts her to bed, that first night at the new house, Kezia asks, " 'Are you going to leave the candle?' " [46]—a simple question based clearly on self-interest. But in "Prelude" she asks, " 'Aren't you going to leave me a candle?' " [47]—and immediately the words are charged with her fear that she will be left to face the dark alone, with a supplication for protection, while the inserted "me" brings to the open the heart of her concern.

Some pages later another small revision produces comparable intensification. At the beginning of the duck-decapitation scene—perhaps the most memorable scene Miss Mansfield ever wrote—Pat has invited the children to come with him to see "how the kings of Ireland chop the head off a duck." "The Aloe" continues: " 'Do you think we *ought* to?' whispered Isabel to Lottie, 'because we haven't asked Grandma or anybody, have we?' 'But Pat's looking after us,' said Lottie." [48] In "Prelude" the passage appears: " 'Do you think we ought to go?' whispered Isabel. 'We haven't asked or anything. Have we?' " [49] The roles of the two children are now radically changed. In "The Aloe," incredibly, Isabel, the dominating and domineering, asks a question as one in doubt; more incredibly, she asks it of little slow-coach Lottie; and most incredibly, Lottie at once produces a satisfactory reply. In "Prelude" Isabel displays none of this moral debilitation: her question, by becoming a general address, assumes the proportions of the sibylline. She knows they haven't asked permission; she states the plain and patent fact and drives it home with her immitigable "Have we?" She is not now seeking light in darkness. True to nature, she is pointing out the paths of good and evil and asking herself and her companions if they are willing to embrace temptation at the cost of probable pain.

By 1916, when she wrote "The Aloe," Miss Mansfield had not yet obtained her mastery of the concise, luminous expression which characterizes her later work. As she herself came to realize, she inclined naturally toward the copious. "This story seems to lack coherence and sharpness. That's the principal thing: it's not at all sharp," she wrote of an unfinished story of the approximate date of "The Aloe." "It's like eating a bunch of grapes instead of a grape of caviare. . . . I have a pretty bad habit of spreading myself at times—of over-writing and understating. It's just carelessness." [50] The "bunch of grapes" has its place also at the literary feast; but for the short story the "grape of caviare" is functionally more appropriate. What might be called the transformation of the grape in Miss Mansfield's technique is strikingly apparent on even a cursory analysis of the two texts under review.

First among Miss Mansfield's aims in the revision of "The Aloe" was the achievement of an economy that should yet avoid sparseness, the economy of the direct, clean-cut line which, with a play of light and shadow, suggests the rounded, living form. To attain such economy she must control many elements. There must be an integration of parts about a natural center. There must be selection, conscious or inspired, of the precise and vivid word. Too much must not be stated, nor too little; the outline must be at once incisive and restrained.

It is not necessary to carry through an extended analysis of Miss Mansfield's method in operation; a few chosen examples will serve. In the passage in "The Aloe" describing Kezia's late-afternoon journey through the empty house before she is picked up by the storeman,[51] the material is vivid, suggestive, and abundant; but the elements are diffuse. The vantage point of observation shifts constantly. At times the author points out objects to the reader—"Mr. and Mrs. Burnell's room," the little tin bathroom which "did not count" as a real room, the view of the esplanade from the bedroom window, the crude interpolation on Kezia's birth. At other times Kezia herself observes and reports. "Prelude" [52] gathers together all dissociated elements and concentrates them in Kezia. "Mr. and Mrs. Burnell's room" becomes "her father's and her mother's room." The pencil rays of light in the empty drawing room—fairy patterns that would appeal to Kezia's imagination—are stressed rather than the familiar wallpaper foliage. Moreover, the atmosphere of desertion has been highly intensified by the insertion of a few vivid details: the flickering light, the zoom of the bluebottle knocking against the ceiling, the carpet tacks wedged into their tenacious bits of fluff. Farther on in the same passage the Dickensian image of the dusk as a slinking thief has been replaced by the childlike "and the dark came," and again the narrative is centered effectively in Kezia.

In this passage also occurs one of Miss Mansfield's rare additions to the original text—the charming bit about the colored squares of glass in the dining-room window through which Kezia looks and sees "a little Chinese Lottie," concentrating in one stroke the essence of childhood fascination. It serves also a very practical purpose, for Lottie, the wandering and dilatory, must be marshaled into view before reassuming an active role in events.

Not only in the adjustment of tonal expression to character did Miss Mansfield work toward a more harmonious prose. In the beautiful description of daybreak the first morning at the new house the scene as it finally stands [53] is the unveiling of the natural world at early dawn. Each word has been chosen to depict the first silence, the first stir and movement, the sound and appearance of the natural world alone. The sleeping people, the "brooding house," the cocks and cattle of the first version [54] have been banished; for this has now become a picture of day-break in a world untouched and uninhabited by human-kind; and since the scene springs from the primeval, the earlier sophisticated conceit of the birds "hanging the garden with bright chains of song" has been excised. The very mood of early morning has been captured, imbued with a serene, expectant purity.

Throughout the revised version this process of excision, accomplishing one or more purposes, has been sustained, with a resultant high economy of expression. In this process redundancy, banality, and repetition vanish. In the duck-decapitation scene, once more, the swift decisiveness of the act demands a swift decisiveness of tone. The first description,[55] although vivid, is diffuse, giving a far less graphic picture than the later condensed account,[56] in which almost simultaneously Pat seizes the duck, lays it across a stump, and up the blood gushes over the white feathers and his hand. Again economy sharpens the prose in a later passage, when Linda analyzes her conflicting feelings for Stanley Burnell. In the first version [57] the force of Linda's fancy—her gift to her husband of her emotions in separate little packages, reserving hatred for the last—is weakened by meandering statement. Reduced to a concise image in "Prelude," [58] it is both characteristic of Linda and excellent.

To thin down the abundance of her prose without a consequent thinning down of meaning required constant alertness to the precise value of each word Miss Mansfield did include. As we glimpsed in her revision of "An Indiscreet Journey," she was setting herself certain requirements: the word she used must be suited to its subject, it must be vivid but unobtrusive, it must be imaginatively suggestive. In the present revision sometimes one, sometimes another, sometimes all of these requirements motivate her changes. Thus Lottie, the timorous and docile, who in "The Aloe" "set up a howl," in "Prelude" "set up a wail"; the tired children in "Prelude" are "taken off to bed," not "trooped off to bed" as in "The Aloe." Frequently, increased vividness is gained by a substitution in a descriptive word or phrase. In "Prelude" the vine tendrils wreathing the kitchen window form "a thick frill of ruffled green," not, as in the earlier version, "a thick frill of dancing green"—and the picture of the square window with its fluted natural curtain takes on new charm. The bushes in the garden with "flat velvety leaves" become bushes with "flat velvet leaves," and by this minute change the sense impression of softness, smoothness, and richness is remarkably increased. Beryl's eyes, "greeny blue with little gold spots in them," are the more memorable for the change to "greeny blue with little gold points." And how much more sinister is the progress of the headless duck in "Prelude" padding away "without a sound" than the original "dreadfully quiet."

One field through which Miss Mansfield swung her sickle far and wide is that of the abundant adjective. In "The Aloe" she had poured forth a profusion of adjectives. Now the most accurate and most colorful was selected, or at times the qualifying words were altogether dropped. In the description of the dawn already noted a more tender beauty is captured through the change from "In the green sky tiny stars floated for a moment" to "In the sky some tiny stars floated for a moment." With the color of the sky left indeterminate and the scattering of stars made more vague, a sense of vastness and elusiveness is summoned up. Again, the "thick fat stalks" of the cabbage roses is simplified to "fat stalks," the "towering fleshy stem" of the aloe to "fleshy stem," the "broad pink garden seat" to "pink garden seat," Pip's bandage with "a big funny sticking-up knot at the top" to a bandage with "a funny knot sticking up at the top."

These changes (and the enumeration could go on for pages) invariably result in an improvement upon prose that was originally warm, colorful, and lively. Only here and there has an obvious crudity necessitated revision. One such passage unintentionally puts Linda in a ridiculous light. Stanley has just arrived from town with his gifts of a pineapple and a jar of oysters. Together they go into the house, Linda carrying the oysters under one arm and the pineapple under the other. Once inside, Stanley grasps her in his arms and covers her face with kisses.[59] The picture of that passionate embrace, including the oysters and the pineapple, arouses a secret smile. In "Prelude" [60] Linda carries each of her parcels in a hand, so that they may at least droop gracefully against her skirts.

The changes we have been noting improve the narrative largely through a stiffening of the basic fiber of the prose; but Miss Mansfield was equally concerned with the achievement of higher subtlety. Some years later, in a letter to a fellow author, she wrote: ". . . but how are we going to convey these overtones, half tones, quarter tones, these hesitations, doubts, beginnings, if we go at them *directly?*" [61] The direct statement necessarily excludes qualification, and it is very likely to exclude implication as well. In all Miss Mansfield's mature work she utilizes the indirect approach. The truth she strove to express becomes thus in part the responsibility of her readers: they must receive the suggestive vibration her words arouse, expand the thought through their own en-

dowment of intuition, understanding, or experience. In
her early career, in the *German Pension* days, Miss Mansfield's penetration was highly acute; but since at that time
her mind was critical and defensive she was more impressed by the incongruities in persons unlike herself than
by the incongruities innate in all existence. In the earlier
stage she seized upon absurdities of behavior for delineation; in the later she pierced below the surface, to the
poignant, the suspended, the unfulfilled. Emotions so elusive require sensitive but controlled treatment. Successful
handling depends as much upon omission as upon statement; and like most young writers Miss Mansfield had to
school herself to discriminate. A chief fault of the *Pension*
stories is their underlining of the obvious.

In "The Aloe" the implication inherent in dramatic
scene is handled with extraordinary skill; but the underlining of the obvious detail is still present at points. In
"Prelude" this note has been consistently muted, so that
"the sense of mystery, the radiance, the afterglow" Miss
Mansfield sought suffuses the whole narrative. Usually
the revision involves simply the dropping of a line or two,
as at the close of the duck-decapitation scene after Kezia's
tempestuous outburst on her first knowledge of slaughter.
Pat has taken Kezia up in his arms in the attempt to quiet
her sobs. Burrowing into his shoulder, she raises her hands
to his face and discovers that he wears little round gold
earrings. "She was very much surprised. She quite forgot
about the duck. 'Do they come off and on?' she asked
huskily," [62] the scene ends in "The Aloe." In "Prelude" [63]
the intrusive "She quite forgot about the duck" is discarded. It is not necessary to underscore the sudden shift
in Kezia's attention. To a small child the fact that men
wear earrings can be as intense a shock, in its way, as the

first visual experience of blood; and the connection between the two merging discoveries is sufficiently established in that Kezia asks her question "huskily."

Occasionally Miss Mansfield achieves implication by
the conscious blurring of a passage originally concrete.
In "The Aloe" Kezia's "*It*"—that haunting, fear-born
image—is fully described in all its features.[64] In "Prelude" [65] her terror is only very generally defined as a
lurking predatory shape, becoming thus far more expressive, for to each child such terror assumes different and
incommunicable form; and Kezia's awful nameless "IT"
that lies in wait through its very vagueness comprehends
all embodiments.

Miss Mansfield's maturing sense of technique, as we
have seen, was rooted in the principles of clarity, economy, and tonal felicity, of the most suggestive and "dens-
est" dramatic expression; her whole maturing interest in
the exploration of the subtleties of inward experience.
Her craft by now was largely mastered. The prelude, the
time of her apprenticeship, was over. She was ready to
begin.

CHAPTER FOUR

The Soul's Desperate Choice

IN NOVEMBER, 1917, after an attack of rheumatism which confined her within doors, to her furious exasperation, Miss Mansfield made a week-end visit to Lady Ottoline Morrell at Garsington Manor. The night of her arrival was extremely cold. When she reached the house she was numb with a severe chill. Within a few days after her return to Chelsea she developed pleurisy.

Through the winter she remained in her studio at Church Street, much of the time in bed, with her Japanese doll Ribni for an innocent companion. Her doctor's final verdict was that she must seek a milder climate; one of her lungs was weak; she must never spend a winter in England again. Once she was strong enough to travel he would furnish the medical certificate required by the Foreign Office for permission to leave the country. Miss Mansfield was delighted. She hated English winters, with their whistling drafts indoors and thick cold fogs outside; and this was an English winter in time of war, with a coal shortage, the supply of gas prescribed, the constant threat of air raids. Happily she prepared to leave for the sunshine of Bandol. Recovery was only a matter of climate. Bandol lived in her mind as a haven of fair skies and blossoming flowers. She felt "almost terrifically well again," [1] eager for departure. On January 8, 1918, she set out, alone, for France.

The journey from Paris to Bandol was agonizing. Railway service, already disrupted by war conditions, was badly impeded by a heavy snowstorm. Protracted delays, inability to procure food, the swarming crowds of passengers, a rough brawl among a mob of soldiers, turned the trip into a nightmare. Exhausted and seriously ill, Miss Mansfield at last reached Bandol, to find the little Mediterranean town painfully altered in her two years of absence. Familiar establishments had changed hands. Strange faces met her when she registered at the Hôtel Beau Rivage, where she had formerly stayed. The shopkeepers had forgotten her. The very sun seemed alien, for it was still winter in Bandol, bitterly cold, with a moaning wind. The war, too, had laid its blight upon the little seaport. The streets were filled with soldiers and sailors; destroyers and submarines rode at anchor in the beautiful bay. When Miss Mansfield visited again the Villa Pauline and saw, at least there, all untouched, all as it existed in memory, yet all forever lost, her anguish overflowed.

She longed for instant return. She was sick, lonely, desolate, passionately irked by the restrictions preventing her immediate departure: for even if she had been well enough to travel she must remain abroad for the three months specified in her certificate as necessary for her recovery. Time lost its stability; it turned diabolic, hanging on, lengthening out without end.

Toward the end of January, almost in a night, the weather turned to summer. The almond trees burst into bud; the lanes were bordered thick with flowers. The warm sea lay quiescent, shimmering and lovely. Miss Mansfield gained a little strength, though the longing for release ate at her heart constantly. Outwardly her days passed almost without action. She rose late and retired early; after lunch she took a slow walk; she read; she wrote her long daily letters to Murry, reflecting the look of sea and sky, the lift of wave and wind. Now and again she talked with one of her casual acquaintances in Bandol; but her life was empty of companionship except for that of Juliette, the maid at the hotel who devoted herself to Miss Mansfield's care. Juliette had a fresh sincerity and charm that won Miss Mansfield's heart. She was like a sturdy flower, "a double stock—tufty, strong, very sweet, very gay." [2]

Physical exhaustion now kept Miss Mansfield from the writing which remained, through all misery and pain, the dominating purpose of her life. Nevertheless she forced herself to the effort, unsatisfactorily at first. Then, after smiting vainly with her rod, she felt the barren rock gush forth. Inevitably the stream was permeated at its source by the loneliness, frustration, and fear in which her heart was plunged. Her illness, her isolation, above all the dreary prolongation of the war, filled her with despair. She too was at the relentless disposal of the war. The war forced her to remain when she longed to depart. Daily she saw about her the grim stamp of warfare, on the bereaved, on the crippled, on the mutilated. She could not now escape its evil as she had two years before: she could not narrow down the world to her own sheltered existence at the Villa Pauline. After the death of her brother she had transcended personal grief through personal love, drawing into the present, as a haven of tranquillity, the past they had shared together. Now she was dealing with nothing personal. She could draw nothing out of the present but unavailing hate.

After several false starts she had at last begun to write "*Je ne parle pas français*," in a frenzy of excitement. It was, she said, her "cry against corruption." It is as well her cry against abandonment to horror, for the little English heroine of the story is left deserted in Paris, with only her own courage for her support. She herself did not know where her story had come from. She recognized her starting points: a dirty Paris café, the apartment at the Quai aux Fleurs where she had stayed three years before, a "bone" of a character here and there; but in the process of creation she had been possessed. "Prelude" had sprung from a conscious evocation of the past. Not only were all physical details familiar, to the nautical buttons on the little girls' coats, but character in its varying nuances stemmed from a solid grounding in firsthand experience. "*Je ne parle pas français*" broke through from a subterranean source, the projected anxieties of a fearful mind. It is in part a pitiful, in part a sordid story of human helplessness in the face of the destructive elements of life.

With the completion of this story and the fanciful little "Sun and Moon," which Miss Mansfield had dreamed complete in all details, restlessness and exhaustion again set in. In the early part of February Ida Baker, a constant friend since the Queen's College days, had managed to join Miss Mansfield at Bandol on hearing that she was alone and seriously ill. Assured thus of a traveling companion, Miss Mansfield considered means of getting back to England in March. She was tormented by the fear that some new development in the war might prevent her scheduled return. On the morning of February 19 she awoke early and rose to open her windows.

I began to repeat that verse of Shakespeare's: "Lo, here the gentle lark weary of rest" [she wrote in her journal a few hours later], and bounded back into bed. The bound made me cough—I spat—it tasted strange—it was bright red blood. Since then I've gone on spitting each time I cough a little more. . . . How unbearable it would be to die—leave 'scraps,' 'bits' . . . nothing real finished.[3]

To Murry she wrote on the following day:

Since this little attack I've had, a queer thing has happened. I feel that my love and longing for the external world—I mean the world of *nature*—has suddenly increased a million times. When I think of the little flowers that grow in grass, and little streams and places where we can lie and look up at the clouds— Oh, I simply ache for them—for them with you. Take you away and the answer to the sum is O. I feel so awfully like a tiny girl whom someone has locked up in the dark cupboard, even though it's daytime. I don't want to bang at the door or make a noise, but I want you to come with a key you've made yourself and let me out, and then we should tiptoe away together into a kinder place where everybody was more of our heart and size.[4]

It is not by accident that this passage is related to the essential theme of "Bliss"—the immutability of natural beauty in the face of human disaster. That story was completed on February 28, just a week after the letter was written.[5]

In spite of her courageous assurance to Murry of "*absolute faith* and *hope* and *love*," [6] Miss Mansfield lived in panic. Rumors of a great German offensive tortured her with fear. The Channel might be closed, locking her up in France with no possible communication with England. She might never return; she might die. Her nervous anxiety mounted to fever pitch. It was better to risk her health than endure the agony of doubt. Moreover, Miss Baker had been summoned back to England, and she would be left in Bandol alone. Armed with a certificate, which she wheedled from her doctor, stating that her physical condition made her return to England imperative, with Miss Baker she set out on the homeward journey on March 21. Her nerves were strung taut; she was sick with a high fever. With difficulty she reached Paris. On March 23, the day after her arrival there, the long-range bombardment of the city began. All civilian traffic across the Channel was suspended. Postal and telephone communication was broken off. Regulations against strangers in Paris closed down remorselessly. Miss Mansfield was forced to present herself daily to the police, to receive permission to remain; she must negotiate with the Military Permit Office, to receive permission to leave as soon as Channel transportation was reopened. Only after three weeks of delay, on April 11, did she reach home, worn and frail, with the shadow of terror darkening her eyes.

For a few weeks following her return Miss Mansfield lived with Murry in his rooms at 47 Redcliffe Road. She was pleased with her surroundings—the quaint people and odd doorways of the street, the stone figure in one of the gardens carrying a stone tray on his head; but she could not long remain in Murry's two badly lighted rooms. She must migrate again, to seek sunshine and fresh air, while Murry tried to find a suitable house.

On April 29 the divorce proceedings which had gone

into suspension six years before were brought to a successful end, under the direction of the London representative of the Bank of New Zealand, who had served as an agent in Miss Mansfield's affairs since her arrival from Wellington. On the third of May Miss Mansfield and Murry were married, at the Kensington Register Office. J. D. Fergusson the artist, an associate from the *Rhythm* days, and Dorothy Brett acted as witnesses. Within two weeks the Murrys were separated again, for on May 17 Miss Mansfield left for Looe, in Cornwall, to join her friend Anne Rice. Murry, during her absence, was to arrange for their occupancy of a tall grey-brick house in Hampstead (which, for its color and size, they dubbed "the Elephant"), auspiciously, or ironically, overlooking the Vale of Health.

Looe at first seemed perfect—warm and peaceful, drenched with golden sunlight. The hotel, though expensive, was clean, airy, and well staffed. Mrs. Honey, Miss Mansfield's aged Cornish serving-woman, like Grandmother Dyer, knew the secret of unobtrusive, soothing care. Miss Rice came in and out with a gift of flowers or a picture, radiating health and life. In spite of a severe attack of pleurisy on her arrival, Miss Mansfield was sure that she would gain strength quickly in the fresh strong sea-filled air. Yet only three days after she had reached Looe she was writing to her husband: "But you know, *I shall always be homesick*." [7] Her life was falling into a familiar pattern: feverish dependence on Murry's letters, longing for return, overwhelming depression that strained each nerve so that the sound of a pin scratch was torture. Again the world turned hideous.

But the ugliness—the ugliness of life—the intolerable corruption of it all— How is it to be borne [she wrote to Lady

Ottoline Morrell on May 24]? To-day for the first time since I arrived, I went for a walk. Anne Rice has been telling me of the beauty of the Spring—all the hedges one great flower —of the beauty of these little "solid" white houses set in their blazing gardens—and the lovely hale old fishermen. But— the sea stank—great grey crabs scuttled over the rocks— all the little private paths and nooks had been fouled by human cattle—there were rags of newspaper in the hedges . . .[8]

In pain and loathing, she wrote Murry, one must set "an iron shutter over one's heart." [9]

This familiar pattern, this tense coiling of every fiber to the extremity of endurance, sprang from illness, and a deep-rooted sense of frustration. Life was her enemy, Miss Mansfield was coming to believe. She was to be disposed of according to its dictates, packed off to regions of fresh air and light, for the sustenance of her unwilling body; torn up, shipped here and there like an unwanted piece of baggage. Her personal will was set aside. Katherine Mansfield did not bend before domination. She braced herself against the coercive force; she fought back with every particle of her strength; or, exhausted, she lay prone in defeat.

With the warm sun, the sea air, and the wholesome food of Cornwall Miss Mansfield grew stronger. By the beginning of June she was able to venture out a bit. One summer's day she spent with Miss Rice exploring Polperro, four miles from Looe, where she was charmed by the little houses—"houses that might have been built *by* seagulls *for* seagulls." [10] Everywhere the foxgloves blossomed, bringing to memory the Lawrences, rejoicing in the great bunches set about their cottage rooms. But these tranquil hours were only rifts in the dark clouds through which the light shone briefly. As spring slipped into summer the hotel filled with people—aged and gluttonous they all seemed to Miss Mansfield, so that she could scarcely endure a meal among them. Loneliness, homesickness, and despair at the passing of time—unfulfilled time—enveloped her.

Once she had recovered a little she turned, as always, to her writing. Very little work of this Cornwall stay has been preserved. Part Miss Mansfield herself destroyed. Part, to her great sorrow, was lost—a detailed notebook of her observations, perhaps in the manner of Dorothy Wordsworth's *Journal*, which she was reading at this time with great sympathy. Only a few fragmentary pieces and the sketch "Carnation," [11] depicting a French hour at Queen's College, remain.

To her intense relief, late in June Murry joined her for a short holiday; and at the end of the month they returned together to London, to pass a few weeks at Redcliffe Road until their house, the Elephant, at East Heath Road, Hampstead, was ready. Just before they moved Miss Mansfield received word of her mother's death. She recognized now the full courage of her mother's spirit, for she too had entered the world her mother had inhabited in life.

For a year—the only year in her life—Miss Mansfield lived in her own home, with her own possessions about her: books, flowers, a porcelain shepherdess clock, a cat and kittens. The management of the household was given over to Miss Baker, who was dependable, if at times a trial. Katherine Mansfield could not bear intrusion upon privacy. She gave her secrets freely or she gave them not at all. The very intensity of Miss Baker's absorption in her life oppressed her. She must be understood intuitively, not through interrogation. With Murry's young brother Richard, fourteen years her junior, she formed a warm friendship at this time. A charming relationship developed between the two, to be sustained later by correspondence, in which Miss Mansfield's generous and tactful encouragement of the younger Murry's confidence reveals one of the most sensitive expressions of her sensitive mind.

At moments during this year Miss Mansfield was happy. But the figure of disease stalked like a specter through the rooms, poisoning the atmosphere. In October she had been told she must enter a sanatorium immediately. She refused to accept life on those terms. She would die in the confinement of a hospital. She chose to maintain the semblance of a normal life, believing that in her work and in the measure of peace her own home afforded she would find salvation for her spirit at least.

Through almost the entire autumn and early winter of 1918 Miss Mansfield did not leave the house; she was scarcely able to walk up and down stairs. Recurrently, for weeks at a time, she was forced to stay in bed, where she did her best to look as though she were there for "pleasure and not for necessity," [12] as she wrote to Virginia Woolf. But although she could not go out she kept in touch with her friends by letter; and toward the end of October the Lawrences came to London from their cottage in Derbyshire. Mrs. Lawrence was ill, but Lawrence called frequently at the Hampstead house during their brief stay.

Miss Mansfield never saw Lawrence after that winter; but a bright spirit of friendship had been rekindled between them which was fostered through correspondence for the next few months. That the two artists shared a vision of life identical at certain points though unalterably divergent at others is clear in all Miss Mansfield's references to Lawrence. She could share with him his love of the world of nature—flowers and nuts and bird tracks in the snow—his eagerness for living, if not his understanding of life. The war, with its burden of death, had opened forever in Miss Mansfield's mind a chamber of knowledge further lighted by the sense of her own precarious mortality. Like Lawrence she now judged society as trivial, hollow, mercenary, smug, and selfish. With only one life to be lived, and that so much the sport of circumstance, one must live it to the fullest, in truth and simplicity among mankind. Yet blindly people dissipated their allotted days. They deceived; they boasted; they lived coarsely and ignominiously. Even the celebrations of the peace which had at last come Miss Mansfield found despicable—cheap carousing and drunken brawls in a land drained of its youth. "I keep seeing all these horrors, bathing in them again and again (God knows I don't want to) and then my mind fills with the wretched little picture I have of my brother's grave," [13] she wrote to Lady Ottoline Morrell. For Lawrence, too, the world was eaten through with maggots. But for him the cure lay in annihilation and rebirth. Man must be re-created, to strength and wisdom and power, through release from the strangle hold of the intellect, through return to his destined fulfillment in his own body and blood. Miss Mansfield could not accept Lawrence's view, nor could she yet produce one more satisfying to herself. She could only look outward and condemn, look inward and weep.

At the beginning of April, 1919, when Murry was appointed editor of the *Athenaeum* a receptive medium for Miss Mansfield's work was again available. Very slowly, almost imperceptibly, she had been edging forward to a position as an established writer. One or two of the *New Age* stories of 1917 had been notably distinctive. "Bliss," her first story to appear in an impressive journal, had been published by the *English Review* in August, 1918. During that summer also "Prelude" had been issued by the Hogarth Press as a little blue-covered quarto; [14] and although it attracted very little notice in the general literary world, a small group of readers recognized its worth.

The *Athenaeum* at first did not publish fiction, but it offered other scope for Miss Mansfield's activity. From April to August, 1919, under the pseudonym Elizabeth Stanley (Mary Elizabeth Stanley was her father's mother's name), she contributed a group of poems which includes some of her best writing in verse.[15] Assisting her friend Koteliansky, she appeared as cotranslater of the brief *Diary of Anton Tchehov* and *The Letters of Anton Tchehov*,[16] a considerable body of material which ran in the *Athenaeum* through several months.[17] Also, beginning with the first number under Murry's editorship she regularly contributed reviews of current fiction, a work which she carried on, whether at home or abroad, for a period of almost two years.[18]

Her responsibilities as a reviewer Miss Mansfield took very seriously. She was a careful, a conscientious, and at first an eager critic, aroused by the literature of her time to the spirit of crusade. Looking over these reviews—more than a hundred and fifty in all—it seems now a great pity that a gifted writer must have devoted her thought and energy to what is, in the main, an assortment of ephemera. Among the authors a few names have survived as famous—Conrad, Galsworthy, Edith Wharton, Virginia Woolf; more obscurely, another handful exists as representative of the period; but of the entire number of titles, at least three quarters sleep eternally as a dead literature.

Miss Mansfield gained little intellectual or artistic profit from this arduous exercise. She acquired a more thorough knowledge of the mediocrity of current literary taste than she would have had without it—a knowledge which enraged her. As a writer, we have seen earlier, she had already struck out on her own course. All that she might have gained from the *Athenaeum* reviewing was a supplementary confirmation of her disgust with the modern world.

As a literary critic Miss Mansfield was completely subjective. From literature she demanded a correspondence with the vision of life she had conceived under the lessons of her own experience; and because in the Russian masters, particularly in Chekhov, she found a vision similar to her own, she used their works almost without exception as a touchstone of literary failure or success. Only rarely does she make reference to a great English writer. She goes first, and always, directly to her view of life as a standard, next to Chekhov, Dostoevski, Tolstoi.

Upon all that she wrote Katherine Mansfield has left the unique imprint of her personality. Although in these reviews she held herself to her critical function with a fairly steady hand, she could not altogether suppress the stronger impulses of the creative writer. Irrepressibly, her lively imagination, her sense of dramatic scene, her talent for sharp dialogue, her characteristic humor, break through the imposed limits to brief expression in their own right. Certain of her mannerisms, on recurrence, become tiresome, to be sure. She is likely to indulge in a coy playfulness, and she often lapses into the brittle overwitty expression that marks her early work. But more often than not her little essays are interesting and thoughtful; and in their revelation of individual temper they form a minor companion piece to the full portrait drawn in the journals and the *Letters*.

Through the summer of 1919 Miss Mansfield was thus actively occupied. She had her work, the concerns of her home, occasional visits to the outer world when her strength permitted. Days at a time she spent in confinement, receiving now and again a call from a friend. Against the autumn colors of her room, dusky purple and gold, she seemed not wholly real, very white, very thin, with the rings slipping up and down her fingers as she moved her hands.[19]

In this room she lived the life apart which always formed the inner core of her experience, summoning for her company her dead mother and brother; recalling house and gate, lawn and garden, of her childhood home. "Not a soul knows where she is," she wrote of herself in her journal. "She goes slowly, thinking it all over, wondering how she can express it *as she wants to*—asking for time and for peace." [20]

She was not destined for peace. With the heavy rains of summer her racking cough grew worse. Fortunately she was under the care of a sympathetic and wise physician, Dr. Victor Sorapure. Dr. Sorapure, cool, detached, yet kindly, understood his patient well. He realized that the restrictions of a hospital would be as fatal to her spirit as a London winter would be to her body. She must be free to write, to maintain privacy, or the fire of her own misery would consume her health. As the most satisfactory course he advised a stay at the Italian Riviera. Another London winter would be ruinous.

By now Miss Mansfield was ready for a change. Already the routine of the household, with its minor problems and inevitable domestic conflicts, had begun to weary her. Murry's nervous absorption in his work—"throwing himself bodily into the milk-jug after the drowning fly" [21]—the gossip and pompous discussions of his literary circle, proved an increasing strain. She was sleeping badly; her old evil days of depression fell upon her. "Somewhere else," she still believed, she might find tranquillity.

Before her departure Miss Mansfield again saw her father, who came to England in the middle of August with his youngest daughter Jeanne. She now had two sisters in London, for Charlotte, who had been widowed in India in 1916, was living there, and Jeanne remained also. In September, a month after her father's arrival, she left for San Remo, Italy, accompanied by her husband. Soon they found a pleasant furnished cottage, the Casetta Deerholm, at Ospedaletti, some three miles away. Here she was established to her satisfaction, with Miss Baker as companion. At the end of September Murry returned to his work in London and Miss Mansfield took up hers in Italy.

At first—again it must be written!—she was happy. The casetta, on a hillside covered with olive and fig trees, delighted her. Below the great sea thundered; behind rose the towering mountain heights. As "a place to get well in" [22] Ospedaletti, in spite of its plague of insects, seemed ideal. Under the hot sun Miss Mansfield began to grow stronger; the fresh and vigorous landscape, charged with the spirit of the ancient past, soothed and relieved her heart.

Her happiness did not continue long. Even in Ospeda-letti some conduct of affairs was inescapable. At the first rough touch—a gardener's dishonesty—the film over the old open wound was rent. The voice raised its familiar cry of anguish: the world was malignant, brutal, ugly; always one found "this snail on the underside of the leaf." [23] She longed for health, her own home, sympathetic companionship, counting over the six long months to be crossed before she could return. Actually she was turn-ing sick of soul with loneliness. "There is a little boat, far out, moving along, *inevitable* it looks and *dead silent*—a little black spot, like the spot on a lung," [24] she wrote morbidly to Murry.

As October waned the days turned cold and stormy; a bitter wind swept against shore and sea. When Miss Mansfield's father visited her, during his continental travels, he urged her to remove to the sheltered warmth of Mentone, across the French border, on the Bay of Garavan. His presence, with two companions, a Beau-champ cousin and her friend Miss Fullerton, brought a stir of unaccustomed life to the casetta. For a few hours Miss Mansfield was revived, under the illusion of protec-tion and love. "And here on the table are five daisies and an orchid that F[ather] picked for me and tied with a bit of grass and handed me," she wrote after her guests had gone. "If I had much to forgive him, I would forgive him much for this little bunch of flowers." [25]

For a time Miss Mansfield continued at the casetta, first because of her unwillingness to enter a new and larger social sphere, later because an attack of fever prevented any change. Isolation drove her to incessant brooding; the constant beat of the sea against the shore lacerated her nerves. She reconsidered the past, in despair at its repeated frustrations; she looked ahead to the future, and turned her face to the wall. Grief at the long separation from Murry turned to anguish at what seemed desertion, and she reflected bitterly on her new husband, death.[26]

During the first weeks of January, following a short visit from Murry over the holidays, she was prostrated by this engulfing despair. Daily she made brief note of her surrender.

January 8. BLACK. A day spent in Hell. Unable to do anything. Took brandy. Determined not to weep—wept. Sense of isolation frightful. I shall die if I don't escape. Nauseated, faint, cold with misery. Oh, I *must* survive it somehow.[27]

Even so, she prepared and sent off her reviews; still she continued to work. On January 11 she wrote "The Man Without a Temperament," continuing through the day, from early morning until midnight, without interruption.[28] This story, like many of Miss Mansfield's, stemmed directly from intimate experience. It acknowledges the homesickness, enforced passivity, and boredom of the man who chooses to stay abroad with his invalid wife. But "the man without a temperament" is selfless and devoted. He does stay.

Depression, together with intense mental activity, had brought Miss Mansfield to a pitch of constant excitement, with her mind raging in semi-hallucinations. Such an existence, beaten through with the monotonous booming of the sea, was insupportable. On January 21, through the arrangement of her cousin Miss Beauchamp and Miss Fullerton, she left Ospedaletti for the Hermitage, a nursing home at Mentone.

The Hermitage, she soon found, was intolerably noisy. Sleeplessness returned, with "*old Casetta* feelings, like madness. Voices and words and half-visions." [29] At the invitation of her cousin and her friend, who quickly realized the unsuitability of the place, in the middle of February she removed to the villa they had taken for the season at Mentone. Just before she left she heard from her husband that he had concluded arrangements with Constable for the publication of a volume of her stories; and at almost the same time she received her copy of *"Je ne parle pas français,"* which Murry and his brother Richard had themselves printed and bound. Like "Prelude" the little book received scant notice in the press; but at least one critic, J. W. N. Sullivan, proclaimed its unusual qualities in a long review. [30]

Under the generous care of her friends Miss Mansfield's health showed great improvement. At the Villa Flora, with its gardens and atmosphere of ordered peace, she slipped gladly into the warmth of sheltered living. Her fevered vision of the world subsided; the ordinary diversions of life assumed a quiet place in her days—drives in the big car that softly climbed the mountains, along roads through blossoming fruit orchards and fields of flowers; shopping expeditions to Mentone; a visit to Monte Carlo, where the glitter and decadent brilliance of the city horrified yet fascinated her mind. But by the end of March, grateful though she was for the attention of her friends, she began to grow restless, to dream, as she always dreamed with distance, of a stable and protected home life of her own, apart from the "worldly world," with content and leisure as a basis for her work.

In her days of misery at Ospedaletti Miss Mansfield had thought with longing of her Hampstead house, her

room with its books, its brass scuttle, its exquisite shepherdess clock. Now, on her return to England at the end
of April, for a while she resumed with relief a semi-normal
life. Occasionally she attended the theater; when her
health allowed she and her husband entertained at home.
To her pleasure her friends Violet and Sidney Schiff,
whom she had met in Mentone in April, were in London
during this summer. Sidney Schiff (Stephen Hudson) was
the champion of Joyce, the friend of Proust. Half unwill-
ingly, she was being caught up in the larger world again.

Throughout this period, in spite of a decline in health
and the emotional conflict with Murry which soon developed, Miss Mansfield continued her *Athenaeum* work.
In addition to her reviews she had begun to contribute a
story each month when the magazine started to publish
fiction at the beginning of June. "Revelations" and "The
Escape," both uncharitable studies of neurotic women,
appeared, as her first offerings, on June 11 and July 9.
The women of these stories are exposed as rapacious,
selfish creatures, of highly irritable nervous sensibility.
One cannot help thinking that out of her own specialized
knowledge of exacerbation Miss Mansfield, in part, was
here turning her knife against herself.

At times Miss Mansfield faced openly the fact that her
marriage was a basic element in her unhappiness. During
the long separations from her husband she thought of him
with yearning as the one person whose sensitivity and love
could satisfy her need for complete sympathy. But her
deeper sense of betrayal ran like a submerged current that
now and again broke its way above ground. Her illness,
she had noted, the winter before, had turned her "into a
woman," dependent upon a stronger being, whereas earlier
she had always been the one to give strength; and Murry

was unable or unwilling to assume the burden. He had established a life of his own, apart from hers, reserving a niche for the consecrated image of his wife. Miss Mansfield also, when they were apart, clung to her image of the figure she required him to be. On actual confrontation, inevitably the images cracked, and both were miserable.

September came, and with it, again, departure. Miss Mansfield had engaged a house for the winter near the large villa Miss Beauchamp and Miss Fullerton had taken for the season at Mentone. Early in September she left London with Miss Baker, who had been living at the Hampstead house during the summer as mistress-in-charge. By the fourteenth of the month she was happily settled in her new quarters, the Villa Isola Bella, a charming, pale-yellow house with a big mimosa tree in the yard and a beautiful view of the Bay of Garavan. All the rooms were well equipped; order, cleanliness, and harmony presided. Marie, "the kind of cook Anatole France might have," [31] fed Miss Mansfield not in body only: her instinctive, varied, and intense response to life was a constant revelation and delight. Outdoors flowers bloomed in profusion. The air was sweet and sharp. Miss Mansfield grew to love Mentone as she loved only New Zealand.

Before long the hot sun and radiant weather, and more, a deep sense of peace, wrought an improvement in Miss Mansfield's health. Her cough subsided; she felt eager and active, within her circumscribed limits, for life and work. Nothing confirms strength like accomplishment. The knowledge that she was at last coming into recognition as a writer after years of striving of itself must have given her new energy. "Pictures" had been published by *Art and Letters* in the issue of Autumn, 1919, and "The Man Without a Temperament" in that of Spring, 1920. Now, with her stories appearing regularly in the *Athenaeum*,[32] along with those of Max Beerbohm, H. M. Tomlinson, and Virginia Woolf, with her reviews assured an honored place, with her new volume of stories in the hands of her publishers, she was done with struggle and could turn her full powers to the work of creation. This release bore as its fruit an abundance of stories through the following two years. The real body of Miss Mansfield's work, indeed, was written during that space of time. Not only was the path before her now clear for progression; she knew that at any bend the path might terminate. A feverish anxiety underlies the constant application of her last few years.

In December, 1920, just nine years after the publication of *In a German Pension*, *Bliss* was brought out by Constable. It attracted serious attention, for the most part favorable, both in England and later in America, where it was published by Knopf. Reviews acclaimed Miss Mansfield's fine, "infinitely inquisitive sensibility," [33] the "shimmering" world she had created, her high control of form. But Miss Mansfield herself was not satisfied. With one or two exceptions her stories seemed to her trifling or insincere. They represented the winnowing of her writings through nearly a decade; but that decade had been one of spiritual as well as artistic development, and she sought now the embodiment of a deeper sense of life.

From the time of her arrival at Mentone she had been writing steadily. Between October and the beginning of the new year she had completed six stories,[34] among them one of the most poignant in the New Zealand group, "The Stranger," and the long and intricately constructed "Daughters of the Late Colonel." She was dedicated now to the expression of the truth as she had come to realize it through her own experience. For over a year she had been engaged in self-examination, in the effort to formulate her adult belief. By slow and difficult steps she had come to the creed of acceptance, acceptance of her personal life with its personal suffering. Deliberately she excluded the general world as evil; for self-preservation it must be shunned. She must live secluded from the hypocrisy and self-interest she perceived as the dominating expressions of modern man, free to transmit her findings as an artist, her sense of the irreducible value at the core of even painful experience. For herself, she had adopted a single faith on which to found both her life and her work: "to be *good, sincere, simple, honest*." [35] She had reached "after 32 years in the dark" [36] a clarity of vision that brought new and more penetrating affirmation of existence:

And then suffering, bodily suffering such as I've known for three years [she wrote in October, 1920]. It has changed for ever everything—even the *appearance* of the world is not the same—there is something added. *Everything has its shadow.* Is it right to resist such suffering? Do you know I feel it has been an immense privilege. . . . It has taken me three years to understand this—to come to see this. We resist, we are terribly frightened. The little boat enters the dark fearful gulf and our only cry is to escape—"put me on land again." But it's useless. Nobody listens. The shadowy figure rows on. One ought to sit still and uncover one's eyes.[37]

In her constant though largely desultory reading over many years Miss Mansfield returned always to three magnetizing points: Shakespeare, the Romantic poets, and the great Russian novelists. Very probably from her devotion to Shakespeare and the Romantic poets her own expression increased in vividness, range, and flexibility.

Always she noted with delight the rich implication of specific words and images. But primarily her response was emotional, even when she set herself to an analysis of Shakespeare's characters. In Wordsworth, Shelley, and Keats she found much to corroborate her own instinctive attitudes. To Keats particularly, after the inception of her own illness, as to Chekhov, she was very strongly drawn. By temperament she was in a sense his feminine counterpart; now her identification with his struggle to reconcile the knowledge of what life was with the vision of what it might be grew even more highly personal.

From the Romantic poets Miss Mansfield absorbed confirmation of her own rebellion at the dualism in existence, of the transcendent mystery and wonder coenduring with mortal ugliness and pain. The Russian writers made their appeal chiefly to her ethical sense, which in her, as perhaps in everyone, was likewise fundamentally emotional. Dostoevski, Tolstoi, Chekhov she read with greatest sympathy. Her own developing convictions, I believe, were intensified by these confluent forces: the recoil from the general world, the concentration on individual fulfillment, by the Romantic poets; the dispassionate acceptance of suffering by Chekhov; the recognition of the Christian principles of humility and self-abnegation by Dostoevski and Tolstoi.

Miss Mansfield was not a Christian believer; she could not find salvation in orthodox religious faith. She was charged with a sense of devotion; she worshiped nature, she worshiped beauty, she worshiped life, she worshiped art. But she could not worship a personal God, not so much through deliberate rejection as through negative disbelief. To her, as to many of her generation, the general immersion in scientific findings had washed away the concept of a divine creator. In addition, her own experience had each year written upon her mind a denial of a governing deity. If in an hour of ecstasy she felt the human need to express gratitude, she must question: "But to whom? To the Lord who gave me consumption?" [38] Unlike Kafka, to her it seemed purposeless to probe the mystery of a being so cruel, so capricious and destructive. In her efforts to achieve some harmony between the demands of the inner and the outer worlds, she was driven, therefore, entirely upon herself.

I believe the only way to *live* as artists under these new conditions in art and life is to put everything to the test for ourselves [she wrote in February, 1921]. We've got, in the long run, to be our own teachers. . . . Well, as I see it, the only way to do that honestly, dead truthfully, shirking nothing and leaving nothing out, is to put everything to the test; not only to face things, but really to find out of what they are composed. . . . To be *thorough*—to be *honest*.[39]

But though intellectually Miss Mansfield realized her need of a faith by which to live and spiritually she set herself the faith of acceptance, emotionally she responded too acutely to immediate experience for unwavering devotion to her creed. Her wisdom came through flashes of intuition, not as the slow garnering of sustained thought. She rose and sank, and rose and sank again, even as she was engaged in severe analysis of the traces of "sediment" she detected in herself.

Don't I live *in glimpses* only [she wrote a few months later]? There is something wrong, there is something small in such a life. One must live more fully and one must have more *power* of loving and feeling. One must be true to one's vision of life—in every single particular—and I am not. The only thing to do is to try again from to-night to be stronger and better—to be *whole*.[40]

Katherine Mansfield was not, as she has been described, "among the saintliest of women." [41] She was very human. She possessed courage, tenacity of purpose, resiliency, gaiety, and humor; but she had also a capricious temper, a fastidious intolerance, a latent fury which did not always sleep, a sharp—at times corrosive—wit. And within the complex of the woman beat the ardent spirit of a child. It was the child in her which delighted in a special "little language"—"eggwegs," "bregglechik," "bigglechiks," "basticks," "cream*b*." It was the child which, even as she strove to reach a mature philosophy, took increasing pleasure in a familiar retreat, to the world of fantasy she had always loved to inhabit. It was a retreat half serious, half playful, to a child's kingdom, where the little denizens of the animal world—insects, birds, beasts—take on human qualities. The hero of this domain was first the Japanese doll Ribni, into whom Miss Mansfield projected an eccentric, audacious, and amusing personality, later the kitten Wingley, of a more versatile and artistic temperament. And woven through these whimsical imaginings was always a fixed pattern of longing dreams, of a life of freedom, joy, and self-fulfillment.

Yet from this very quality of childlikeness sprang also her capacity for unquenchable delight, most particularly delight in the world of nature. Like Dorothy Wordsworth, she saw the marvelous wherever her eye could reach, from the rising mountain heads to the delicate wild-strawberry leaf threading through the moss. Dorothy Wordsworth was the calmer of spirit, walking the pathways of Alfoxden and Grasmere dedicated and rapt. She partook of nature as her daily food; it sustained her, she could not live on any other fare. Miss Mansfield's response was more excitable. She could never witness the miracle of the world's beauty with a tranquil heart. Even in the early London days her stubborn will was always softened once she moved in the natural world again. Here also one detects the ichor of disease coursing in her veins, to quicken as it destroyed. Her ardor is at times as much delirium as ecstasy. To her, as to Keats, the world was magnified in loveliness once it became a world from which she might on any day depart.

With equal childlike fervor she responded to the natural good she discovered in mankind, though her discoveries came less often as the years passed, and almost always among the working people with whom she was associated in her retired life. In them was virtue, as in Wordsworth's humble folk—vigor, truth, simplicity, a close communion with life: Juliette, the lovable little maid at the Hôtel Beau Rivage, in Bandol; Mrs. Honey of Looe, with her gentle manner and soft Cornish voice; Marie, by far the richest of nature, at the Villa Isola Bella, a Frenchwoman to the bone, articulate, observant, imaginative, a genuine artist in her practical realm.

It was this childlike quality in Katherine Mansfield which gave her nature its enchanting spontaneity, its freshness of perception, its ineradicable hopefulness; but it was this quality also which lay at the source of her great spiritual disquietude. The child persisted—neither to be vanquished nor ignored—fearful yet trusting, eager to love, stricken by rebuff, unequal to the burden of adult suffering. Beyond any question she was profoundly sincere in her embrace of total acceptance as a faith by which to live; but the act was one of imposed will—the soul's desperate choice, to use her own words—which she found well-nigh insupportable.

In February, 1921, when the *Athenaeum* was merged with the *Nation* under Massingham's editorship, Murry joined Miss Mansfield at Mentone. Here they remained together until the end of April. From the start of the new year Miss Mansfield had been extremely ill, confined to her bed for almost two months. She lay watching the peach tree outside her window rouse from its long sleep to break into leaf and flower. "In spite of everything," she wrote to Lady Ottoline Morrell, "one cannot but praise Life." [42] By late April she was able to rise for a few hours each day; but her cough had grown worse, and she was spitting blood again. The wandering journey of the consumptive in search of health—made by Keats, by Chekhov, by Lawrence—must be resumed. At the beginning of May, with the faithful Miss Baker, she left for Baugy, Switzerland, while Murry returned to England to give a course of lectures at Oxford. The door closed on the Villa Isola Bella.

For a few weeks, until the end of May, Miss Mansfield lived at the hotel at Baugy, on the Lake of Geneva, surrounded by the massive Alpine heights, clothed with pines and firs, which rose to mingle with sky. The countryside she found delightful, with its little herdboys among their springing goats, its ancient miniature castles and tidy compact towns, scarcely changed, it seemed, from the Middle Ages; but Montreux and Clarens which lay spread beneath her balcony window were offensive—ugly, solid, hideously respectable, like the people who inhabited them.

Day after day she lay in her chaise longue, reading Chaucer, Marlowe, her beloved Shakespeare. After the concentrated exertion of the fall and winter before, she was creatively as well as physically exhausted. Only one story, "Life of Ma Parker," which appeared in the *Nation* on February 26, had been completed since January. As a totality, however, in a period of a year she had accomplished a remarkable amount of work. Also, the extent of her recognition as a writer was increasing steadily. Now the *London Mercury* had become interested in her stories, publishing "The Stranger" in January and "The Daughters of the Late Colonel" in May.

Doctors must be sought out—she had taken a bad chill and was scarcely able to move; the familiar examination must be undergone again. In mid-May, after a few exasperating interviews with the local physicians, who advised her to rest and think of pleasant things, she motored to Montana to see the leading Swiss specialist in tuberculosis. She still had a chance of recovery, she was told; beyond that he would not commit himself.

At the beginning of June, when her husband rejoined her, Miss Mansfield left Baugy for a temporary stay at Sierre, a little town of orchards and vineyards famed for its extremely dry climate. Here they remained for about three weeks until they found a chateau, set in the midst of an unbroken pine forest, in Montana, some two thousand feet above Sierre. The Châlet des Sapins was isolated from humankind, looking across a valley toward the silvery mountain peaks opposite. Except for Miss Mansfield's cousin "Elizabeth," the Countess Russell, who lived a short distance away, they saw almost no one. For nearly a year they lived here very quietly, above and apart from the world, in harmony now that Murry had at last acceded to his wife's necessities.

The seclusion of this life was in many ways regenerating. By cutting off civilization the irritations and demands of civilized society were removed. Through the confinement imposed by her illness Miss Mansfield had come into a little citadel of peace, relieved of loneliness by the presence of her husband. Together they established a simple, orderly life, cared for by the buxom maidservant Ernestine, both with work to do, with the forests to explore when Miss Mansfield's strength allowed; finding satisfaction in the little homely tasks of jam-making and mending; reading Shakespeare together once again, Jane Austen, Hardy; talking, playing chess or cribbage, discussing fireplace and rooms in the house they planned to build in Montana "in two or three years' time." [43] When Miss Baker on a return trip from England brought back the kitten Wingley Miss Mansfield's satisfaction was complete.

Time flowed swiftly, as the seasons rounded. The starry summer flowers gave way to brilliant mountain ash; pears and apples filled the autumn trees; nights grew colder; then the first soft scattering of snow brought the winter in.

But in spite of ease from strain, and deep assuagement at living close to nature, Miss Mansfield was not essentially at peace. Freed from loneliness and worry, set, as it were, for her own judgment against the judgment of the mountain summits, she turned to rigorous self-scrutiny, castigating in herself the sin of pride, the old sire of the others—pride in her accomplishment, pride in her own sensitivity. She must cleanse herself to purity in order to transmit the truth, she believed. "I must try and write simply, fully, freely, from my heart," she resolved in November. ". . . And especially to keep in touch with Life—with the sky and this moon, these stars, these cold, candid peaks." [44]

Though through the summer she had suffered frequent illness, apart from her chronic condition, she had come again into a period of abundant productivity. By the end of October fully half the stories included in *The Garden Party* were written. A number of these form part of a series she had agreed to supply the *Sphere*, which came out at intervals from August through December,[45] to her amused dismay with illustrations. But with these stories, once they were finished, she was sharply dissatisfied. Most of them, indeed, do not rank among her finest work. Some are very slight; some merely skim the surface. They do not draw upon the deepest insight she could command. "It's a kind of playing," she herself acknowledged. "I want to put *all* my force behind it, but somehow, I *cannot!*" [46] Very possibly the sense of pressure, the necessity of writing to a fixed order, resulted in this diminution of force. For when she turned again to New Zealand for her deeper satisfaction, she wrote, during this same period, some of her most memorable work: "The Garden Party," [47] the poignant "Doll's House," [48] the long and limpid "At the Bay." [49] To Dorothy Brett after finishing this last story she wrote:

It is as good as I can do, and all my heart and soul is in it . . . every single bit. . . . It is so strange to bring the dead to life again. There's my Grandmother, back in her chair with her pink knitting, there stalks my uncle over the grass; I feel as I write, "You are not dead, my darlings. All is remembered. I bow down to you. I efface myself so that you may live again

through me in your richness and beauty." And one feels
possessed.[50]

At the same time she wrote to Violet Schiff: "I think I
really judge a place by how vividly I can recall the past.
One lives in the Past—or I do. And here it is living." [51]

"One must have a miracle," [52] Miss Mansfield wrote in
December, 1921, echoing Dostoevski. In spite of the battle
fought and won repeatedly—the acceptance of physical
pain as the condition of her life—she still longed for the
miracle of her recovery. Reports of the Russian specialist
Manoukhin, who was reputed to cure tuberculosis by a
systematized X-ray treatment, had reached her during the
autumn. On her inquiry Dr. Manoukhin wrote encourag-
ingly about her case. Again hope soared. She believed, even
while she dared not believe. Through January she waited
impatiently, gathering strength for the trip to Paris, to
Manoukhin's clinic. She was beset with colds, chills, and
fever. Nevertheless she kept at her work, to earn money
toward the expense of the treatment. In that one month
she completed two stories, "A Cup of Tea" [53] and "Taking the Veil," [54] as well as beginning the long, unfinished
"Doves' Nest." No longer was money the pressing problem of her life; she could readily earn enough. She sought
now the ability to walk swiftly, to run, to move among
those inconspicuous in good health.

On January 30, with Miss Baker, she left for Paris, to
make arrangements for a course of Manoukhin's treatments in May. Paris was to her now only one of the de-
tested cities of the world, filled with noise and brutal
people.

Oh, how I love gentleness [she wrote shortly after her arrival]. All these people everywhere are like creatures at a railway station—shouting, calling, rushing, with ugly looks and ways. And the women's eyes—like false stones—hard, stupid—there is only one word, corrupt. . . . Of course, I don't want them to be all solemn or Sundayfied. God forbid. But it seems there is so little of the spirit of love and gaiety and *warmth* in the world just now.[55]

Ten years before she had been eager to drain the full draught of Parisian life. Now only Manoukhin could have drawn her to mingle in its turbulence. The courteous Russian doctor inspired her with instant trust. On his advice she undertook his course immediately; and since the treatments were to run through fifteen weeks her husband joined her early in February. On his arrival, when Miss Baker had returned to England, their family routine was transferred to the Victoria Palace Hotel, on the Rue Blaise Desgoffe. In the quiet granite building she lived imprisoned for two months, going out only to Manoukhin's clinic at the Trocadéro; watching, fascinated, the caged canary at the window opposite shrilling his delicate song above the city stones; playing chess with Murry, discussing books with him at tea.

In her general revulsion from the contemporary world Miss Mansfield rejected also the modern spirit as it expressed itself in literature. The broad genre of social and psychological realism, or social moralism as exemplified by Shaw, she found completely sterile as art. With the counterpoising genre of experimentalism she was little better satisfied. It was blighted, in her opinion, by a paralyzing self-consciousness which resulted in ostentation, pretense, and perversity. Very probably much of the work that came her way in the postwar deluge warranted

her opinion. One must remember also that in her years of
Athenaeum reviewing she was called upon to wade
through quantities of inferior work, of the familiar sort
that comes and goes each season. Yet at heart I believe
her interest in contemporary writing in her latter years
was only perfunctory. Though her infrequent comments
are often perceptive, they are usually lukewarm. Eliot,
whose work she must have known through his several
contributions to the *Athenaeum* under Murry's editorship, she noticed only to remark that she considered
"Prufrock" "by far and away the most interesting and
the best modern poem." [56] Proust, whose novel was only
about halfway in print when she came to read him in
1921, apparently at Sidney Schiff's urging, aroused her
warmest sympathy, though one would have thought that
his nostalgic melancholy, his fine dissections of human
experience, would have evoked more excitable enthusiasm
than she expressed. Joyce, whom she read seriously also
late in 1921, she found repellent. The "feeling of wet
linoleum and unemptied pails and far worse horrors in the
house of his mind" [57] was too strong for her fastidious
nature, though she made a sincere effort to be just. Apparently *Ulysses* worried and disturbed her. First she condemned it, then she recanted, then she tried to balance the
two attitudes. At last she gave up the struggle completely.
"The further I am away from it, the less I think of it,"
she stated finally. "As to reading it again, or even opening
that great tome—never!" [58] Toward Lawrence, with
whom in many ways she felt a greater affinity than with
any other writer of her generation, she had a more sharply
divided response. She could neither understand nor accept
his "doctrine of mindlessness," as she called it; to her his
whole philosophy of human regeneration involved a de-

nial of the highest development in humankind—the imagination, the delicate, evaluating sensibility. Nevertheless she sincerely admired the honest passion which charged his work and his rare gift of vigorous poetic realism. Lawrence, to her mind, was obsessed, but at least he believed in and battled for his obsession, and that, among the "half-female, frightened writers-of-to-day," [59] distinguished him as a real creator.

There is little ambiguity about Miss Mansfield's literary tastes. Though she herself was of her time in what she wrote, she was also out of her time, immersed in her own spiritual and artistic preoccupations. To the body of work which was emerging as the chief literary expression of that time she was basically unsympathetic. One must keep in mind the fact that on their first appearance the monuments of a period are not always recognized or understood. A literary generation has matured since the 1920's, devoted to painstaking works of explication. Nevertheless, through her husband's interests she must have been drawn into the first currents of discovery. Her real concern was elsewhere, with the writers of earlier centuries, those who fed her spirit with its essential nourishment.

A few weeks after Miss Mansfield reached Paris, in March, 1922, *The Garden Party* was brought out by Constable in England, later by Knopf in America. On both sides of the Atlantic the book evoked widespread critical response. Its author was now firmly established "as one of our most notable writers," [60] the *English Review* stated. Of "The Stranger" Edward Shanks wrote: "It is one of the best stories in the English language." [61] Notice after notice commended the penetration of Miss Mansfield's insight, the poetic quality of her prose, the concentrated brilliance of her technique, though a number objected to the "disagreeable" subjects she chose to write about. Even before the publication of *The Garden Party* Miss Mansfield's talent had won extensive recognition. Thomas Hardy had suggested that she write more about the two pathetic sisters in "The Daughters of the Late Colonel"; Galsworthy had written his appreciation of "At the Bay," on its appearance in the *London Mercury* at the beginning of the year. The *Nation* and the *Sketch* importuned her for stories; the editor of a modern anthology had scaled her mountain heights to request a contribution; younger writers sought her criticism of their efforts. Miss Mansfield took her success with genuine humility. She was gratified, in a quiet way, at reaching the hearts of those who expressed pleasure in her work; but she had too deep a sense of artistic integrity to be carried away by public praise. Her chief concern was to serve her gifts with more fidelity than she had yet achieved.

Meanwhile in Paris she was pinning her desperate faith on Manoukhin's treatments, wondering if after all Coué were not the magician who could work her miracle, grasping at "anything, anything to be out of the trap—to escape, to be free." [62] She was far from free. She was chained to the prison of her body—racked now by burning fever, neuritis, throbbing headaches, as a result of the X-ray applications; chained even to her writing in order to earn money for Manoukhin's extremely high fees. In February she had planned out the contents of a new book, listing seventeen stories, of which three were already completed, and one, "The Fly," was finished on February 20. Of the remainder a few were begun and abandoned. "The Fly," written at the height of the violent reaction to Manoukhin's treatments, incorporates a despair even more hopeless than that of "*Je ne parle pas français*." There is no note of pathos or anguish in this story, but a relentless, grim depiction of the caprices of destiny.

Toward the end of her Paris stay, when the initial effect of Manoukhin's treatments began to wear off, Miss Mansfield was able to enlarge her life to a small extent. Simply to leave the hotel, to drive out through the flowering Bois, to feel the springtime warmth, renewed her hope and energy. Through a friend, at her request she was introduced to Ivan Bunin, whose "Gentleman from San Francisco" she greatly admired; but her real reason for wishing to meet the Russian author was that he had known Chekhov, whom she always thought of as a personal friend. But Bunin proved disappointing. Yes, he had known Chekhov, that writer of graceful things—long ago —many years ago. Then he turned the conversation to his own work.

Soon the encircling network of invitations, telephone calls, appointments, became highly fatiguing, and worse, a wedge alienating inner from outer self. Miss Mansfield knew that she must escape in order to be able to write again. On the completion of Manoukhin's course, at the end of May, she and her husband returned at once to Switzerland, to a pleasant hotel at Randogne, in the neighborhood of Montana. Shortly after, Miss Baker joined them to take charge of their practical affairs. Since Manoukhin's efforts apparently had been successful Miss Mansfield planned to repeat his course the following October. For the present her life resumed its familiar pattern of close communion with nature, self-analysis, and work. Settled in the remote mountain hotel, free to deliberate, she felt happiest now when entirely alone.

At the beginning of July Miss Mansfield decided to leave Randogne for the Sierre valley, while her husband remained at the hotel above, joining her at week-ends. The separation was not the issue of conflict. She had entered upon a period of concentrated inward experience in which she must have solitude, as she strove to grasp the final key to existence which would free her from self-division. Illness by imposing its own inflexible laws had released her from the common obligations of life. The ordinary manner of living had become irrelevant; it no longer offered room for the requirements of the ailing spirit and unsleeping mind. A year earlier she had still believed that the human being could find salvation only in another mortal, through love on earth, since faith in God was gone for her generation. Yet sin remained, which could be absolved only by the forgiveness of one who understood greatly because his love was great. The divine power must be subsumed in the human. Now she had passed beyond that belief, to the knowledge that no mortal creature can bear the burden of divine responsibility, neither the one nor the other in any human relationship. Yet sin remained. Only one avenue was left. She must find absolution within herself, through self-purification, in solitude.

Miss Mansfield had not elevated herself to sanctity. She had not become inhuman. On the contrary, she had entered a realm where the significance of the human was so intense, where the secret of human entity so consumed her thought, that the ordinary circumstances of daily life lost their meaning. Her intellect was still actively concerned with the true meaning of art; her heart was still warm with affection for her family and her friends. She wrote at this time some of her longest letters; but they are letters which, for all their consideration of current happenings, are preoccupied with the principle by which she had come to believe life must be lived, the principle of purity attained through unremitting effort by the individual soul. Only thus could she serve the truth as a writer. "Calm yourself. Clear yourself," she had written the previous October. ". . . One must learn, one must practise to *forget* oneself. I can't tell the truth about Aunt Anne unless I am free to look into her life without self-consciousness. Oh God! I am divided still. I am bad. I fail in my personal life. I lapse into impatience, temper, vanity, and so I fail as thy priest." [63] From the time she had left Italy, a year and a half before, the conviction had been growing in her mind that the physical body is merely one manifestation of the spirit, that the healthy spirit creates a healthy body as it creates healthy emotion and healthy thought. In this belief, toward which she had herself been groping slowly but tenaciously, she was encouraged by her attentive reading of a little-known book, *Cosmic Anatomy*, in the early months of 1922.[64] Among other modern corruptions the author (who uses the pseudonym "M.B. Oxon") attacks the regulation of life by the conscious intellect, with a resultant atrophy of man's potential capacity for balanced, healthy feeling, and urges a freer, responsive identity with the "push and flow of cosmos." This expansion of the deeper "consciousness" Miss Mansfield equated with a state of spiritual exaltation and therefore of total health.

Adherence to this belief had not yet changed Miss Mansfield's attitude toward her work, though she had written only "The Fly" and "Honeymoon" [65] since her arrival in Paris the February before. She could still observe with her old acuteness her associates at the hotel, finding in an aged American traveler and his companions the material for her unfinished "Father and the Girls." She

KATHERINE MANSFIELD, 1921
From a photograph in the possession of J. Middleton Murry

could still lose herself in her long Jamesian story, "The Doves' Nest," which she had been writing at intervals since the previous January. She could still ponder the secret of loneliness in her last complete story, "The Canary," [66] which she finished early in July. "So many ideas come and go," she noted in her journal. "If there is time I shall write them all. If this uninterrupted time continues." [67]

Toward the end of August the Murrys left Switzerland for England. Miss Mansfield was anxious to consult Dr. Sorapure, whose opinion she trusted, before undertaking a second course with Manoukhin in the fall. She had long been convinced that her heart was diseased, and she was sure that its action was jeopardized by the X-ray treatments. Dr. Sorapure's examination brought a moderately good account: her heart was organically sound, he reported, and even her general health seemed considerably improved.

For the six weeks of her London stay [68] Miss Mansfield took two rooms in the apartment of her friend Miss Brett, keeping her presence secret from all but her most intimate circle. She saw again her father, who had recently arrived in England; she saw her sisters Charlotte and Jeanne and her few cherished friends. She looked again upon London and knew that she was done with it forever. Living in England was like living in a chimney, she said, choked with the fumes and carbon of false standards. The clever people, the "mind-probers" as she called them, who evaded any commitment to life by chatting of minor eighteenth-century poetry, wearied her as much by their solemnity as by their pretentiousness. When she returned to Paris she was thankful to leave the city which had drawn her beyond denial, from island to far island, a dozen years before. But there was still the future stretching ahead in which to practice the beliefs to which she was now dedicated. With a future, one must plan. She thought of the new book she would have ready, to appear the following spring; of a winter in Italy with her husband, after the Paris treatments were over; of the trip to New Zealand for which her heart longed.[69]

On October 2, with Miss Baker, she crossed to Paris and took rooms at the modest hotel at the Place de la Sorbonne where she had stayed during the bombardment four years earlier. She began Manoukhin's treatments; but she had now lost all faith in their efficacy. She felt no stronger; her cough grew worse and worse.

In London during the summer of 1922 the experiment in communal living at the Gurdjieff Institute,[70] near Fontainebleau, was being publicized by Gurdjieff's chief spokesman, P. D. Ouspenski, the Russian mathematician and journalist. Gurdjieff, a Russian subject of Greek parentage who became an exile after the Revolution of 1917, was reputed to have traveled widely in the East, studying especially the religious rites and exercises of the monastic orders of Turkistan, Mongolia, Tibet, and India. He had early gathered a group of disciples, made up chiefly of uprooted members of the Russian intelligentsia, whom he established, after many shifts, at Avon, France, in 1922, together with the additional members Ouspenski had attracted through his London lectures.

Roughly stated, Gurdjieff's object as a psychic leader was to develop a harmonious personality in man through the balanced functioning of his intellectual, emotional, and physical "centers," releasing him thereby from the bondage to imposed habit which distorted or destroyed his true potentialities. In practical application his system required of its followers a life of extremely plain living, of strenuous but varied manual labor, and of creative expression through craftwork and rhythmic exercises. Gurdjieff himself devised a series of mental and physical tests for each individual member and determined the psychical instruction he should receive. The men and women who had joined his institute, at this time about seventy in all, were utterly subordinated to his control. They regarded him with awe and veneration dominated by fear, as the direct minister of a divine power, with a knowledge of divine mysteries.

On reaching London in August Miss Mansfield had at once arranged for an interview with Ouspenski.[71] Gurdjieff, she was sure, offered precisely what she was seeking: spiritual rebirth to a calmness and stability of wisdom which would serve as an integrating center of the self. Even as she was suffering her customary violent reaction to Manoukhin's course, she was investigating the life of the institute. Her faith in medical treatment was now completely gone. Manoukhin was no man of miracles. He had cured many people; some he could not cure, and of these she was convinced she was one. Her cure must be effected by inward means, through discipline in self-abnegation and humility, and in the Gurdjieff Institute she believed she had found a way of life which would foster her spiritual advance.

I am a divided being with a bias towards what I want to be, but no more [she wrote to Koteliansky from France]. And this it seems I cannot improve. No, I cannot. I have tried. . . .

So I am always conscious of this secret disruption in me—
and at last (thank Heaven!) it has ended in a complete revolution and I mean to change my whole way of life entirely.[72]

Miss Mansfield did not plunge precipitately into this
new experiment. She gave the matter intense consideration. Under Manoukhin's care the preceding spring she
had been reduced to total inactivity. Since that time she
had written nothing beyond larger or smaller fragments.
To live with any satisfaction she must work, and to work
she must be healthy. By health she meant the capacity to
enjoy natural strength and energy in a life rooted deep
in the actual earth—to work with her own hands, to assist
the growth of animals, flowers, plants, growing thereby
herself—to become, in her own words, *"a child of the
sun"*; [73] and from this direct and fruitful expenditure of
self to be released from racking disunity into her fullest
emotional and creative powers; above all, to be freed from
dependence for happiness upon any other source than her
own equanimity. A pitiful anguish beats through the
journal records of her struggle—the fear and hope and
desperation of the trapped creature that will not believe
it is inexorably trapped.

In her hotel room, enisled amidst the busy surge of city
life, she could glimpse through her window the solitary
tower of Saint Jacques, which she had seen also from her
windows at the Quai aux Fleurs seven years before, rising
still in dedication though its edifice had been destroyed.
In this room, alone, she made her decision. On October 16 she entered Le Prieuré, an old monastic estate at the
edge of a forest, about thirty miles from Paris. She was
convinced now that she must be reborn into an entirely
new life. "I have to die to so much," she wrote to her husband; "I have to make such *big* changes. I feel the only

thing to do is to get the dying over—to court it, almost.
. . . For with all my soul I do long for a real life, for
truth, and for real strength." [74] But conviction was not
enough. She had come to realize that she needed guidance.
In Gurdjieff she believed she had found her guide.

Katherine Mansfield joined the Gurdjieff Institute with
an earnest faith in the regenerative power of its form of
life. She now gave herself up entirely to the process of
spiritual cure. Her writing, for the present, she abandoned
completely. "I do not want to write any stories until I am
a less terribly poor human being," [75] she told Koteliansky
shortly after entering Le Prieuré. Through physical
weakness she could take no part in the communal life of
the institute, but she could watch, absorb, and ponder. A
platform was constructed for her high in a building which
had been converted into a stable, for Gurdjieff believed
that the exhalations from cows—spiritual as well as physical—were beneficial to the tubercular. Here she lay on
a mattress and cushions several hours each day, gazing at
the lively patterns which a fellow member had painted on
the plaster ceiling just above her platform. When she was
able, she would sit in the workshop, watching the neat
action of hammer and saw, or would walk out to the
garden and the barnyard to observe the energetic labors
of her associates.[76] "It's so full of life and humour that I
wouldn't be anywhere else," [77] she wrote to her husband
a few days after her arrival. One remembers the first
bright faith with which she embraced each of her new
ventures, and cannot still the voice of doubt. Indeed, her
letters a few weeks later hold a hint of skepticism. "Of
course, it is true that life here is quite different," she wrote
early in November, "but violent changes to one's individuality—of course, they do not occur." [78] More openly,

she wrote still later that she was not sure she would continue at the institute. She had gained from the experience; but she had begun to question Gurdjieff's power.

For three months Miss Mansfield lived in retirement at Avon. She was facing now, with a new attitude, the conflict between the actual and the ideal which had riven her asunder for years. Except for her hours of exaltation, she had never been able either to compromise with or to accept the actual. She could rise above it at moments; she could feel and formulate her spiritual creed; but she had fluctuated in a constant struggle which has as its most moving element the superhuman aspiration to which she set herself. In the fourteen years since she had left Wellington she had met, again and yet again, the blasting of illusion. She had wrenched herself free from her native country, to find the country of her hope and faith crumble. She could not return; she had passed beyond the point of return. She must seek or make a world now within herself.

Orage, the friend of her early London days, who had urged her to come to Avon, was also a member of the institute. Again they talked together. Miss Mansfield discussed her new attitude toward her work. "One must become more in order to write better." [79] she told him. In time she would embody in her stories what she herself had slowly learned—that the only value is the ancient and indestructible value of self-knowledge. At present the task at hand was to attain self-discipline. For the first time in her life she strove to reach out of herself into the entity of others. She had made this effort previously as a writer, but never as a woman among living women and men. On the contrary she had recoiled in painful shock from ugliness, brutality, and stupidity. Now she perceived that she must begin anew, must "learn to live—really live—and in relation to everything—not isolated." [80]

She stood, she believed, on the verge of realization of her faith, and thus believing she did so stand. Her larger vision was never impaired. On January 9, 1923, her husband arrived at the institute to visit her for a week. That evening as she was going to her room she suffered an attack of coughing which brought on a violent hemorrhage. While Murry ran to get a doctor, she sat on the edge of her bed, pressing her stained hands over her mouth. Within half an hour she was dead.

She was buried in the communal cemetery at Avon. Through over a score of years the friends who never knew her in life have come to her grave, to read the words of Hotspur, which she had always loved, inscribed on the stone: "But I tell you, my lord fool, out of this nettle, danger, we pluck this flower, safety."

CHAPTER FIVE

Katherine Mansfield

IN THE CLOSING YEARS of her life, as we have seen, Katherine Mansfield formulated a theory of art conceived entirely in subjective ethical terms. Perhaps the best condensation of its substance is found in her own words: "Lord, make me crystal clear for thy light to shine through," [1] though we must recognize the prayer as that of the secular mystic, not the dedicated believer. Fundamentally, she did not depart from her artistic purpose as she stated it in 1918, at the time she was writing *"Je ne parle pas français"*: to transmit to the best of her powers the radiant beauty she saw in the world about her and to set down her "cry against corruption." [2] In the later period, however, the transmission of beauty in itself, as commensurate with truth, was to serve as her moral protest, and she intensified to an extreme her demand for purity in the transmitting instrument.

It is by now a commonplace of literary history that the first decades of our century, particularly the years after the first world war, form a period of transition. The fixed order had disintegrated; old values and old loyalties had fallen. The established body of truth—the corpus of traditions, conventions, beliefs—had not only been hewn asunder but scattered to the four winds. The seeking mind was driven in upon itself, to construct among the fragments its own vision. We have thus the flowering of individual expression, shaped by individual temperament out of individual experience, to be tested as true or false by individual temperament and experience. We have thus the early Eliot, Lawrence, Joyce, Kafka, Proust.

Miss Mansfield's mind perceived in sharp, intuitive flashes; her apprehension was never the result of long, contemplative thought. Her "individual truth" therefore is transfixed within the experience of a moment, within the immediate, and is expressed in isolated form, by the method of presentation André Maurois has called *"une coupe dans le temps"* [3]—the swift, illuminated glimpse into a character or situation at a given moment, the revelation of the kernel of meaning within the husk of the ordinary, the trifling, the banal. To be successful this method demands highly conscious utilization. A careful pattern of the parts which constitute the whole must be shaped so that the central meaning, conveyed by indirection, emerges unobscured, with the required manipulation of details inconspicuously achieved. And since the emotions probed are likely to be elusive, clarity of their communication depends upon a linking of the vague with the concrete.

From the time of the publication of *Bliss* in 1920 the relationship of Miss Mansfield's technique to that of Chekhov has been emphasized. In a broad sense this identification is correct. Chekhov had perfected a quarter of a century before the type of story on which Miss Mansfield came to concentrate—the presentation of the significant within a fragmentary happening. It should be remembered, incidentally, that Chekhov's collected work includes over six hundred stories, which he handled in various ways, according to their demands. We find also the story with the carefully wrought plot, such as "The Bet," the slight sketch, the *novella* or short novel. "After the Theatre" delineates an adolescent mood in four pages; "Three Years," covering a hundred and fifty, traces the changing nature of love over a protracted period of time— nor are these pieces unique examples. Most often, however, he does convey his artistic perceptions through the medium of the isolated segment of experience. Chekhov's world too was one of upheaval, with the fixed social and moral orders giving way—a disordered world of nihilism, emancipation, reform, revolution, still preserving the outline of an established structure through the coercive or palliative measures of a deteriorated governing force.

Miss Mansfield herself recognized and stressed the unusual affinity of her temperament with Chekhov's. For at least three years before the final shaping of "Prelude" she had been studying his writings attentively. She read him with that delight of recognition with which one mind embraces another closely akin, particularly when such kinship demolishes the barriers of time, race, and mortality. "She admired and understood Tchehov's work as few English writers have done," Mr. Murry has written. ". . . But her method was wholly her own, and her development would have been precisely the same had Tchehov never existed." [4] It is futile to state as fact the issue of circumstances contrary to fact. Chekhov had existed; Miss Mansfield did read and reread him throughout her adult years. The Russian writer stimulated and confirmed her own maturing conception of her art, as she herself acknowledged. It is perhaps possible that her development would have been "precisely the same" if Chekhov had never existed. Nevertheless, her close study of his work, her perception of the fine overtones of meaning conveyed through his fluidity of form, surely clarified her own concept of the short story.

Both Chekhov and Miss Mansfield saw humanity in terms of the particular individual—the single atom of the confusing mass that could be fixed and analyzed. Each drew his subject matter directly from his fund of personal experience. Without question Chekhov's range is incomparably the greater, for his sympathies were broader and he lived actively in the world. He was by profession a doctor whose work brought him into close contact with many aspects of Russian life. He was interested in science, in political and social reforms, as well as in literature— in the improvement of penal conditions, in the organization of famine relief among the peasants, in the establishment of schools, the construction of roads, the founding of libraries and hospitals. As a landowner he knew the life of provincial Russia; as a writer he knew the artistic circles of Moscow and Petersburg; as an invalid he knew the secluded retreat of Yalta in the Crimea. His mind by native endowment was acute, appraising, unprejudiced, observant, compassionate. Life presented him with an abundance of material on which to draw, and he found no incident too trifling for his scrutiny.

Miss Mansfield has at times been derogated as a conscious imitator of Chekhov who had exhausted what was at best a tenuous talent at the time of her death. This judgment is hasty as well as vain. Her understanding of her own best powers came relatively late, so that only in her last years of virtual isolation did she attain fullest command of her material. Admittedly in comparison with Chekhov she has explored only a limited sphere of experience; but within that limitation she has produced stories of incisive meaning, and in the group of New Zealand stories she has created a set of characters who continue to live by their provocative vitality.

The broad likenesses between Miss Mansfield's work and Chekhov's have been often remarked. Most importantly, one ventures to say, she observed in him the method of narration she came to adopt exclusively—the apparently casual interlinking of a number of incidents to form a texture through which the real intention of the writer shines. In "The Kiss," for example, Chekhov sketches in at considerable length the wearisome routine of the military battalion of which Ryabovitch is an officer, so that, though he never directly states the fact, Ryabovitch's immersion in his delusive romantic dreams seems both inevitable and pitiful, given his nature as Chekhov has previously established it: his confirmed timidity, his unassertive pleasure in women, his mournful resignation to the minor social role he plays. As in a great many of his stories, Chekhov is here examining the longing for richness, beauty, and sympathy in the hearts of the inarticulate and nondescript. He keeps his distance from his material; he says no word for Ryabovitch or against him. But through the presentation of his character as shy, passive, and sensitive, of the tedious petty responsibilities of his life as staff captain, of his separation from his coarser-grained companions, Chekhov imbues his narrative with his compassion for one who is doomed by his own weakness to a life of emotional aridity. Frequently Chekhov conjoins

incidents by the device of contrast or reversal, more succinctly employed in the shorter pieces than in "The Kiss":
in "A Gentleman Friend," the "charming Vanda," seeking help in evil days from a former cavalier, a dentist, finds
herself professionally hurried into the dentist's chair; or
again, more subtly, in "Old Age" the vigorous brutality
of active life is set against the sterile inanition of physical
decay.

Miss Mansfield's technical execution will be examined
in detail later. Here it will suffice to make a few general
observations on Chekhov's narrative method and hers and
to remark the characteristic attitude of each writer toward
his material. Neither one is greatly interested in event as
event, or even in the primary emotion inhering in an
event. Though Chekhov often deals with violent subject
matter—destructive passion, crime, betrayal, hate—his
concern is never with action in itself but with the emotional repercussions of action on the characters involved.
The modulation thus is always subdued; when the sensa-
tional is dealt with it is presented, as it were, in another
room. Thus in "Enemies" the death of Kirilov's son and
the elopement of Aboguin's wife are employed second-
arily, to give rise to the theme that suffering does not always unite men but can produce hostility and bitterness.
Miss Mansfield does not often write of violence, but, like
Chekhov, she usually presents her material not for the
overt meaning of the happenings but to make a tangential
point, slanting the elements of the central situation to ex-
tract an oblique theme. The story of Mouse's elopement
and abandonment in "*Je ne parle pas français*" is shaped to
illuminate the peculiar depravity of Raoul Duquette's
character; "The Garden Party" juxtaposes social gaiety
and sudden death to reveal the bewildering shock a young

girl suffers at the knowledge that in life such incongruities can coexist.

Chekhov's prime artistic aim, he stated again and again, was to write with complete objectivity. This objectivity he achieves by means of impersonal treatment of his subject matter—straightforward narration, concise description, at times direct exposition—conveying not only the story but the implications within the story through his acute sense of the value of suggestive incident. Frequently he presents his material through the medium of a first-person narrator who tells the story either about himself or about someone he has known, establishing thus a close immediacy between the reader and the subject without the intrusion of the author's voice.

Miss Mansfield's chief modifications of Chekhov's method issue from her employment of devices developed in a later day, most importantly the formal flashback and the interior monologue, both of which radically affect the handling of time. By means of these devices Miss Mansfield can so order her elements that her immediate situation exists intact; past time and future are strained through the meshes of the present, with a resultant high condensation of material. Chekhov must hold to chronological progression, slipping lightly over the years, when need be, by a simple phrase. Further, the utilization of the interior monologue creates another distinction. Chekhov must take the reader from the outer aspect of his subject to the inner; Miss Mansfield can transport the reader directly within.

If we examine more closely the texture of each writer's work, many detailed similarities appear. Both achieve characteristic effect through swiftness and lucidity of presentation; both are sensitively alert to the multiple value of minor action, detail, and dialogue. Both take the plunge direct into the heart of a subject. "When one has written a story," Ivan Bunin reports Chekhov as saying, "I believe that one ought to strike out both the beginning and the end. That is where we novelists are most inclined to lie." [5] Every reader of Miss Mansfield's stories must have been struck by her frequent use of an opening sentence that presupposes knowledge of anterior events: "And then, after six years, she saw him again," [6] "And after all the weather was ideal," [7] "The week after was one of the busiest weeks of their lives." [8] Nor is she any more discursive in her conclusions. "The Doll's House" falls away into silence after Our Else's single, simple remark, which concentrates the entire pathos of the story. "Bliss" ends sharply on the climax of Bertha Young's discovery of her husband's unfaithfulness. "At the Bay" does not end at all; it merely stops. The particular day in the life of the Burnell family the author has chosen to present comes to a close, and with it the story closes. Any formalized conclusion would be artificial—in Chekhov's words a lie.

Like Chekhov Miss Mansfield possessed the gift of capturing in brief and vivid terms the living aspect of natural scene. Chekhov merges his descriptive passages smoothly into the body of his narrative, closely relating human emotion and environment, using always unpretentious language. ". . . beauty and expressiveness in nature are attained only by simplicity," he wrote to Gorki, "by such simple phrases as 'The sun set,' 'It was dark,' 'It began to rain.' " [9] Miss Mansfield's descriptive passages are more picturesque than Chekhov's, more concentrated and more lyrical. She frequently employs poetic imagery, which Chekhov rarely uses; she apprehends nature intensely, in minute detail, and, except in the New Zealand stories, is more likely to gain her artistic effect through impressionistic emphasis of such detail than through the general interfusion of natural scene which fills Chekhov's stories. When Chekhov writes of the freshly fallen snow he describes the first fall of snow at any time, in any city: the smell of snow in the air, the sound of snow crunching softly underfoot, the fresh light blanketing that gives the world a virginal appearance.[10] Miss Mansfield, describing a snowfall, emphasizes distinctive detail in localized scene: the window boxes "full of great sprays of white coral," the lawn "covered with a wavy pattern of cat's paws," the "thick, thick icing on the garden table," the withered pods of the laburnum tree sheathed in white, the dark leaf of ivy showing here and there.[11]

This difference in perception, of course, determines the quality of all the sense impressions conveyed by each writer, not merely the descriptions of natural scene. Miss Mansfield's stories are most often set indoors, in a drawing room, a tearoom, a room in a hotel, with a reduction of scope thereby which allows for high particularization of detail: the blue teapot, the gold cushions, the antlers of firelight in the grate, the Japanese vase of paper daffodils. Setting is usually bright; music sounds; textures—silks, velvets, luxurious leather—brush the hand. Material objects are visualized with minute precision: a toilet set adorned with tiny apples, an exquisite enamel box looking as though it had been "baked in cream." Chekhov's stories may take place anywhere—in a peasant hut, a hospital, a wealthy home, on the platform of a railroad station, in the forest, on the steppe. Whatever the setting he uses, the tonal quality is almost uniformly subdued. Colors are gentle—mild yellows, greys, blues; rain and snow fall often; evening and autumn scenes recur. Descriptions of appearance—of material objects or of characters—are never sharp in their particulars, though remarkably expressive as a totality. No writer has surpassed his extraordinary skill in conveying the essence of a whole through a few representative details—the pathetic-comic insignificance of Ryabovitch is concentrated in the glancing descriptive bit, "a little officer in spectacles, with sloping shoulders, and whiskers like a lynx's"; [12] the mean squalor of a dirty peasant hut pervasively colors a sordid incident by the casual mention of the cheap clock ticking on the wall, the half-frozen flies buzzing in the icon corner, the rustle of cockroaches under the benches, the smell of soot in the air.[13]

The chief difference between Miss Mansfield's descriptive technique and Chekhov's lies thus in Chekhov's stress on the significant combination of general detail and Miss Mansfield's stress on the significant combination of particularized detail. Chekhov is always unobtrusive; appealing always directly to the senses, he suffuses his narrative evenly with a muted atmosphere. Miss Mansfield too appeals directly to the senses, in brief and precise terms; but because by nature she perceived the immediate world as both concentrated and reduced, observing generally the unusual rather than the characteristic detail, the impression she transmits has a highly individual intensity which we do not find in Chekhov. This difference of perception, underlying everything each author wrote, constitutes a broad distinction between Chekhov's work and hers.

Carried beyond the point of sensory apprehension, this difference underlies also a differing conception of life. Chekhov's view again is muted; whatever his private uncertainty or unrest, he never varied in expression from the attitude he formulated at the age of twenty-eight: "We shall not play the charlatan, and we will declare frankly that nothing is clear in this world. Only fools and charlatans know and understand everything." [14] In Chekhov's work the total pattern traced emerges as an enigma. Life is beyond human comprehension. One must resign oneself to acceptance of its frustrations and evil, with bewilderment, with melancholy, with compassion. In Miss Mansfield's work the total pattern emerges as a dichotomy—the irreconcilable cleavage between the rich potentialities of life and the inescapable brutalities of human experience which must evoke despair.

The similarity of Miss Mansfield's technique to Chekhov's has always been heavily stressed. Its similarity to the technique of Joyce in the epiphanies of *Dubliners* has not been equally remarked. Miss Mansfield may have been familiar with *Dubliners*, after its belated publication in 1914, though she has left no recorded reference to the book—which on her part would indicate a neutral response. It is not to suggest possible "influence" that *Dubliners* is mentioned here, but to note the coincidence of Joyce's concept of the short story and Miss Mansfield's and to compare the methods of the two writers in the execution of their work. It is not beyond possibility that an ancestor common to both may be interred in previous time. George Moore, at the suggestion of John Eglinton, had written a group of stories directly modeled upon Turgenev's *Sportsman's Sketches*, published in 1903 as *The Untilled Field*. These stories, which examine the life of the oppressed Irish peasant in something of the way *Dubliners* examines the life of the oppressed city dweller, might very well have been known to Joyce, and of course Turgenev's work was thoroughly assimilated by Chekhov.

According to Stephen Dedalus in *Stephen Hero* the epiphany constitutes the moment of insight into an entity, on the surface trivial, commonplace, or even dull, revealed by means of an aesthetic ordering of its parts, so that it is beautiful in structure and significant in meaning, or rather so that the structural ordering of the parts conveys the beauty of harmony and the beauty of meaning. In this form, concise and self-contained, the element of time must be stringently reduced. Whatever is necessary and relevant to the significance of the story must be compressed within the brief scope of the crucial moment of the "showing forth." Since the entire object is the revelation of inner meaning, success in handling depends on pressure, so to speak, on the degree of significance extracted from a given subject by means of high condensation. Thus interpreted, "epiphany" might equally distinguish most of Katherine Mansfield's stories, and very many of Chekhov's as well.

Naturally, marked differences occur in the execution of the three writers. Chekhov, as we have noted, employs the conventional devices of an earlier generation. Technically considered, his originality consists in the selection of the separate parts which, united, form the web which captures an elusive theme. Joyce's stories have neither the muted quality of Chekhov's nor the high clarity of Miss Mansfield's. His method is closer to that of Maupassant— a severe reduction of the material to its essential substance, presented with entire objectivity. The stories seem to tell themselves, in clear, firm, concentrated prose. In general his situations have less bulk than those most commonly found in Chekhov and Miss Mansfield: a young boy learns of the death of an old defeated priest, his friend; a confirmed drunkard undertakes a religious retreat; a group of young men carouse after a race. But within the static situation the emotional significance has been molded to high intensity; the impact on the reader is forcible and keen.

Like all good writers of fiction Joyce skillfully employs the conventional devices of contrast, functional dialogue and functional action, particularly characterizing detail of action or appearance. Like Chekhov and Miss Mansfield he opens his story in the heart of a situation; when the meaning has been revealed the story at once ends. Structurally, as in the work of the other two writers, the strength of the whole depends upon the arrangement of the constituent parts. In "Clay," for example, which has a thematic relationship to Katherine Mansfield's "Miss Brill," the narrative is merely the account of the visit of an old woman to her nephew's home on Allhallow Eve. Step by step, without a word of comment or explanation, we are taken with Maria, rather *by* Maria, through the experience—her anticipation of the event, her preparations before she leaves, her purchase of a gift of plum cake, her little encounter with a tipsy old gentleman on the tram, the simple festivities at the Donnellys'. In the superstitious game she plays with her nephew's children, Maria's selection of the saucer of clay which presages her death receives no more emphasis than any of the other incidents, for to Maria it is merely another, rather confusing incident in her day. What Joyce intends is not to lead up to a sharp climax but to lay bare the pathos in Maria's cramped existence. Each trivial detail of her experience which he relates forms the crucial substance of her life. The reader participates in her experience directly and is concurrently aware of the pitiful discrepancy between the experience as it actually is and the enlargement it undergoes in the meager dimensions of her world. At the end, when she sings "I Dreamt That I Dwelt," quavering out her dream of wealth and love and pride, we scarcely need Joe Donnelly's tears to indicate the ironic contrast.

In "Miss Brill" Miss Mansfield presents an elderly spinster who ekes out a narrow living in Paris by genteel, inconsequential work. The focus placed on Miss Brill is even more concentrated than Joyce's focus on Maria, for Miss Brill, a solitary figure throughout the story, is revealed wholly by means of the interior monologue in association with external scene. Like Maria, Miss Brill is intensely absorbed in the limited happenings which make up her life, but here the absorption is highly conscious on her part, actually exploited. She sits in the Jardins Publiques with the band playing a gay Sunday-afternoon program, alert to every detail in the scene about her: the conductor is wearing a new coat, she observes; two old people sitting beside her disappointingly are silent—the park-bench conversations have been lapsing in interest of late; little unfinished stories are enacted before her eyes by the passersby, by the young, the fascinating, the heartless. Miss Brill, excited by her fancy that she also is an "actress" among the rest, playing her part week after week, feels a rush of confused emotion—an exultation and sadness, a longing to participate more strongly in the dramatic whole. The story ends on the sharp note of her complete exclusion: a young couple, checked in their crude love-making by her presence, ridicule her appearance; her momentary illusion of sharing in the drama of life is destroyed.

The theme of "Miss Brill" thus emerges from a carefully linked series of incidents, for the author gives no comment or explanation. But the story fails to achieve the poignant impact of "Clay." Maria simply acts and *is;* the pathos of her life exists in the bare fact of its being. Miss Brill, hyperconscious, semihysterical, through feverish examination herself emphasizes the meaning of each trivial happening in her afternoon, so that the very instrument of implication—the running stream of feeling—here gives rise to the obvious, or at least the mechanical. Joyce has focused on an external situation, with a central figure within the situation who is revealed by the events. Miss Mansfield has focused on a central figure who creates the situation within and about herself.

This application of focus forms a chief difference in the methods of the two writers. All the stories of *Dubliners* except "The Dead" are primarily concerned with the meaning contained within a situation (with Joyce, of course, "situation" does not mean complexity of events). "An Encounter," to select one of the most static, presents the discrepancy between the excited anticipation two boys experience before a day of roaming and the realization of aimlessness, fatigue, and sinister threat in the actuality. "Ivy Day in the Committee Room," a much longer story, likewise focuses on situation. Through the desultory stillborn conversation in the barren committee room which culminates in the quickening of emotion once Parnell is named and Mr. Hynes reads his conventional memorial verses, Joyce reveals the sense of loss of purpose, of central meaning, in the life of the adherents once the leader is gone.

In general Miss Mansfield's focus is on the individual figure. Every detail of the presentation is selected to convey the emotional timbre of a central character, an intensification of the individual to which the situation itself is subordinate. Among the stories included in *Bliss* a number of the earlier pieces show a fumbling control of this technique. In "Psychology" in particular the uncertain focus proves distracting. Now we are taken inside the consciousness of the man, now of the woman, as they meet in her studio for tea; now we seem to be following an identical stream of thought or feeling in both; now the author makes a statement which carries an unexpected satiric overtone. Since the central experience relates to the woman character, one has thus a sense primarily of the situation, amidst a dispersal of its emotional force. The later stories, even those contained in the same volume, limit the range of focus to a single figure, with situation designed to expose emotional experience or character. In "Bliss" Harry Young's infidelity is subsidiary to the destruction of Bertha Young's intoxicating bliss in sudden shock; in "A Cup of Tea" Rosemary Fell's adventure with the starving shopgirl is turned to expose Rosemary's feline egocentricity; in "Poison" the whole narrative is shaped to depict the worldly figure of Beatrice through the consciousness of her former lover, who tells the story, at the same time that it defines the narrator himself, both as he is now and as he used to be. By Miss Mansfield's method a more highly particularized character is presented than we find in *Dubliners*, though not necessarily therefore always a deeper one. The only figure on whom Joyce has focused comparably is Gabriel Conroy in "The Dead." In this longest and finest of his stories Joyce builds his structure on a succession of minute epiphanies: Gabriel at his aunts' evening party, seen in relationship to the little servant girl, to his maiden aunts, to Gretta his wife, to various of the guests, so that gradually we are inducted into his irritable, introspective temperament. Not only is Gabriel thus depicted;

the focus swerves at times to other of the figures, to establish the general atmosphere which contributes to Gabriel's
emotional agitation at the end. Like Ryabovitch in the
opening section of "The Kiss," Gabriel moves against
a background of quickening excitement—dancing, eating, drinking, social gallantry. Throughout Joyce preserves his habit of impersonal narration, his controlled objectivity; but in this story he goes beyond the accurate
representation of the significant. As T. S. Eliot has remarked, he assumes an "ethically orthodox" attitude
toward his material; he offers, through implication, moral
comment.[15] Gabriel undergoes spiritual development, in
the melodic closing scene. He sees that he has been self-
centered, petty, and demanding, that all too often life consists of various forms of death; that it is better to die in
the fullness of passion than to fade out in the desiccation
of old age, that actually the dead die in the body only,
so long as they are still embraced by living memory in
the world.

Within the broad theme of the story, implicit in the
title "The Dead," resides the special theme of Gabriel's
relationship to his wife. He realizes that he is an exile from
a world Gretta possesses, the world of her earlier life with
its portion of emotion and experience. David Daiches has
already drawn attention to the thematic likeness of this
element in the story to Katherine Mansfield's "The
Stranger," [16] which deals also with the inviolable world
a wife inhabits—not to be invaded even by passionate
love; least of all to be invaded by the demands of passionate
love. Unlike the leisurely development of "The Dead,"
Miss Mansfield's presentation is sharply condensed. Tension is established in the first paragraphs by the unex-
plained delay of the steamer, hanging motionless in the

distance, which is bringing Janey Hammond home after a year of absence. With a stroke of high economy Miss Mansfield opens the story when the period of waiting is nearly over, so that her central figure, Mr. Hammond, seen thus under acute and prolonged stress, emerges with intensified force. He is never still; he marches up and down among the little crowd of people, constantly addressing one or another, twirling his umbrella, pulling out his expensive watch, energetic, nervous, impetuous. In the first two or three pages, through the depiction of Mr. Hammond's excitement, all the necessary exposition is introduced: his active, dominating, essentially simple nature; something of Janey's elusive quality; the time, the place, the circumstances. As the steamer begins to move the story also moves forward, with a constantly heightening emotional tempo as the moment of reunion draws nearer and is at last attained. Point by point, the subsequent incidents establish the crux of the story in the temperamental distance separating husband and wife: Mr. Hammond's conflicting pride and jealousy as Janey lingers to say good-by to her traveling companions; his irritable uneasiness at her insistence on a private word with the ship's doctor; his mounting impatience to get her to himself; Janey's charming, cool diversion of his demands, accomplished with slightly amused, slightly ironic affection, her eagerness to go directly home to the children, her barely perceptible hesitation before she accedes to his importunities. At the end the narrative swings round in a full circle. Janey explains that the steamer was delayed because of official duties in connection with a death at sea—an invalid passenger had died the night before, a young man, a stranger, whom she had befriended. She had been alone with him. " 'He died in my arms,' " [17] she says quietly. Rocking under the full knowledge of his frustration, of the mysterious barriers of reserve which he can never penetrate but which fall, almost casually, for others, Mr. Hammond is left alone with his stranger in the chilly room. It was not Miss Mansfield's intention to make a moral point in this story (or in any other). She was concerned, as I believe Joyce was primarily concerned in "The Dead," with the condition of human loneliness, which even though it may at times give rise to exaltation is nevertheless grounded always in the knowledge of human pain.

As Joyce built "The Dead" on the structural unit of the epiphany (and was to build his larger works on the same unit, weaving into an intricate vast meshwork individual moments of revelation), Miss Mansfield builds her longer stories on the unit of the single, highly economical, significant scene. In "Prelude," as we have noted, she first utilized this technique. *"Je ne parle pas français,"* her second story of considerable length, from the nature of its subject matter demanded a variation of the method. The material here serves a dual purpose: to give the central story of the tortured relationship between Dick Harmon and his sweetheart Mouse and to portray in full the figure of Raoul Duquette, who represents the perversion and refined brutality often encountered in modern bohemian circles. Therefore she has placed the focus on Duquette, who tells the story in the first person in the form of a confessional-monologue. Through his own words he is gradually exposed: the young French literary hanger-on, egotistical, self-analytical and self-conscious, cruel, unscrupulous, at heart slavish and insecure. Through the flow of his recital the Dick-Mouse story unfolds in a fairly simple course. Starting in the present with an establishment of the immediate scene in a cheap French café, Duquette sketches in his own history, touching obscurely on the central story to come, then reverts to the past, giving a hint of Dick Harmon's excessive attachment to his mother which is to destroy his relationship with Mouse. One brief scene follows another, striking now and again the pathetic Mouse leitmotiv, *Je ne parle pas français*, and each separate scene, incisive and compact, embodies both a portion of the story and a further view into the murky depths of Raoul Duquette's character. Both elements are essential to the purpose of the story. The full portrait of Raoul Duquette is necessary both to sharpen by contrast the genuine suffering of Dick Harmon and Mouse and to convey the extremity of Mouse's betrayal, since at the end she is left friendless in Paris except for his depraved interest.

In "At the Bay," her third long story, Miss Mansfield returned to the subject matter and technique of "Prelude." As we have seen, in "Prelude" the focus shifts from one member to another of the Burnell family, fluidly moving to illuminate the several figures in their complex inter-relationships. Similarly, in "At the Bay" one character or another always dominates the selected scene, but here the real focal unit of the story is the temporal division of the single day Miss Mansfield has chosen to describe. Through the cycle of the hours she carries her family; early morning, late morning; early afternoon, late afternoon; evening, night. This is the framework Virginia Woolf chose some years later for *Mrs. Dalloway*, but in Miss Mansfield's story the technical device is not equally emphasized. Morning, afternoon, and evening are simply the unobtrusive settings for her episodes; yet the entire narrative is steeped in the atmosphere of that summer day. Time seems to pass with the natural rhythm of actuality, conveyed through sense impression rather than mechanical device. In *Mrs. Dalloway* the bells of London ring throughout the novel—"First a warning, musical; then the hour, irrevocable." [18] We are forever caught up in the clangor of a dozen city clocks, and each half-hour or hour thus marked off contains its precise segment of narrative. In "At the Bay" it is as though the slow finger of shadow moved across the face of a sundial, gently and silently.

"The Daughters of the Late Colonel," Miss Mansfield wrote to Richard Murry, was "the outcome of the *Prelude* method—it just unfolds and opens." [19] In this story the focus centers on the two spinster sisters, Constantia and Josephine, in a series of scenes which shows them in relationship to various members of their narrow world, but in a more complicated pattern than Joyce employs in "The Dead." Though formally the temporal compass of the story is a single week, time flows back and forth, interlacing past and present. "The week after was one of the busiest weeks of their lives," the narrative begins. Then it is as though curtain after curtain were drawn back, revealing their life in the present, in the immediate past, in the distant past that had made them what they are. We see the timid, subjugated spirits of the sisters, clinging yet to their pitiful pleasures and pitiful shreds of dreams, shrinking before the domination of their invalid father, the arrogant independence of their servant Kate, the contemptuous superiority of Nurse Andrews. By this means we are guided far into the recesses of the hidden natures of the two, for each scene is a moment of revelation which is linked by terminal association to the opening of the scene following. This story on its first appearance in the *London Mercury* was labeled "a dismal transcript of inefficiency" [20] by the *Saturday Review*. "It's almost terrifying to be misunderstood," Miss Mansfield wrote. ". . . All was meant, of course, to lead up to that last paragraph, when my two flowerless ones turned with that timid gesture, to the sun. 'Perhaps *now* . . .' And after that, it seemed to me, they died as surely as Father was dead." [21]

The successful revelation of "moments of being," to use Mrs. Woolf's phrase, requires a conscious utilization of every device that will insure economy. Expository information cannot exceed a minimum or it will outweigh the whole. Both Joyce and Miss Mansfield have little concern with anterior events relating to a story; nevertheless a degree of orientation into the given circumstances is imperative. Very often Joyce allows expository material to remain implicit. The young boy of the first three stories of *Dubliners,* to take a minor example, lives not with his parents but with an uncle and aunt, a fact which is never explained but which is introduced very early in the first story, for it contributes to a full understanding of the dreamy, introspective lad. At times Joyce furnishes the necessary grounding conventionally by a succinct passage of direct explanation. At other times he establishes his points by indirect means. In "Counterparts" the setting in a law office, the approximate year and season, the relationship between Farrington and his superior Mr. Alleyne, emerge in the first page or two from the concentrated body of the narrative, through the employment of dialogue or concrete detail which at the same time serves to define character and to move the story along.

Miss Mansfield also is highly adept in turning the elements of her material to more than one purpose, particularly in the rapid establishment of exposition through oblique reference. "A Dill Pickle," one of the earliest stories in her mature technique, opens with one of her

curtain-rise sentences—"And then after six years she saw
him again"—condensing a whole history into nine words:
a relationship between a man and woman has been broken
off, or at least suspended; it was intimate and important,
for "she" is conscious of the exact period of time that has
elapsed. From thence onward, with no overt statement,
the former intimacy between the two is developed as
earlier events filter through the static situation in the present. Their conversation circles constantly, and very naturally, about the past, every reference drawing up in the
mind of each an associated incident which establishes the
source of their conflict in conflicting temperament. The
story is centered in Vera's consciousness. It is she who
remarks internally on all that is said, who recalls the evidences of his brashness that offended her delicate nature,
yet who now perceives, or thinks she perceives, her innate
need of his more sympathetic qualities. Meanwhile the
man chatters on at length, corroborating both the impression of his character that Vera's thoughts convey
and the impression of Vera herself which these same
thoughts transmit. Very clearly, "A Dill Pickle" reveals
an adaptation of the technique of the semidramatic pieces
Miss Mansfield was also writing at this time. But the
handling of the intricate material in this story is not yet
smooth; linkage of part to part at times is obvious. "In the
warmth, as it were, another memory unfolded," [22] Miss
Mansfield states baldly at one point.

In "Poison," written three years later, in November,
1920, the technique is under firm control. Miss Mansfield
herself in one of her letters has analyzed her technical
procedure:

The story is told by (evidently) a worldly, rather cynical
(not wholly cynical) man *against* himself (but not alto-

gether) when he was so absurdly young. You know how young by his idea of what woman is. She has been up to now, only the *vision*, only she who passes. You realise that? And here he has put all his passion into this Beatrice. It's *promiscuous* love, not understood as such by him; perfectly understood as such by her. But you realise the vie de luxe they are living—the very table—sweets, liqueurs, lilies, pearls. And you realise? she expects a letter from someone calling her away? *Fully* expects it? That accounts for her farewell AND her declaration. And when it doesn't come even her *commonness* peeps out—the newspaper touch of such a woman. She can't disguise her chagrin. She gives herself away. . . . He, of course, laughs at it now, and laughs at her. Take what he says about her "sense of order" and the crocodile. But he also regrets the self who, dead privately, would have been young enough to have actually wanted to *Marry* such a woman. But I meant it to be light—tossed off—and yet through it—Oh, subtly—the lament for youthful belief.[23]

"You realize" is the key to the method. In the first page or so of the story the situation is rapidly set by the inclusion of the few details which establish the "vie de luxe," by the repeated "we" and "as always" to indicate its extension back in time, by Beatrice's impatient exclamation when she finds the postman has not come. Particularly significant is Beatrice's fastidious habit of dropping into French when she speaks of such common matters as food or the weather or "playfully," as the narrator satirically puts it, of her love for the young man. At this point the story is ready to unfold; what we need as background has been given, swiftly, succinctly, by means of details which serve also other functional ends.

The fabric of Miss Mansfield's stories is thus very tightly woven. Every separate thread, intertwining among the others, has a value of more than one specific kind. Concrete detail, of course, counts very heavily, not only to establish setting and to define character but as basic to the expression of theme. Miss Mansfield does not often describe the physical appearance of her characters. She conveys a sense of being, of age and essence, with swift, impressionistic strokes, often through the use of color—of dress, of eyes or hair, of ornament—and of imagery. She rarely uses the exact technique of the objective realist. Joyce, like Chekhov, is highly skilled at realistic portraiture, constructing out of a few details the memorable embodiment of a figure—Little Chandler with his small white well-manicured hands, his childish white teeth, his fair silken hair and moustache; Farrington with his great bulk, his dark wine-colored face and eyes with dirty yellowish whites. To a far greater extent than Joyce, however, Miss Mansfield draws skillfully on the device of characterizing minor action. Probably the most revealing gesture throughout *Dubliners* is the way a man takes down his glass—cautiously, furiously, boldly, sadly. For the rest, the characters chiefly sit or walk and talk, so that any particularity of action stands out with high significance—Lenehan's skipping gait as he keeps alongside Corley's burly frame in "Two Gallants"; Mr. Alleyne's habit of shooting his fragile, hairless head up over the pile of papers on his desk in "Counterparts." Although Miss Mansfield's characters are more constantly in motion than Joyce's, they never move about aimlessly. Monica Tyrell in "Revelations," a hypersensitive neurotic, shrinks, shudders, agonizes at every jarring sound; Harry Young in "Bliss" rattles and slams his way about the house in bouncing male exuberance; Ma Parker, reviewing the miseries of her life, seeks to escape remembrance through the physical activity of cleaning the literary gentleman's dirty flat.

Even the constant daydreams in which Miss Mansfield's characters indulge are made dynamic by such characterizing details.

Perhaps the most valuable function to which Miss Mansfield turns detail appears in the device which she had hit upon as early as 1908 in "The Tiredness of Rosabel," the externalization of feeling by associating it with some fitting concrete correlative. By this device she avoids direct statement; the emotion she wishes to convey resides in the association of the object and the character. With one stroke she thus deflects the full tide of emotion and corroborates character, as she anchors to a solid substance the elusive feeling she wishes to transmit. Mouse in *"Je ne parle pas français,"* exerting control under grueling strain, speaks very little; she merely clings to her little grey muff, strokes it in silence, keeps her hands tight within it, as if it were the one thing in the world on which she can depend. Vera's former lover in "A Dill Pickle" catches up one of her gloves as she rises abruptly to leave, clutches it "as if that would hold her," [24] draws it gently through his fingers in the softened mood of regret, then suddenly, swiftly, returns it and scrapes back his chair. Mr. Salesby in "The Man Without a Temperament" turns, turns the heavy signet ring on his finger throughout the story, the circle of bondage confining him to the controlled boredom and homesickness which Miss Mansfield never directly states. Constantia in "The Daughters of the Late Colonel" centers her longing dreams about the stone image of Buddha on the mantelpiece, inscrutable and mysterious, which seems on the verge of revealing his secret after her father has died; but at the end she turns away from the Buddha "with one of her vague gestures." [25]

This method of cutting through the tangle of a complex and sometimes elusive emotion, swiftly and incisively, is excellent, but it is not infallible. At times it breaks down through being carried to an extreme. In "Miss Brill" Miss Mansfield indicates the emotional starvation of her character by Miss Brill's semi-personification of her fur piece. Early in the story Miss Brill talks to it, caresses it, thinks of it as "little rogue." Then at the emotional climax of her self-dramatizing reverie a silly girl ridicules this detail of her dress. Hurrying home to her room, Miss Brill sits for a long time on her bed, beside the box in which she keeps the fur piece. "She unclasped the necklet quickly; quickly, without looking, laid it inside. But when she put the lid on she thought she heard something crying." [26] Here the association of emotion with the external object has been pushed to an identity which Miss Brill herself points out, and we are conscious of excess. Likewise in "The Singing Lesson" the parallel between Miss Meadows' grief at her abruptly broken engagement and the melancholy "lament" her class is singing is manipulated too obviously; moreover, the sentimental phrases of the song which coincide with her emotion sentimentalize the whole; and the turnabout after Basil's telegram of recantation to a joyful paean is highly mechanical. "The Singing Lesson" is one of Miss Mansfield's least successful stories.

But in general Miss Mansfield's handling of the device is skillful. The associated object plays a natural part in the whole, hovering between functional detail and symbol. It is not usually employed as a distinct symbol, as it is in Mrs. Woolf's "Slater's Pins Have No Points," in which Fanny Wilmot's rose represents beauty, the blunt pin she has dropped represents practical sense, and the notes struck by the two symbols weave about the figure of

Julia Craye in a fuguelike design. Without question Mrs. Woolf's story is a highly finished virtuoso piece, with the complex material remarkably controlled; but, apart from her lapses, Miss Mansfield's touch, freer, more suggestive, more flexible, evokes a deeper emotional response.

Miss Mansfield thus is the impressionist painter, communicating her individual vision of a subject by a stroke here carefully related to a stroke there. Joyce is the objective realist, faithfully reproducing the external aspect of his subject which conceals its hidden significance. His clear, sharp, accurate detail, his infrequent use of metaphor, his strict impersonality of narration, convey his meaning through a neutral instrument. Miss Mansfield, in contradistinction, has shaped an instrument which is irradiated with the color of her own sensibility. This difference in general tone goes back to a fundamental difference in temperament. Joyce consciously set himself to present his material denuded of any personal attitude: life is painful enough to speak for itself. Miss Mansfield also strove to achieve complete objectivity. In Chekhov again she found the formulation of her aims: fidelity to life, the ugly being as real as the beautiful but not, as Chekhov was careful to insist, more real than the beautiful; detachment, the preservation of emotional equilibrium; restriction to the artist's proper sphere—to state the problems he perceives, not to solve them, which is the occupation of the scientist. Certainly Joyce sets out to solve no problems; certainly he preserves rigorous distance from his subject matter. Even the presumably autobiographical stories of adolescence, the first three of the book, are put in the form of recollections. The experiences recounted are now over; shock and fury have subsided; worse has happened. One can look back with detachment, with a sense of balance, with irony. Distance from a subject gives it clarity and proper proportions. With strength of feeling, the emotional content—in *Dubliners* the loss, oppression, and sterility Joyce perceived in the lives of his fellow men—can attain intolerable force. A deep knowledge of suffering underlies these stories, however severely the personal attitude is exorcised. Nevertheless, one would not wish a reduction of literary method to a single kind; the very eradication of the personal constitutes a personal attitude, which may extend to coldness. The warm humanity which infuses without softening Chekhov's work, the puzzled irony, the lightening touch of humor, create a different but equally expressive medium, capable of subtle modulations. Far more directly than Chekhov's writings, Miss Mansfield's stories reflect the qualities of her own temperament. Spontaneous, extremely personal in all relationships, she deals always with the individual, viewed through the intensifying glass of her own vision. Like Joyce in *Dubliners*, she is frequently concerned with death in life; but Joyce's deaths are in general the issue of social forces, which one can examine dispassionately, whereas she explores the region of her own spiritual dwelling place, in which reasonless fate or interacting human needs inflict suffering.

Katherine Mansfield's art has been most often characterized as "feminine"—by such diverse critics, among others, as T. S. Eliot, André Maurois, Katherine Anne Porter, and H. E. Bates. Not all the critics who emphasize this term have stopped to give their definition of its meaning. Mr. Bates, however, has stated at some length what it signifies to him. Although he considers Miss Mansfield's work with sympathy, his basic criticism is leveled at her "style," which he defines as "delicate and rippling," her favorite device being "a kind of mental soliloquy, fluttering, gossipy, breathless with question and answer." [27] The dangers which Miss Mansfield does not avoid, he states, are a confusion of the writer's voice with the voice of her character; monotony, since the tone never varies; and finally, a recognizable sameness about very different figures, until they are all "chattering overgrown schoolgirls busy asking and answering breathless facile questions about love and life and happiness." [28] In an account covering the history of the modern short story fine critical points naturally cannot be included. But Mr. Bates seems to have given Miss Mansfield's work only superficial consideration, based apparently on her most frequently reprinted stories.

It is true that in many of Miss Mansfield's stories the prose rhythms have a rapid, lilting beat. At its best this tempo is swift and buoyant; at its worst it is uneven and hysterical, as in "The Singing Lesson" and parts of "Bliss." The points Mr. Bates neglects are that the appropriateness of this tone to the subject matter of a story must be considered and that the adoption of the same tone by the author in the expository or interconnective material as in the interior monologue may not actually be a flaw. In general, in presenting her stories Miss Mansfield assumes a vantage point of observation just outside the limits of a given scene. Here she can examine her subject at close range, readily slip in and out of the consciousness of her figures, and make rapid connections between interior and exterior view. Joyce in his passages of interior monologue displays his usual acute sensitivity of ear in adapting the idiom he employs to the nature of his subject. To Eveline, uncertain, driven to confront a critical issue, he gives a very simple mode of expression, as befits a young unsophisticated girl; to James Duffy, cold, aloof, egocentric, intellectual, a formal polished tone; to the romantic lad in "Araby" the most poetic imagery in the book. Then, by a deft transition he resumes his ground outside the character and the prose becomes again wholly impersonal.

Miss Mansfield, like Virginia Woolf, sustains throughout a story one persisting note. Mrs. Woolf, focusing always on inner consciousness, rapidly transcribes in stylized language the sensations she wishes to depict: Mabel Waring's agony of self-consciousness in "The New Dress," which washes up and catches within it Mabel's essential temperament as well as her earlier history; Fanny Wilmot's flutter of emotion as she gropes for her rose, which serves also to mirror the inscrutable figure of Julia Craye. Miss Mansfield frequently reverses Mrs. Woolf's method. Instead of transmitting thought or feeling through a formalized literary medium, she casts the whole narrative into the informal tone she employs for the expression of interior consciousness. "A Cup of Tea" opens thus:

Rosemary Fell was not exactly beautiful. No, you couldn't have called her beautiful. Pretty? Well, if you took her to pieces . . . But why be so cruel as to take anyone to pieces? . . . She had a duck of a boy. No, not Peter— Michael. And her husband absolutely adored her. They were rich, really rich, not just comfortably well off, which is odious and stuffy and sounds like one's grandparents. But if Rosemary wanted to shop she would go to Paris as you or I would go to Bond Street.[29]

Obviously this expository passage cannot be intended as a reproduction of Rosemary's own stream of thought. It is the author who is speaking, in the very cadence she employs later for Rosemary's interior monologues: "Yes, she liked it very much. She loved it; it was a great duck." [30] By using Rosemary's own quick, telescoped idiom in the passages of exterior portrayal Miss Mansfield turns against her character the blade of Rosemary's own brittle, shallow sophistication. The tone here is another weapon of exposure.

Miss Mansfield had no affection for the modern metropolitan young woman. Almost without exception the young women she presents are callous, temperamental, selfish, and unreasonable. They demand the servile, undeviating attention of their men; their hypersensitive nerves cannot endure the slightest strain. It is in the delineation of these self-conscious, egocentric beings that she utilizes the syncopated accent of their own speech— for Rosemary Fell, Monica Tyrell, Isabel in "Marriage à la Mode," the woman in "The Escape." Bertha Young in "Bliss" to my mind exemplifies a misapplication of this tone; she seems not so much detestable as immature and stupid, an impression I do not believe Miss Mansfield meant to convey. Bertha expresses her excitement in an overwrought, gushing manner which alienates sympathy; and Miss Mansfield on her part joins in with her:

He tossed the coat away, put his hands on her shoulders and turned her violently to him. His lips said: "I adore you," and Miss Fulton laid her moonbeam fingers on his cheeks and smiled her sleepy smile. Harry's nostrils quivered; his lips curled back in a hideous grin while he whispered: "Tomorrow," and with her eyelids Miss Fulton said: "Yes." [31]

The note of hysteria is here sounded too crudely. One is so much distracted by the image of Harry Young with nostrils quivering and lips distorted that Bertha's emotional shock passes almost unobserved.

If Miss Mansfield had little charity for her own sex, she had also little admiration for the male. The men she depicts are either insufferable in conceit or pitiable in frustration. The difference between the two types is primitive; those of the first, who receive fullest attention, torment their women; those of the second are tormented by their women. Frequently the men are youthful or effeminate; occasionally they are both. Reggie in "Mr. and Mrs. Dove" is not only callow but emotionally disturbed, so that his "fluttering" tone is not incongruous with the subject, although this story, indeed, does not rank among Miss Mansfield's best. For Raoul Duquette, again the adaptation of tone serves the purpose of exposure. As a promising young writer, the author of *False Coins*, *Wrong Doors*, and *Left Umbrellas*, Duquette uses a self-conscious literary idiom, dissecting his conceits as well as his character as he relates the narrative. Further, he is sexually perverted, so that his feminine turn of phrase and thought is intrinsic to his nature.

I am little and light [he describes himself] with an olive skin, black eyes with long lashes, black silky hair cut short, tiny square teeth that show when I smile. . . . I confess, without my clothes I am rather charming. Plump, almost like a girl, with smooth shoulders, and I wear a thin gold bracelet above my left elbow.[32]

That flashy bird of plumage Mr. Reginald Peacock, the emotional teacher of voice, is also highly effeminate. Again tone and subject unite successfully, with the qualifying modulations carrying his fundamental cruelty and pompous conceit, though as one of the earlier stories the technique here is not always firm.

For the sensitive young girl, not yet woman, no longer

child, Miss Mansfield felt especial sympathy. Laura at the garden party, Leila at her first ball, the unnamed fledgling set against the corrupt milieu of Monte Carlo, stand midway between the conflicting worlds of childhood and maturity. Here the light, flying lilt of the prose admirably transmits the virginal quality of their anticipation, their gaiety and eagerness, their sudden recoil from the unexpected shock of life. It seems a little perverse of Mr. Bates to have selected as representative of Miss Mansfield's "style" as a whole passages from the interior monologues of the two adolescent girls Laura and Leila.

In a substantial number of the other stories the modulation of expression to the subject matter is skillfully achieved. "The Canary," like "The Lady's Maid," sustains in the monologue form a note of bleak resignation to old age and loneliness:

. . . Company, you see—that was what he was. Perfect company. If you have lived alone you will realize how precious that is. Of course there were my three young men who came in to supper every evening, and sometimes stayed in the dining-room afterwards reading the paper. But I could not expect them to be interested in the little things that made my day. Why should they be? [33]

Again, in "Pictures" Miss Ada Moss's soliloquies carry the resentful bewilderment and self-deluding evasions of the respectable woman driven to seek out disreputable ways; and in "Life of Ma Parker" the choice of sordid detail, reduction of imagery, and adaptation of idiom merge to establish the appropriate tone for the battered old charwoman whose history is related:

. . . From Lennie's little box of a chest there came a sound as though something was boiling. There was a great lump of something bubbling in his chest that he couldn't get rid of. When he coughed the sweat sprang out on his head; his eyes bulged, his hands waved, and the great lump bubbled as a potato knocks in a saucepan. But what was more awful than all was when he didn't cough he sat against the pillow and never spoke or answered, or even made as if he heard. Only he looked offended.[34]

One should consider also the two long unfinished pieces, "A Married Man's Story" and "The Doves' Nest," which, placed side by side, offer a striking contrast. "A Married Man's Story," while immediately recognizable as "Mansfield," differs in expression from any other of her narratives. The sentences are longer, more involved in construction, conveying a tone of measured gravity excellently suited to the coldly analytical detached first-person narrator. "The Doves' Nest," on the other hand, is imbued with charming sprightliness, delightfully adapted to the young girl Milly and her featherbrained mother, while it also moves slowly and fully, with a solidity of grounding that the concentrated shorter stories lack.

This is not to argue that Miss Mansfield's work possesses either high variety or extensive range, or that she is always successful in execution within the limits of her scope. William's unhappy soliloquies in "Marriage à la Mode" are scarcely masculine; nor do the thoughts of old Mr. Neave in "An Ideal Family" sound aged and weary enough for a disappointed "successful" man. (These stories, it may be remarked in passing, as well as the sentimental pieces "Sixpence" and "Taking the Veil," belong to the series Miss Mansfield wrote by agreement for the *Sphere* within a period of five months.) But if one wishes to establish an accurate understanding of Miss Mansfield's accomplishment, it seems just to apply more careful attention to her faults and her virtues than Mr. Bates apparently has given in his dismissal of her "style" as unvaried school-girl soliloquy.

In my judgment, a chief characterizing element in Miss Mansfield's work resides not so much in prose tempo or rhythm as in the kind of perception which invests her material. Her vision of the world was the vision of child-hood, which perceives in highly vivid and meaningful detail, making fresh imaginative associations, so that her writing is touched with a delicate Dickensian quality. In even greater abundance these gossamer grotesqueries pervade her letters and her journals. Now and again an interesting evolution from these sources can be traced. In May, 1919, Miss Mansfield wrote from her Hampstead house to Virginia Woolf: "The vicar called upon me yesterday and asked if he might come occasionally and administer a *little* Private Communion to me at any time . . . just a drain of wine, I suppose, and a crumb of bread. Why a little? It puzzled me greatly." [35] When a year and a half later she wrote "The Daughters of the Late Colonel" she had not forgotten her mystification. Mr. Farolles, the vicar, calling upon Constantia and Josephine the after-noon of their father's death, offers his assistance. " 'And if either of you would like a little Communion, either or both of you, here *and* now, you have only to tell me. A little Communion is often very help—a great comfort,' he added tenderly." [36] Then with characteristic humor Miss Mansfield spins out the little incident:

But the idea of a little Communion terrified them. What! In the drawing-room by themselves—with no—no altar or anything! The piano would be much too high, thought Con-stantia, and Mr. Farolles could not possibly lean over it with the chalice. And Kate would be sure to come bursting in and interrupt them, thought Josephine. And supposing the bell rang in the middle? It might be somebody important—about their mourning. Would they get up reverently and go out, or would they have to wait . . . in torture? [37]

Again, in a letter describing her trip to Switzerland in May, 1921, Miss Mansfield wrote: "The manager, who is very like a goldfish, flashed through the glass doors and our journey was over." [38] In "Honeymoon," written several months later, she extended this little image to enliven the manager of the hotel where George and Fanny stop for tea: "The sleek manager, who was marvellously like a fish in a frock coat, skimmed forward." [39] The manager's mouth opens and shuts "as though he was ready for another dive under the water"; [40] in his professional affability he "grimaced and smirked and flicked his serviette like a fin." [41]

At times this quality of fanciful perception coincides functionally with the depiction of a character, as it does with Constantia and Josephine. Particularly apt is this integration in "A Married Man's Story," as the narrator, reviewing his lonely childhood, describes his terrifying vision of his mother, standing in her night clothes beside his bed, whispering that she has been poisoned by his father.

Did that visit happen? Was it a dream? Why did she come to tell me? Or why, if she came, did she go away so quickly? And her expression—so joyous under the frightened look—was that real? I believed it fully the afternoon of the funeral, when I saw my father dressed up for his part, hat and all. That tall hat so gleaming black and round was like a cork covered with black sealing-wax, and the rest of my father was awfully like a bottle, with his face for the label—*Deadly Poison*. It flashed into my mind as I stood opposite him in the hall. And Deadly Poison, or old D.P., was my private name for him from that day.[42]

Developed at its most extensive, this fanciful quality appears in Linda Burnell, whom Miss Mansfield consciously endowed with her own imaginative gifts. Lying alone in her room, Linda has a paralyzing sense that the inanimate things around her are slowly coming alive, not only the larger pieces like furniture but the smaller objects.

How often she had seen the tassel fringe of her quilt change into a funny procession of dancers with priests attending. . . . For there were some tassels that did not dance at all but walked stately, bent forward as if praying or chanting. How often the medicine bottles had turned into a row of little men with brown top-hats on; and the washstand jug had a way of sitting in the basin like a fat bird in a round nest.[43]

This whimsical fancy is entirely in keeping with the sustained tenor of Linda's reveries, in which the actual constantly undergoes the permutations of the world of dreams. Nor is it unsuited to the nature of Raoul Duquette to formulate his first impression of Mouse: "She came upon you with the same kind of shock that you feel when you have been drinking tea out of a thin innocent cup and suddenly, at the bottom, you see a tiny creature, half butterfly, half woman, bowing to you with her hands in her sleeves"; [44] or to note of her costume—the long dark cloak edged at the neck and armbands with grey fur, the close-fitting little furry cap—" 'Carrying out the mouse idea.' " [45] But when this quality of imagination recurs in various characters somewhat indiscriminately, one begins to question its persistent appearance: Bertha Young's notion in "Bliss" that Mrs. Norman Knight without her amusing coat is like "a very intelligent monkey—who had even made that yellow silk dress out of scraped banana skins. And her amber ear-rings; they were like little dangling nuts"; [46] William's "horrible vision" in "Marriage à la Mode," as he takes his present of a melon to his little son, of "one of Isabel's young poets lapping up a slice, for some reason, behind the nursery door"; [47] Miss Meadows' acid judgment of a fellow teacher in "The Singing Lesson": "Everything about her was sweet, pale, like honey. You would not have been surprised to see a bee caught in the tangles of that yellow hair." [48] Sharp, arresting, frequently delightful as these flights of fancy are, they endow a number of characters with accidental similarity in that they all possess Miss Mansfield's own imaginative perception.

This quality of perception is closely linked with Miss Mansfield's capacity for intensely concentrated sensuous experience, which she transmits also in her writing. Her stories are flooded with light; the wind blows, the sea washes; flowers are scattered about abundantly; music plays, bells sound; the busy throb of cities beats its way into the mind. For the most part, the world she has created is a brilliant world of vivid motion and bright color. Motion she conveys chiefly through the use of energetic verbs—*twinkle, flash, dart, sparkle, glitter, gleam, glide, spin*—so that her prose takes on a buoyant, iridescent quality. This quality inheres even more strongly in her characteristic choice of images. Predominant above all others is the "bird-wing" image, which occurs in almost every story, sometimes with several variations in the same piece. Blossoms have leaves like moth's wings or perch among the branches of a tree "like red and white birds." [49] Voices beat like birds; emotion presses in the breast "like two fanning wings." [50] Two birds sing in the kettle at teatime; the air is "feathery" with snow; at the garden party the guests flutter about like bright birds arrested in mid-flight. Fenella's grandfather looks "like a very old wide-awake bird"; [51] Our Else is a little white owl; Mr. Salesby thinks of his invalid wife as "a broken bird that tries to fly and sinks again and again struggles" [52] (the image Miss Mansfield uses of herself in the intimate poems of 1919); Janey in "The Stranger" is characterized throughout as a light, airy being who may at any moment fly away. This recurrent image imbues the prose with a delicate agitation that is heightened by the most persisting secondary images—the flower, the leaf, the fern, the star, the candle flame, the flicker of fire. Most frequent among these images—appearing almost as often as the bird-wing metaphor—are those based upon a parallel with some aspect of the sea, often with the curious dual effect of both expansion and reduction through the nature of their specific details. Dick Harmon is likened to a sailor, dreamy and abstracted away from his ship; Fenella on her voyage sees the houses on the distant shore clustered together like shells on the lid of a box; the big summer hats of the women in "At the Bay" look like immense shells; Mouse after her betrayal speaks in a voice "like the voice you might imagine coming out of a tiny, cold sea-shell swept high and dry at last by the salt tide." [53]

Miss Mansfield always relates details of setting to the emotional mood of her stories, not only through the choice of season in which events occur—the expectancy of flowering spring to Bertha Young's expectancy of bliss; the exhausting heat of summer to William's exhausting emotional frustration in "Marriage à la Mode"—but also less directly through a pervasive "natural" imagery which most often draws its parallel from some aspect of weather or light. In general these images play a functional role in the depiction of scene, unobtrusively heightening the central mood and theme of a story. They do not commonly appear as an overt symbol, as they do, rather too deliberately, in "The Daughters of the Late Colonel." Constantia and Josephine, toward the end of this story, realizing that at last they have been freed from spiritual bondage by their father's death, experience a wavering aspiration for a more abundant life. "On the Indian carpet there fell a square of sunlight, pale red; it came and went and came—and stayed, deepened—until it shone almost golden." [54] As the sisters stand wondering, hoping, longing, the sun "pressed through the windows, thieved its way in, flashed its light over the furniture and the photographs," [55] illuminating the worn relics of the past which still imprisons them. When the moment of aspiration shrivels, a big cloud blots out the sun as the story ends.

For the most part, in the other stories emotional mood is attached to details of imagery with less obvious intent. Remoteness or detachment is at times conveyed through an association with moonlight: Pearl Fulton, Harry Young's cryptic charmer, appears to Bertha Young as pale, silver, cool, with "moonbeam fingers"; Linda Burnell's sense of the distance separating her from her husband Linda herself phrases as "being strangely discovered in a flood of cold light" [56] at the rising of the moon. Fear or desolation is most frequently associated with the dark, the cold, with rain or snow: the frightening shadows of night descend to terrify Kezia and her playmates; Ma Parker is left with her misery in the icy wind and rain; cold rain and the dark "spinning down like ashes" [57] stir Rosemary Fell to self-pitying loneliness; the fire flickers, falls and dies, the room grows colder, as Mr. Hammond receives from Janey his intolerable pain. Conversely, the warmth of love and security is represented again and again by the glow of firelight or lamplight—sometimes glimpsed from the outside—the protecting walls that shut out the night.

A subordinate group of images, which serve to intensify an unpleasant or commonplace atmosphere, draw their parallels from familiar objects in domestic living. Monica Tyrell, wrenched out of sleep on a "frightful windy morning," sees through the window "a huge pale sky and a cloud like a torn shirt dragging across." [58] Ma Parker, cleaning up the unsightly rubbish in the literary gentleman's flat, notices through the dirty window the clouds in the wintry sky "frayed at the edges, with holes in them, or dark stains like tea." [59] The servant girl in "Prelude" prepares afternoon tea in the warm kitchen, with a blowfly buzzing and the clock ticking "slow and deliberate, like the click of an old woman's knitting needle." [60] Fat Mrs. Samuel Josephs in the same story envelops Lottie "like a huge warm black silk tea cosy," [61] asthmatically soothing her grief. Reggie's mother in "Mr. and Mrs. Dove" is brusque and sharp, like her own garden shears. Plump old women are "old dusty pincushions"; lean old women "worn umbrellas."

What immediately strikes one in a study of Miss Mansfield's imagery is her concentration on the miniature, a quality which extends to her entire handling of imaginative detail. The woman in "Psychology" pictures herself and her companion as reduced figures in a scene so small it might have been painted on the blue teapot lid. Reggie, lighting Anne's cigarette, sees "the tiny flame glow in the pearl ring she wore." [62] The tableau on the lid of the enamel box which enchants Rosemary Fell is meticulously reproduced—the "minute creature" under a flowery tree embraced by a creature still more minute, whose hat, with green ribbons streaming, hangs like a geranium petal from a branch. The tiny manuka blossoms which fall on Linda as she sits on the lawn beside her infant boy are described with similar exactitude: "Each pale yellow petal shone as if each was the careful work of a loving hand. The tiny tongue in the centre gave it the shape of a bell. And when you turned it over the outside was a deep bronze colour. . . . Who takes the trouble—or the joy—to make all these things that are wasted, wasted." [63]

This fascination by the very small is a quality found more often in women than in men, but it distinguishes most generally the curious and observant child. Like a child's, too, is Miss Mansfield's representation of ugliness or evil, in the reduced dimensions of an insect—the snail or spider usually—or an animal. The hateful Mrs. Harry Kember in "At the Bay" swims off like a water rat; the two obnoxious women guests at the hotel in "The Man Without a Temperament" keep their knitting beside them in coils like two snakes. Danger, almost always identified with sexual passion, invariably appears as a frightening animal. At times the terror is nameless—the cry of the beast in the jungle that disturbs the man and woman in "Psychology"; but most often it takes concrete form as a cat or dog. Miss Moss's downfall in "Pictures" is foreshadowed by her glimpse of an old brown tailless cat which appears in the street from nowhere and greedily laps up a splash of milk. Similarly, Bertha Young sees the exquisite beauty of the flowering pear tree disfigured by the two dragging cats that creep before it through the garden bed. Raoul Duquette is repeatedly characterized as a sharp-nosed fox terrier, sniffing and prowling about the defenseless Mouse, who by her very name is defined as a small, helpless, hunted creature. Thinking, as always in metaphor, Linda Burnell pictures her husband as a rushing Newfoundland dog, brutally assaulting her body in his passionate attack (though "in the daytime," in his submissive hours, she "really was fond of him").[64]

In this scheme of things, this ruined Eden, the large symbols Miss Mansfield uses—the bird, the tree, the insect—accord perfectly. Two doves, one always in front of the other running forward with a little laughing cry, the other always following faithfully, bowing and bowing, symbolize the relationship between Reggie and Anne. In "Bliss" the central symbol is the lovely pear tree, which to Bertha Young represents her life and which embodies Bertha's own virginal quality. Again, in "The Escape" a tree serves as the central symbol, a tree with "a great arc of copper leaves that gave back the light and yet were sombre." [65] As the man looks into it, freed for the time from his wife's nagging, it seems to overspread the sky, motionless in the quivering heat, with from somewhere within the sound of a woman's voice singing. The voice disturbs the peace and silence; he struggles against the sudden oppression he feels. Then the voice ceases, and he is again enfolded in peace. Here, as I understand it, the man's "escape" is through mystical identification with the complete, harmonious pattern of life represented by the tree, which the delusive charm of woman shatters; but occasionally the vision can be glimpsed and for a time retained.

In "Prelude" the aloe figures importantly. As the story stands, Linda notices the aloe on her first morning at the new house, the "cruel leaves," the thick stem plunging into the earth. "The curving leaves seemed to be hiding something; the blind stem cut into the air as if no wind could ever shake it." [66] When Kezia asks if the tree ever bears flowers, Linda smiles, half shutting her eyes, and answers: " 'Once every hundred years.' " [67] Toward the end of the story Linda walks in the garden with her mother. They stand before the aloe, which in the bright moonlight seems like a ship with oars lifted riding the grassy waves. Linda imagines that the ship draws nearer, that she is caught up and carried away, beyond the gardens and fields, leaving house and family behind. As she walks on with her mother, she notices again the long sharp thorns edging the aloe leaves. "Nobody would dare to come near the ship or to follow after," [68] she thinks. As in her earlier fancy of driving away from her family without looking back, Linda's essential nature is here incorporate. For the aloe is Linda herself, set about with sharp thorns, firmly rooted in her determination to preserve herself apart, unapproachable in external appearance, but with the possibility of bearing "once every hundred years" the flower of selfless love. Originally Miss Mansfield designed the aloe for a larger role in this story. One of her working notes reads: "They cut down the stem when Linda is ill. She has been counting on the flowering of the Aloe." [69] She had planned also to have the birth of the infant son, who "must mean the world to Linda," [70] take place in "the last chapter." Both Linda and the aloe tree remain unchanged at the end of "Prelude"; but in "At the Bay," though the aloe is not mentioned, the little son has been born.

The third recurrent symbol in Miss Mansfield's stories draws upon insect life. Jonathan Trout, describing his

incarceration as an office worker to Linda, pictures himself as an insect that has flown into a room and dashes itself
against walls and windows in an effort to get free.

"Why don't I fly out again? There's the window or the door
or whatever it was I came in by. It's not hopelessly shut—is
it? Why don't I find it and be off? . . . For some reason"
—Jonathan paused between the words—"it's not allowed,
it's forbidden, it's against the insect law, to stop banging and
flopping and crawling up the pane even for an instant." [71]

The insect is created in multitudes; he is born, exists for
his little time, or is destroyed by any one of a thousand
accidents. He is at the mercy of a capricious force that
has brought him into being and determines his extinction.
As far back as 1918 Miss Mansfield wrote, under the head-
ing "The Fly":

Oh, the times when she had walked upside down on the ceiling, run up glittering panes, floated on a lake of light, flashed
through a shining beam!
    And God looked upon the fly fallen into the jug of milk
and saw that it was good. And the smallest Cherubim and
Seraphim of all, who delight in misfortune, struck their silver
harps and shrilled: "How is the fly fallen, fallen!" [72]

Elsewhere in her journals and letters she uses this metaphor again, and it also occurs briefly in "The Voyage."
Perhaps the image was refreshed in her mind during her
reading of Shakespeare at the end of 1921, shortly before
she wrote "The Fly," by the lines in *Lear:*

> As flies to wanton boys are we to th' gods.
> They kill us for their sport.

Or she may have come upon Chekhov's "Small Fry,"
with which her story has several close similarities.

In general Miss Mansfield employs lesser symbols skillfully, so that they form an intrinsic element of a story and
carry their symbolic and thematic significance at the same
time. The little lamp in "The Doll's House" plays its part
as a concrete little lamp, as enchanting in its miniature
perfection to Kezia as it was to Kathleen Beauchamp when
Mrs. Heywood sent her present to the three little Beauchamp girls; in "Prelude" the aloe forms a natural part of
the established scene; and Jonathan Trout's insect metaphor in "At the Bay" is wholly in keeping with his habitual
manner of speech. But when she deliberately shapes a story
about a symbol she is not always equally adept. The parallel in "Mr. and Mrs. Dove" between the two doves and
Reggie and Anne is made by Anne herself, emphasized
and underscored again in the title. In "Bliss," also, Bertha
Young herself makes clear the symbolic intention: "And
she seemed to see on her eyelids the lovely pear tree with
its wide open blossoms as a symbol of her own life." [73] In
"The Fly" the central symbolism is confused. Obviously
the boss stands for a superior controlling power—God,
destiny, or fate—which in capricious and impersonal
cruelty tortures the little creature struggling under his
hand until it lies still in death. At the same time the boss
is presented as one who has himself received the blows of
this superior power through the death of his only son in
the war. Thus the functional role which the boss plays
in the story does not fuse with the symbolic role, a division which probably accounts for the various unsatis-
factory interpretations of the symbolism in this story,
further complicated by the secondary theme attached to
the boss: the atrophy of feeling the poor of heart even-
tually experience.

The world Miss Mansfield has created is constructed by

a woman's intellect out of the emotional apprehension of a child. It is Kezia's world in the New Zealand stories, overflowing with natural beauty, exhilarating to see, touch, taste, hear, smell, enchanting in the sunlight but mysterious and frightening in the dark. In the face of danger Kezia seeks the glow of lamplight, the encircling walls of home. But the walls cannot really offer protection; the beast of danger lurks outside, and sometimes in, the slinking animal shapes which terrify a child. "I adore *Life*, but my experience of the world is that it's pretty terrible," [74] Miss Mansfield wrote in 1921. This dualism she could never resolve into a harmony; it underlies the entire body of her work. Only in "The Fly" does she give up the struggle and submit.

From the emotional content of Miss Mansfield's stories, the attitude toward life acquired through adult insight and experience, emerge a few persisting themes, basically unchanged, as has been already noted, from their incorporation in her earlier experimental work. These themes are essentially those of the writers of her generation: a preoccupation with loneliness and frustration, with sexual maladjustment, with purposeless suffering, with the falseness, ostentation, and sterility of modern sophisticated life, with the denial of emotional fulfillment to all classes of men. Put thus broadly, this statement comprehends the early thematic substance of T. S. Eliot. Again, implicit in her work, appearing and disappearing like a winding thread, is a dispersed expression of the great Proustian theme: that in the shift and flux of time, through the invasion of other values, other demands, other interests, no human relationship remains unchanged; at the moment of its consummation it is being altered, to be lost until re-animated from the past. Naturally, the communication of these themes is determined by the sensibility behind the shaping mind; and it is here that the most careful judgment of Miss Mansfield's achievement is required.

Historically Miss Mansfield's position in literature, though minor, is secure. Of course no general literary trend can be attributed to a single motivating force. The confluence of interacting elements—social, political, psychological, philosophical, as well as literary—is always highly intricate. Yet it may not be arbitrary to single out as standing at the head of the broad stream of development in the modern short story Miss Mansfield and the Joyce of *Dubliners*. This is not to neglect the earlier important contribution of Maupassant in France, later of the Irish writers after Joyce, especially O'Faolain and O'Connor, of A. E. Coppard in England and Sherwood Anderson in America. It is merely to point out that the dominating form of the serious short story in English for the last quarter century has been a form incorporating elements of the work of both Joyce and Katherine Mansfield, which has extended on the one hand to the stringent economies of Dorothy Parker and Ernest Hemingway, on the other to the psychological subtleties of Elizabeth Bowen and Eudora Welty, lapsing in latter days to the arid accomplishments in the genre known as the *New Yorker* story.

But the true test of a writer is more than his position in the stream of historical development. The value of his creation exists apart from time, as an artistic entity. Before considering Miss Mansfield's achievement in this sense it is well to remember that the body of her mature work comprises under forty stories, written, except for

"Prelude," in a period of five years; and that in spite of some unevenness this work reveals a progressive strengthening, not only in details of technique but in imaginative insight, though the quality of this insight remains unchanged and the original circumscription of view is not much enlarged. To me it seems more relevant to examine Miss Mansfield's actual accomplishment for its significance and worth than to deplore the acknowledged limitations of her scope. Enough attention has already been paid to her specific lapses, variations, and failures; the infusion of her own temperament into her writing is a prime source of weakness, but a weakness over which she was gaining firm control, as her last stories indicate. In a final evaluation I believe one should regard especially that portion of an artist's work in which his fullest potentialities have been realized.

High among Miss Mansfield's abilities is her gift for entertaining satire, a gift which she drew upon most abundantly in her early arrogant years and which gives an astringent note to many of her later stories. Consistently this satire is directed against the charlatans and poseurs of the artistic circles with which she was familiar —through the figures of Raoul Duquette, Mr. Reginald Peacock, Isabel's crass egotists in "Marriage à la Mode," the agitated minor poet and the affected Norman Knights in "Bliss"; and it is as wittily pertinent today as it was twenty-five years ago. In the expression of this talent, Katherine Anne Porter has remarked, lay Miss Mansfield's true artistic medium. "Mistakenly," Miss Porter has written, "she fought in herself those very elements that combined to form her virtue: a certain grim, quiet ruthlessness of judgment, an unsparing and sometimes cruel eye, a natural malicious wit, an intelligent humor." [75] In my judgment, skillfully presented as these anatomizings are, it is not this ability which gives play to Miss Mansfield's finest gifts. These gifts find their highest expression in a quality in her work less easily defined, a quality by which she achieves a quickening of her readers' apprehensions, a sharpening of imaginative perception as well as the capacity for sensuous response, the power "to view as a subtle symbol what they otherwise would regard merely as a stray fact," as one critic has put it.[76]

This power of persuasion resides in all Miss Mansfield's finest work; and it goes back to an insight, penetrating, intensifying, yet extremely delicate, which perceives most acutely when it is applied to the lonely reaches within the inarticulate. However moving the depiction of Ma Parker's misery, until she is driven to question "What have I done? What have I done?" however pitiable the downfall of foolish, well-intentioned Ada Moss, it is in those other stories which probe the nature of the several deaths in life—in "The Daughters of the Late Colonel," in "The Canary," surpassingly in "The Doll's House" and "The Stranger"—that Miss Mansfield's vision is at its most sensitive. It is this insight which recognizes that the pathos of the empty life lies in its irremediable waste; that the experience of anguish can be very bitter even though it is not on a dramatic scale; that the ordeal of grief is hard, but the slow ordeal of resignation harder—recognitions which most of us would accept as true to our own knowledge. These are negative recognitions, it may be said; nevertheless they constitute perceptions which can enlarge our own fund of sympathy.

At its strongest and fullest this insight informs the group of New Zealand stories which stands as Miss Mansfield's highest accomplishment. Taken together, this group com-

prises a substantial body of material. Besides "Prelude,"
"At the Bay," and "The Doll's House," which present the
Burnell family directly, six other stories [77] involve the
same scene and many of the same characters. Fragmentary
as the various pieces are in which the Burnells, in one guise
or another, appear, they present a constantly widening
view of individual human nature which yields up uni-
versal human significance. We perceive in a series of
flashes, it is true, but we do absorb a remarkable depth of
knowledge about this New Zealand family. Kezia at seventeen may appear as Laura Sheridan; Stanley may be called
Mr. Hammond, Linda may be called Janey Hammond or
Mrs. Sheridan: we know very well who they are. So distinct is our sense of their being that in the unfinished story
"Six Years After," in which the husband and wife are
given no names at all, we scarcely notice that they lack the
designations Stanley and Linda.

In part this fullness of character portrayal is achieved
because the characters have space in which to grow. We
understand Linda the better, naturally, for seeing her
respond to the sensitivity of her brother-in-law Jonathan
Trout with her own sensitivity, for watching her break
through her dislike for her children to a reluctant tenderness for her infant son, in a scene of exquisite beauty—a
scene which makes all the more poignant the grief of the
mother in "Six Years After" who hears the voice of her
dead son calling her over the grey sea. Our sympathy for
Stanley is likewise heightened as we observe him baffled
and irritated by the easy-going, ineffectual Jonathan
Trout, whom he regards as a failure and who yet, he
senses uneasily, has some clue to happiness Stanley himself cannot grasp, even though Jonathan is too weak to
follow it.

The scenes devoted to the children, the Burnell sisters, their cousins Pip and Rags, the disreputable Kelveys of "The Doll's House," reinforce character similarly. As moving as "The Doll's House" is in isolation, its fullest poignance is revealed only when it is related to "Prelude" and "At the Bay." The Kelveys are the outcasts of the village; their mother is a washerwoman, their father has disappeared. But they are endowed with human instincts, as Kezia, the compassionate and stubborn, understands. They long to see the new doll's house, like all the other children. In breaking the prohibition to invite them into her yard Kezia is setting herself against superior command; and we see in the other stories the bewildering realization the children are forced to make that their world, with its own laws of good and evil, is not the world of the adults. It is the shock the children suffer at this conflict with adult reality that places them, for all their enchanting vigor, in a haunting, pathetic light. Excitedly they witness the beheading of a duck; but their excitement turns to fright and nervous irritation once the silent body has fallen over motionless; here is a new and tangible horror: something which a moment ago breathed, ate, swam, now lies dead in its gush of bright red blood, and the sensitive child shrieks "Put head back!" in the effort to restore the dimensions of her own familiar world.

The figures in these New Zealand stories, further, are set in a very definite environment, as concrete as Joyce's Dublin. We know the house, the gardens, the paddocks; we know what these people wear, what they eat, and where they sleep. But neither spatial enlargement nor concrete grounding would in themselves make for the unequaled depth and lucidity of the characters. The source of their distinction lies in the subtle penetration with which Miss Mansfield as a woman viewed the experience of her childhood, which she retained in living memory within herself. Willa Cather has observed, in a fine essay on "Prelude" and "At the Bay," that in these stories the author "communicates vastly more than she actually writes." [78] Miss Mansfield's secret can never be wholly captured: what she somehow manages to convey is that emotional vibration between character and character which we know through intuition in actual life, those filaments of intimate experience which determine the nature of our being and therefore of our happiness. "It isn't as though one sits and watches the spectacle," Miss Mansfield wrote after finishing "The Stranger." "That would be thrilling enough, God knows. But one is the spectacle for the time." [79] This "spectacle" she has shaped into stories that are poignant but strong, firmly fashioned even at their most delicate. If this quality of creation is to be termed feminine, it fulfills, in my opinion, a necessary function in literature.

Katherine Mansfield was not a writer of magnitude. She dealt with passion, with high tragedy and comedy, no more than she dealt with robust adventure. In the gallery of characters she has created, a number are merely variations on a few established types (but in the main they are sprightly variations). Among the others, Raoul Duquette, the daughters of the late colonel Constantia and Josephine, Linda and Stanley Burnell, the grandmother, the New Zealand children, assume a vitality rarely met in the sphere of the short story—and I think I would add Miss Ada Moss. Each stands the test of repeated encounters, one of the severest tests, surely, that one can apply to a fictional character.

The enlargement of perception one receives from Miss

Mansfield's finest work is of the kind one gains from association with an imaginative and gifted child, who sees, freshly and sharply, imponderables of meaning within the compass of the small. But she was also a woman who had suffered in the world, and it is not often that the untouched apprehension of the child fuses perfectly with the view acquired through the circumstances of her life. When it does we have a form of expression which intensifies to lasting value a portion of human experience, through the instrument of original vision, and which is therefore authentic art.

NOTES

PRELIMINARY NOTE. For the biographical material in this study I am indebted to a number of main sources, to which, except for direct quotations, I now make general acknowledgment. The principal facts of Miss Mansfield's life until she left New Zealand for England in 1908 I have taken from Sir Harold Beauchamp's *Reminiscences and Recollections* (New Plymouth, N. Z., 1937), published for private circulation, which has been made accessible to me through the kindness of Mrs. Mackintosh Bell (Vera Beauchamp Bell), of Ottawa, Ontario. Supplementing this account, I have drawn upon *The Life of Katherine Mansfield* (London, 1933), by Ruth Elvish Mantz and J. Middleton Murry, a biography which carries Miss Mansfield's life up to 1912, approximately the point at which her *Letters* and *Journal* open. For the body of biographical facts between 1912 and 1919 I have drawn upon Mr. Murry's (incomplete) autobiography, *Between Two Worlds* (New York, 1936). From 1912 on, however, I have utilized all possible factual material in Miss Mansfield's *Letters, Journal,* and *Scrapbook,* basing my account of the years from 1919 to 1923 largely on these sources. These last three volumes, of course, have served me throughout for the comprehension and interpretation of Katherine

Mansfield's personality, in ways too finely shaded for bibliographical acknowledgment.

CHAPTER I. KATHLEEN BEAUCHAMP

1. "The Pine-Tree, the Sparrows, and You and I," *Queen's College Magazine*, XXII (December, 1903), 74–76; "Die Einsame (The Lonely One)," *ibid.*, XXII (March, 1904), 129–131; "Your Birthday," *ibid.*, XXIII (December, 1904), 203–205; "One Day," *ibid.*, XXIV (July, 1905), 294–299; "About Pat," *ibid.*, XXIV (December, 1905), 344–347. Of these five stories, "About Pat" is reprinted in *The Scrapbook of Katherine Mansfield*, ed. J. Middleton Murry (New York, 1940), pp. 3–7 f., with the omission of the two opening and the closing paragraphs.

2. The Beauchamp line of descent, according to family belief, goes back to Richard Beauchamp, who accompanied William the Conqueror to England in 1066, to engage in the Battle of Hastings, and who received both honors and material rewards from the first Norman king of England. John Beauchamp (b. 1781) married Ann Stone, one of the six daughters of Samuel Stone and his wife Mary Sneyd, whose mother claimed descent from a Saxon family prominent in England in the days of King Alfred. The Stone family included twelve children, of whom the six daughters were remarkable for their beauty. Like her sister Harriet (who married Leslie), Ann Stone sat as model to C. R. Leslie, notably for his portrait of the Widow Wadman, in "The Widow Wadman and Uncle Toby." This picture was exhibited with the empire loan collection in the New Zealand National Gallery in August, 1936. Either Harriet or Ann figures in two pictures now possessed by the royal family: "Lady Jane Grey Refusing the Crown" and "The Coronation of Queen Victoria."

3. Samuel Pepys mentions, in November, 1660, a "gilt tankard" bought at "Mr. Beauchamp's, the goldsmith" at a cost of £200. (*The Diary of Samuel Pepys*, ed. Henry B. Wheatley [London, 1924], I, 262, 267.) For further reference to Mr. Beauchamp see *ibid.*, III, 146, 333.

4. Charles Robert Leslie was born in London on October 19, 1794, the son of American parents of Philadelphia. His father, a friend of Benjamin Franklin, died in 1804, leaving a seriously impaired estate. From childhood Leslie had shown an active interest in painting. While still a youth he attracted notice among wealthy Philadelphians, who raised funds to send him abroad for two years. He sailed from New York in November, 1811, with letters from Sully to Benjamin West and other artists.

In London Leslie studied under West and Washington Allston. It was through Allston that he became acquainted with Coleridge. He was also an intimate friend of Washington Irving. Apparently he was a genial, affectionate, well-liked companion: he knew many of the most eminent writers and artists of the day—Lamb, Scott, Wordsworth, Sidney Smith, Samuel Rogers, Constable, Flaxman, Wilkie, Landseer, Etty, and Turner, among others.

After his marriage to Ann Stone in 1825 Leslie was closely associated with John Beauchamp's family, then living in Hornsey Lane, Highgate, in northwest London. Through his introduction the Beauchamps met John Constable, whose boys delighted in the forges, metals, crucibles, and cinders of the Beauchamp workshop. (*The Letters of John Constable, R.A. to C. R. Leslie, R.A. 1826–1837*, ed. Peter Leslie [London, 1931], pp. 102 f.) Perhaps Katherine Mansfield's grandfather, Arthur Beauchamp, as a boy heard his painter uncle relate various of the incidents described in his *Autobiographical Recollections:* how he introduced Coleridge to *Knickerbocker's History of New York,* reading which Coleridge "must have sate up the greater part of the night" (I, 34); how he journeyed to Scotland to paint Sir Walter Scott, whose nature he warmly admired but who had "things hanging on the walls of his dining-room, which no eye possessing sensibility to what is excellent in art could have endured" (I, 93 f.); how he breakfasted one morning with Wordsworth, Samuel Rogers, and Washington Irving and brought them all to his own house later for conversation (I, 240).

In 1848 Leslie was appointed professor of painting at the Royal Academy (he had been made an associate in 1820). His best work represents humorous scenes from Cervantes, Molière, Shakespeare's comedies, and the eighteenth-century novelists. In his time he was well known for his portraits also. In 1838 and 1841 he was summoned by Queen Victoria to paint two scenes of court ceremony. He died on May 5, 1859.

Leslie's published works include *Memoirs of the Life of John Constable, Esq., R.A.* (1843); *Hand-book for Young Painters* (1855); *Autobiographical Recollections,* ed. Tom Taylor (1860); and *Life and Times of Sir Joshua Reynolds,* begun by Leslie and completed by Tom Taylor (1865).

5. John Beauchamp's family consisted of eight sons and one daughter, of whom the second son and the daughter died young. Arthur Beauchamp, the sixth son, was born at Hornsey Lane, Highgate, on October 4, 1827. By nature he was a wanderer. His first real position at Sydney, in the firm of his brother Henry Herron, irked him beyond endurance by its routine and multiplicity of detail. He soon left, to embark on varied business ventures of his own. At the beginning of his career, by the death of Jane Beauchamp, his father's sister, he had

inherited a considerable number of shares of New Zealand lands. He did not settle in New Zealand immediately, however. First he tried his fortune, both as general merchant and as prospector, in the newly opened gold fields of Victoria. It was during this period, in June, 1854, that he married Mary Elizabeth Stanley, of a family of silversmiths originally of Lancashire. Courageously she went with him from one mushroom settlement to another, with the patience and endurance which sustained her throughout the exigencies of a hard life. Three sons were born between 1855 and 1858, each in a different town.

At length Arthur Beauchamp abandoned the gold fields and in Melbourne entered upon his lifelong occupation of storekeeper and auctioneer, an employment well suited to his gifts of shrewdness, wit, and imaginative fluency. But the climate of Melbourne, he found, undermined the health of his young children. His two eldest sons died in infancy.

In 1861 with his wife, his third child Harold, and a fourth infant son, Arthur Beauchamp set sail in the *Lalla Rookh* on a merchant venture to New Zealand. He had already made a similar merchandising voyage earlier, on first leaving his brother's firm in Sydney. After the successful disposal of his cargo he made his way to Picton, opposite Wellington, across Cook Strait, at the head of the South Island, where his brother Cradock seems to have settled previously. Apparently he had exchanged his property sections in Wellington for others at Picton— a bad bargain, for while Wellington land values increased Picton shares remained stagnant. Once in Picton, established as storekeeper and auctioneer, he entered the political life of the little town. In a community where able men were not abundant his ready, picturesque speech and wide experience of colonial life qualified him well for public office. For two years, 1864–66, he served as Picton representative on the Provincial Council of Marlborough, and from 1866 to 1867 as representative in Parliament. The demands of his private business, however, led him to resign the latter office after one session.

Picton, after an initial burst of energy, was destined for a slow, retired, steadily declining life. Arthur Beauchamp, in the succeeding years, shifted from one settlement to another, engaging, with a few variations, in his established profession of general merchant and auctioneer. Toward the end of his life, in 1907, after forty years he returned to Picton, where he died in 1910 at the age of eighty-two. He had lived, for longer or shorter periods of time, in some eighteen communities since his twenty-first year.

6. Harold Beauchamp was born at Ararat, Victoria, on November 15, 1858.

7. Through the kindness of Mrs. Mackintosh Bell it has been my privilege to read a considerable number of Miss Mansfield's letters to her father. The strength and constancy of her affection are manifest throughout the group.

8. *The Letters of Katherine Mansfield*, ed. J. Middleton Murry (New York, 1929), I, 265.

9. Annie Burnell Dyer was born at Sydney, New South Wales, on March 24, 1864.

10. *Letters*, I, 185.

11. Vera Margaret, born at Hill Street, Wellington, on October 22, 1885; Charlotte Mary, born at Wadestown, Wellington, on July 9, 1887, in the first house built by Mr. Beauchamp for his family; Kathleen Mansfield, born on October 14, 1888, at 11 Tinakori Road, Wellington, where Mr. Beauchamp, finding the wind of Wadestown intolerable, had built his second house; Gwendoline Burnell, born at 11 Tinakori Road on October 11, 1890 (who died of infant cholera at the age of three months); Jeanne Worthington, born at 11 Tinakori Road on May 20, 1892; Leslie Heron, born at a private hospital in Wellington on February 21, 1894.

12. *Letters*, I, 187.

13. In the *Life* the name is spelled "Barry"; but in a letter from Barrie Waters to Sir Harold Beauchamp, now in the possession of Mrs. Bell, the name is signed as given here.

14. *Letters*, II, 400.

15. "Omana Chimes," "Katherine Mansfield at School," *New Zealand Exporter Annual*, October 10, 1929.

16. Willa Cather, *Not Under Forty* (New York, 1936), p. 131.

17. "Enna Blake," *High School Reporter* (Second Term, 1898); "A Happy Christmas Eve," *ibid.* (Second Term, 1899). (Typescripts supplied by Mr. Morris.)

18. Marion Ruddick, a Canadian child whose father had come to New Zealand in the government service. At her first meeting with Marion, Kathleen with great pride produced the copy of the *Reporter* containing her first story. Many years later, in London, when the friends were together again, Miss Ruddick recalled this incident. "What a little horror I must have been!" said Katherine Mansfield. (Marion Ruddick, "Incidents in the Childhood of Katherine Mansfield," typescript in the possession of Mrs. Bell.)

19. The Beauchamp family sailed in January, 1903, reaching England in March. For his large party consisting of his five children, himself and his wife, Belle Dyer, and Sydney Dyer, Mrs. Beauchamp's brother, Mr. Beauchamp engaged the entire passenger accommodation of a small vessel, the *Niwaru*. Belle Dyer, who remained in London

as unofficial chaperone to the Beauchamp girls, married in England the following year.

20. Mrs. Howard Ambrose, of Hamilton, Ontario, formerly Isobel Creelman, who attended Queen's College during the time the Beauchamp girls were there, recalls that Kathleen always seemed reserved and "different"—like the "deep notes" of the 'cello she played. One stanza of the poetry Kathleen was writing at this time impressed her so morbidly that she remembered it even after many years:

> "I hope I may die in the darkness
>   When the world is so quiet and still,
>   And my soul pass away with the shadows,
>   Ere the sun rises over the hill."

(From a conversation with Mrs. Ambrose.)

21. See p. 206, n. 1, above.

22. Reprinted in part in the *Life*. Kathleen began her "novel" in May, 1906. The *Life* (p. 215) erroneously gives the year as 1907.

23. *Life*, p. 180.

24. *Ibid.*, pp. 162 f.

25. *Journal of Katherine Mansfield*, ed. J. Middleton Murry (New York, 1927), p. 54.

26. The family group was now smaller. Leslie, the twelve-year-old son, was away at school. Grandmother Dyer had removed to the home of her eldest daughter, where she died on the last day of December, 1906, before Kathleen had visited her after her return.

27. From a letter in the possession of Mrs. Bell.

28. "Vignettes" and "Silhouettes" were published in *The Native Companion* in October and November, 1907, respectively. (See p. 26.) Two more, "Vignette—By the Sea" and "Vignette—Westminster Cathedral," in typescript, are in the possession of Mrs. Bell.

29. Tom L. Mills, whose account of the incident includes a brief description of Kathleen Beauchamp at this time: "I discovered in this literary Beauchamp a girl bright, well read and informed on general topics, obviously a thinker, and not the least bit diffident about her writings. She was quite convinced in herself that she could write—that she had the gift to write." (Tom L. Mills, "Katherine Mansfield," *New Zealand Railways Magazine*, VIII [September 1, 1933], 6.) Mr. Mills states that two manuscripts were sent out, one to Australia, to *The Native Companion*, and one to London, and that both were accepted and paid for; but he does not give the name of the London periodical in which this early work appeared. The *Life* (p. 274) states that three manuscripts were sent to *The Native Companion* and were accepted; the London publication is not mentioned.

30. At Queen's College Kathleen decided on "Katherine Mansfield"

as her nom de plume. For her friend Ida Baker she selected the name Lesley Moore, shortened later to L.M. In his article "Katherine Mansfield" (*The Sewanee Review*, XLVIII [April–June, 1940], 263), Mr. Arnold Whitridge expands the initials to "Little Mouse," without explanation, although there seems no reason to question the account given in the *Life* (p. 185).

31. *The Native Companion* (November 1, 1907), p. 229.

32. *Ibid.* (December 2, 1907), p. 265.

33. *Life*, p. 283.

CHAPTER II. ET EGO IN BOHEMIA

1. *Letters*, II, 343.

2. According to Mr. Murry Miss Mansfield lived with her first husband only a few days; according to Sir Harold Beauchamp she remained with him a few months.

3. *Journal*, p. 1. The date "1910" supplied by Mr. Murry for this entry is wrong if his assignment of the fragment to the Bavarian stay is correct. In the spring and early summer of 1910 Miss Mansfield was at Rottingdean, England. (*Letters*, II, 292, and dated frontispiece to the *Life*.)

4. "To Stanislaw Wyspiański." Typescript supplied by Mr. Morris from the limited edition of this poem, printed in 1938 by the Favil Press for Mr. Bertram Rota, of Bodley House, Vigo Street, London.

Stanislaw Wyspiański (1869–1907) was one of the greatest Polish dramatic poets of the late nineteenth century. This poem was evidently an outcome of Miss Mansfield's friendship with a group of Poles during her Bavarian stay of 1909–10.

5. Mr. Murry states that apparently at this time Miss Mansfield made a second unsuccessful attempt to live with her husband. He bases his statement on Mr. Orage's recollection that Mr. Bowden accompanied Miss Mansfield to the office of *The New Age* (*Life*, p. 328).

6. It is commonly agreed by Mr. Murry and other critics that Orage first appreciated and encouraged Miss Mansfield's talent. In a vituperative pamphlet, however, *The Old "New Age": Orage—and Others* (London, 1936), Miss Beatrice Hastings, a subeditor of *The New Age* from 1907 to 1914 and an intimate associate of Orage during that period, asserts her claim to that honor, on the grounds that she had "entire charge of, and responsibility for, the literary direction of the paper, from reading and selection of MSS. to the last detail of spacing and position" (p. 3).

With Orage, Miss Hastings had become Miss Mansfield's friend after *The New Age* had become interested in the young author. Mr.

Murry speaks of this friendship with her editors as "the one period of her life between 1908 and 1911 upon which she constantly looked back with delight. She stayed with them frequently in a cottage in Sussex, and had the joy of being among her own kind" (*Life*, p. 328). In the present pamphlet, although by this time both Orage and Miss Mansfield were dead, Miss Hastings writes of each with abusive animosity. Her eventual rupture with Orage had evidently left her an outraged and embittered woman.

The list of Miss Mansfield's contributions to *The New Age* reads as follows:

"The Child-Who-Was-Tired"	February 24, 1910
"Germans at Meat"	March 3, 1910
"The Baron"	March 10, 1910
"The Luft Bad"	March 24, 1910
"Loneliness" (poem)	May 26, 1910
"At 'Lehmann's' "	July 7, 1910
"Frau Brechenmacher Attends a Wedding"	July 21, 1910
"The Sister of the Baroness"	August 4, 1910
"Frau Fischer"	August 18, 1910
"A Birthday"	May 18, 1911 *
"The Breidenbach Family in England"	August 17, 1911 †
"The Modern Soul"	June 22, 1911
"The Festival of the Coronation" (uncollected)	June 29, 1911
"The Journey to Bruges"	August 24, 1911
"Being a Truthful Adventure"	September 7, 1911 §
"Love Cycle" (parodies in verse; uncollected)	October 19, 1911
"A Marriage of Passion" (uncollected)	March 7, 1912
"At the Club" (uncollected)	March 7, 1912

* Incorrectly listed by Ruth Mantz in *The Critical Bibliography of Katherine Mansfield* (London, 1931), as May 18, 1910 (pp. 31, 101).

† Although this story was published without the author's signature, it seems definitely assignable to a place among Miss Mansfield's contributions to *The New Age*. The item is not mentioned in the *Critical Bibliography*.

§ Incorrectly listed in the *Critical Bibliography* as September 17, 1911 (pp. 51, 101).

7. William Orton, *The Last Romantic* (New York and Toronto, 1937), pp. 269–286. Concerning this section of Mr. Orton's book Mr. Morris has written to me: "I have letters both from Murry and from Orton stating that the whole chapter is genuine including a page or two of journal saved from destruction and also some poems, some published for the first time."

8. Orton, *The Last Romantic*, p. 276.

9. In his *Reminiscences and Recollections* Sir Harold Beauchamp lists every voyage he and his wife made to England. There is no record of a trip between that of 1911 and that of 1919, the year after Mrs. Beauchamp's death.

10. Miss Mansfield's verse has been collected in *Poems by Katherine Mansfield* (New York, 1924). Scattered additional poems appear in the *Scrapbook*. Two early poems were published in Australian magazines: "In the Botanical Gardens," under the pseudonym Julian Mark, in the Melbourne *Native Companion* in December, 1907, and "A Day in Bed," signed K. M. Beauchamp, in the Sydney *Lone Hand* in October, 1909. "November," written for her sister Vera's birthday and originally entitled "October," appeared in the London *Daily News* on November 3, 1909.

The child verses included in *Poems*, written in 1907, may be dismissed briefly. They are no better and no worse than might have been written by any high school senior of incipient talent. Since they stem largely from childhood recollections their chief value is that they offer a further authentic glimpse into Miss Mansfield's early history.

Of the poems dated 1909–10, six again spring directly from childhood recollections and relate closely (though incidentally) to the later New Zealand stories based upon Miss Mansfield's early experience. Here Kathleen Beauchamp, her little brother, and the beloved grandmother appear in a series of intimate little pictures. Again the poems are valuable chiefly for the added bits of detail which blend into the background of the group of New Zealand stories. The remaining poems in this section show little distinction of idea, form, or imagery.

Over one half of the poems dated 1911–13 comprise the group printed in *Rhythm* in 1912–13. These are the poems, according to Mr. Murry, which Mr. Orage found unsuitable for *The New Age*, a rejection which made Miss Mansfield so sensitive about her verse that she resorted to a pseudonym when her poems appeared in *Rhythm* and later in *The Athenaeum* under Mr. Murry's editorship (*Poems*, p. 12). Undoubtedly there is truth in this statement. Yet Miss Mansfield had a very close association with *Rhythm* after the acceptance of her first contribution. She supplied several poems and often more than one story for each issue, as well as contributing reviews and being listed among the edi-

torial staff. Just as she withdrew from too frequent personal appearance under the pseudonym she adopted for some of her stories, Lili
Heron, she may have assumed the pseudonym Boris Petrovsky signed
to many of her poems in part for equal reasons of modesty. Similarly,
when her poems were appearing in *The Athenaeum* in 1919 and 1920
under the pseudonym Elizabeth Stanley, she was also contributing
reviews and stories regularly.

The *Rhythm* poems, unrhymed impressionistic verses, though unquestionably sincere, seem rather juvenile, not because the emotion
from which they stem is childish but because of their diffuse overflow
of longing or ecstasy, the absence of precision of diction or precision
of form. The remaining pieces grouped with these poems are either
trifling or banal.

A particular charm attaches to one or two of the poems which Miss
Mansfield wrote at the Villa Pauline, in 1916, during the time she was
working on "The Aloe." She was living in that period in a luminous
glow of serenity. "Voices of the Air," with its controlled but flexible
form, its sharp yet delicate detail, is perhaps her most memorable poem.
The remainder, except for the sonnet to her dead brother, are merely
incidental verse.

In her later years, after 1919, Miss Mansfield turned to poetry most
often for the expression of secret anguish. Of these poems "The
Wounded Bird" in its naked self-revelation is the most moving; "Sorrowing Love" the most felicitous, with its restrained melancholy
cadence of lament, echoing the words of the forsaken Ophelia and
the song of *Twelfth Night*, "Come away, come away, Death."

Miss Mansfield has written a number of striking lines of poetry;
her gift for the vivid epithet, the sharp, distinctive detail, is manifest
in her poetry as well as in her prose. But her poetry as a whole stands
merely as a minor footnote to the real body of her work.

11. The list of Miss Mansfield's contributions to *Rhythm* reads as
follows:

"The Woman at the Store"	Spring, 1912 *
"Very Early Spring" (poem)	
"The Awakening River" (poem)	
"The Meaning of Rhythm" (an essay in	June, 1912
collaboration with J. M. Murry; un-	
collected)	
"The Sea Child" (poem)	

* Incorrectly listed in the *Critical Bibliography* as Spring, 1911 (pp.
51, 102).

"Seriousness in Art" (an essay in collab-   July, 1912
    oration with J. M. Murry; uncollected)

"Tales of a Courtyard" (uncollected)   August, 1912

"The Earth-Child in the Grass" (poem)   September, 1912
"How Pearl Button was Kidnapped"
"Spring in a Dream" (uncollected)

"New Dresses"   October, 1912
"The Little Girl"
"Sunday Lunch" †

"To God the Father" (poem)   November, 1912

"The Opal Dream Cave" (poem)   December, 1912
"Sea" (poem)

"Ole Underwood" §   January, 1913
"Jangling Memory" (poem)

"Sea Song" (poem)   March, 1913
"There was a Child Once" (poem)

† This item, which is signed merely "By the Tiger," is not mentioned in the *Critical Bibliography*. It appears in the *Scrapbook*, pp. 10–14.

§ Incorrectly listed in the *Critical Bibliography* as January, 1912 (pp. 52, 102).

12. See the list of contributions to *The New Age*, p. 212, n. 6, above.

13. Dated by Mr. Murry, *The Little Girl and Other Stories* (New York, 1924), p. 16. Published in *Rhythm* (October, 1912) under the pseudonym Lili Heron.

14. What is probably the first professional criticism of Miss Mansfield's work appeared in *The New Age* for May 4, 1911, on the issuance of the first six numbers of *The Open Window* as a bound volume. In a leading article Alfred E. Randall deals with the artistic efforts of the contributors with little sympathy. Of Katherine Mansfield's story he exclaims: "O, Shaw! where is thy sting? O, Grimm! where is thy victory?" (*Literary Supplement*, *The New Age*, N.S., IX, 1.)

15. See the list of contributions to *Rhythm*, n. 11, above.

16. Dated by Mr. Murry, *The Little Girl*, p. 54. "New Dresses" apparently was designed for *The New Age*, for in the version in *Rhythm* (October, 1912) the unmistakably British characters are hung with names relating to the *Pension* sketches—"Andreas Binzer," "Frau Binzer," "Dr. Erb"—names which Miss Mansfield assigned also to the characters of "A Birthday."

17. Dated by Mr. Murry, *The Little Girl*, p. 85. Published in *Rhythm* (October, 1912) under the pseudonym Lili Heron.

18. *The Little Girl*, pp. 50 f.

19. *In a German Pension* (New York, 1926), p. 28.

20. *Ibid.*, p. 45.

21. *Ibid.*, pp. 71 f.

22. Although "The Journey to Bruges" and "A Truthful Adventure," according to Mr. Murry's dating (*The Little Girl*, pp. 24, 35), were written in 1910, they were not printed in *The New Age* until August 24 and September 7, 1911, respectively.

23. "Katherine Mansfield and Chekhov," *Modern Language Notes*, L (June, 1935), 394–396 f.

24. *In a German Pension*, p. 66.

25. Dated by Mr. Murry, *The Little Girl*, p. 9.

26. In the original version of "New Dresses" (*Rhythm* [October, 1912]), the names assigned the characters, later the Carstairs, are identical with those of the Binzer family in "A Birthday." With this knowledge as a clue, one is made certain of what he has sensed all along—that the Binzers of "A Birthday" are not really Germans at all, but British and Beauchamps. "A Birthday" thus joins the little body of work foreshadowing the later New Zealand stories.

27. *In a German Pension*, p. 112.

28. Neither "The Swing of the Pendulum" nor "A Blaze" was published before its inclusion in *In a German Pension*.

29. *In a German Pension*, p. 174.

30. *The New Age*, N.S., X, 447.

31. See the list of contributions to *Rhythm*, pp. 214–215, n. 11, above.

32. See the list of contributions to *Rhythm*, pp. 214–215, n. 11, above.

33. Hugh Kingsmill, *Frank Harris* (London, 1932), p. 9.

34. Hugh Kingsmill, *The Life of D. H. Lawrence* (New York, 1938), p. 83.

35. For an account of *Rhythm* and *The Blue Review* see Appendix, pp. 227–229, below.

36. H. S. Ede, *Savage Messiah* (New York, 1931), p. 3.

37. Horace Brodzky, *Henri Gaudier Brzeska, 1891–1915* (London, 1933), pp. 153, 161.

38. Ede, *Savage Messiah*, p. 136.

39. "Pension Séguin," *The Blue Review* (May, 1913); "Violet," *ibid.* (June, 1913); "Bains Turcs," *ibid.* (July, 1913).

40. "The Georgian Renaissance," *Rhythm* (March, 1913).

41. "The Soiled Rose," *The Blue Review* (May, 1913). Republished in *The Prussian Officer and Other Stories* (London, 1914) as "The Shades of Spring."

42. *The Letters of D. H. Lawrence*, ed. Aldous Huxley (New York, 1932), pp. 159–162.

43. Francis Carco, *Montmartre à vingt ans* (Paris, 1938), p. 183.

44. *Letters*, I, 7.

45. *Journal*, p. 6.

46. *Ibid.*, p. 8.

47. "Seriousness in Art," *Rhythm*, II (July, 1912), 49.

48. *Letters of D. H. Lawrence*, p. 809.

49. *Scrapbook*, p. 24.

50. *Journal*, pp. 19, 20, 21.

51. Catherine Carswell, *The Savage Pilgrimage* (London, 1932), p. 22.

52. Unpublished until its inclusion in *The Little Girl* in 1924.

53. *Journal*, pp. 26 ff.

54. M. Carco (*Montmartre à vingt ans*, p. 177) identifies himself unequivocally with Raoul Duquette. Miss Mansfield herself wrote, however, in a letter to Murry of February 4, 1918 (*Letters*, I, 108): "The subject, I mean *lui qui parle*, is taken from F. and M., and God knows who." Throughout his autobiography, one may observe, Mr. Murry refers to M. Carco by the initials of the fictitious Raoul Duquette, "R. D."

55. These passages are included in the chapter on Katherine Mansfield in *Montmartre à vingt ans*, pp. 185, 187, 198 f., 202, corresponding to the identical material in *Les Innocents* (Paris, 1916), pp. 98, 109, 200.

56. *Montmartre à vingt ans*, p. 184.

57. *Ibid.*, p. 196. In *Bohème d'artiste* (Paris, 1940) M. Carco tells again the story of his complicated relationship with the Murrys, ending with a fuller account of their last meeting in Paris, a chance encounter in the spring of 1922, than he gives in *Montmartre à vingt ans* (pp. 204 f.).

58. *Letters*, I, 8.

59. Unpublished until its inclusion in *Bliss* in 1921.

60. *Letters*, I, 9.

61. *Ibid.*, p. 10.

62. This novel, which may be the *Maata* of which a synopsis and the two opening chapters remain, was later abandoned (*Journal*, p. 18). In *The Mystery of Maata* (Wellington, N. Z., 1946) P. A. Lawlor tells of his unsuccessful efforts to induce a Maori woman named Maata Mahupuku, whom he identifies as Katherine Mansfield's Wellington school friend, to let him see the manuscript of an unpublished novel, *Maata*, which she asserted was in her possession. He can only conjecture the substance of the manuscript, however, and how it came into Maata's hands.

63. *Letters of D. H. Lawrence,* p. 255.

64. *Ibid.,* pp. 256–263. In the preface to *Reflections on the Death of a Porcupine* (Philadelphia, 1925) Lawrence repudiates the seriousness of his faith in the *Signature* venture. Nevertheless his letters of that period indicate the sincerity of his belief at the time.

65. Published in *The Signature* (October 4, 1915; October 18, 1915).

66. Published in *The Signature* (October 18 and November 1, 1915), under the pseudonym Matilda Berry.

CHAPTER III. "PRELUDE"

1. *Letters,* I, 32.
2. *Letters of D. H. Lawrence,* p. 300.
3. *Letters,* I, 56.
4. *Journal,* p. 44.
5. *Ibid.*
6. Beauchamp, *Reminiscences and Recollections,* p. 205.
7. *Letters of D. H. Lawrence,* pp. 309, 314, 324, 336, 340, 341, 345.
8. *Ibid.,* p. 341.
9. *Letters,* I, 61.
10. *Letters of D. H. Lawrence,* pp. 355 f., 357.

It was during the Murrys' stay at Higher Tregerthen that Lawrence began to write *Women in Love,* in which Katherine Mansfield and Murry figure as Gudrun Brangwen and Gerald Crich. The novel is concerned exclusively with the emotional relationships of its characters; no actual incident from Miss Mansfield's life is included except that of her discomfiture of Lawrence's literary deriders at the Café Royal. (Murry, *Reminiscences of D. H. Lawrence* [London, 1933], pp. 95 f.; *Between Two Worlds,* p. 352; *Women in Love* [London, 1921], pp. 402–408.) Thus the book need be given no more than passing mention here. Discussions of the Murrys as related to Gudrun and Gerald Crich may be found in *Between Two Worlds,* pp. 411–415, and Kingsmill, *Life of D. H. Lawrence,* pp. 132 f.

11. John Middleton Murry, *God, Being an Introduction to the Science of Metabiology* (London, 1929), p. 18.

12. Whether Mr. Murry never knew or has forgotten that Miss Mansfield returned to *The New Age* after 1912 one cannot say. With the exception of "Stay-laces," published on November 4, 1915, the various contributions appeared between May 3 and October 4, 1917. Although three of the stories in the group ("Two Tuppenny Ones, Please," "Late at Night," and "The Black Cap") are included in *The Little Girl* and are dated as of 1917, Mr. Murry has made no mention of Miss Mansfield's reappearance in *The New Age* in his own writings or in his annotations to Miss Mantz's *Critical Bibliography.* The text

of the *Critical Bibliography* thus needs correction at several points. The list of Miss Mansfield's contributions to *The New Age* in 1917 reads as follows:

"Two Tuppenny Ones, Please"	May 3, 1917
"Late at Night"	May 10, 1917
"The Black Cap"	May 17, 1917
"In Confidence" (uncollected)	May 24, 1917
"The Common Round" (uncollected in this version)	May 31, 1917
"A Pic-nic" (uncollected)	June 7, 1917
"Mr. Reginald Peacock's Day"	June 14, 1917
"M. Séguin's Goat" (translated from the French of Alphonse Daudet; uncollected)	September 6, 1917
"An Album Leaf"	September 20, 1917
"A Dill Pickle"	October 4, 1917

13. *Letters*, I, 68.

14. *Ibid.*, p. 70.

15. *Ibid.*, p. 71.

16. "Pension Séguin," "Violet," "Bains Turcs." See p. 216, n. 39, above.

17. "Pension Séguin," *The Little Girl*, p. 95.

18. "Violet," *ibid.*, p. 106.

19. *The Little Girl*, p. 151.

20. *Journal*, p. 27.

21. *The Little Girl*, p. 157.

22. See p. 218, nn. 65, 66, above.

23. *The New Age* (November 4, 1915).

24. Consideration of "Mr. Reginald Peacock's Day," "An Album Leaf," and "A Dill Pickle" is reserved for the later chapter on Miss Mansfield's mature work.

25. *Bliss and Other Stories* (New York, 1921), p. 160.

26. *Journal*, pp. 43 f.

27. *Letters*, I, 74 f.

28. *Bliss*, p. 17.

29. See *Journal*, pp. 50–53 f., 58–59; *Scrapbook*, pp. 45–57, 64–67.

30. *The Aloe* (London, 1930), pp. 5–13. The Samuel Josephs family may be identified with the Walter Nathans, who lived next door to the Beauchamps, at 13 Tinakori Road, Wellington.

31. *The Aloe*, pp. 26–27.

32. *Scrapbook*, p. 47.

33. *The Aloe*, pp. 57–65 f.

34. *Ibid.*, pp. 121–131.

35. Nan Pym in "Prelude." *The Aloe*, pp. 155–156.
36. *Journal*, p. 50.
37. *Life*, p. 162.
38. *The Aloe*, pp. 75–77 f.
39. *Ibid.*, p. 86.
40. *Bliss*, p. 34.
41. *The Aloe*, p. 91.
42. *Bliss*, p. 37.
43. *The Aloe*, pp. 45 f.
44. *Bliss*, p. 21.
45. *The Aloe*, pp. 150 f.
46. *Ibid.*, p. 37.
47. *Bliss*, p. 15.
48. *The Aloe*, p. 109.
49. *Bliss*, p. 48.
50. *Scrapbook*, p. 70.
51. *The Aloe*, pp. 13–16.
52. *Bliss*, pp. 5–6.
53. *Ibid.*, p. 19.
54. *The Aloe*, pp. 42–43 f.
55. *Ibid.*, p. 112.
56. *Bliss*, p. 50.
57. *The Aloe*, pp. 141 f.
58. *Bliss*, p. 62.
59. *The Aloe*, p. 93.
60. *Bliss*, p. 38.
61. *Letters*, II, 476.
62. *The Aloe*, p. 115.
63. *Bliss*, p. 52.
64. *The Aloe*, pp. 17 f.
65. *Bliss*, p. 7.

CHAPTER IV
THE SOUL'S DESPERATE CHOICE

1. *Letters*, I, 80.
2. *Ibid.*, p. 111.
3. *Journal*, p. 77.
4. *Letters*, I, 116.
5. *Ibid.*, p. 123.
6. *Ibid.*, p. 116.
7. *Letters*, I, 152.
8. *Ibid.*, p. 157.
9. *Ibid.*, p. 156.

10. *Ibid.*, p. 172.

11. Although Mr. Murry dates "Carnation" as having been written in 1917 (*The Little Girl*, p. 208), Miss Mansfield's reference to the story in a letter of May 29, 1918 (*Letters*, I, 162), seems to assign it definitely to the stay at Looe.

12. *Letters*, I, 192.

13. *Ibid.*, p. 195.

14. Although the date of publication of the Hogarth Press "Prelude" is given as May 16, 1918, in the *Critical Bibliography* (p. 32), on May 12, 1918, Miss Mansfield wrote of her story to Dorothy Brett: ". . . they say it will be ready by June (*Letters*, I, 146), and in a letter to Mrs. Woolf of May 29 she approves the cover paper and design selected (*ibid.*, p. 163).

15. In January, 1920, Miss Mansfield reappeared under the same pen name with two additional poems.

16. *The Athenaeum* (April 2, 1920).

17. Published, in thirteen installments, from April 4 through October 31, 1919. Publication of this work in book form was forestalled by Constance Garnett's edition of Chekhov's letters in 1920.

18. These reviews were published posthumously in book form in 1930 under the title *Novels and Novelists*.

19. Sylvia Lynd, "Katherine Mansfield," *The Weekly Westminster Gazette*, I (January 20, 1923), 12.

20. *Journal*, p. 105.

21. *Letters*, I, 206.

22. *Ibid.*, p. 217.

23. *Ibid.*, p. 230.

24. *Ibid.*, p. 231.

25. *Ibid.*, p. 250.

26. "The New Husband," *Scrapbook*, pp. 145–146 f.

27. *Journal*, pp. 140 f.

28. *Ibid.*, p. 141.

29. *Ibid.*, p. 146.

30. *The Athenaeum* (April 2, 1920), p. 447.

31. *Letters*, II, 321.

32. The full list for 1920 includes: "Revelations" (June 11), "The Escape" (July 9), "Bank Holiday" (August 6), "The Wind Blows" (reprinted from *The Signature;* August 27), "Sun and Moon" (October 1), "The Young Girl" (October 29), "Miss Brill" (November 26), "The Lady's Maid" (December 24).

33. Conrad Aiken, "The Short Story as Poetry," *The Freeman*, III (May 11, 1921), 210.

34. "The Stranger" and "Poison" in November, "The Daughters of the Late Colonel" in December (*Letters*, II, 346, 354, 359), in addition

to *The Athenaeum* stories published between October 29 and December 24, 1920. (See n. 32, above.)

35. *Journal*, p. 177.

36. *Letters*, II, 340.

37. *Ibid.*, p. 334.

38. *Ibid.*, I, 256.

39. *Ibid.*, II, 363.

40. *Ibid.*, p. 381 f.

41. Thomas Moult, "Katherine Mansfield," *The Bookman* (London), LXIII (February, 1923), 227.

42. *Letters*, II, 367.

43. *Ibid.*, p. 401.

44. *Journal*, p. 200.

45. "Sixpence" (August 6), "Mr. and Mrs. Dove" (August 13), "An Ideal Family" (August 20), "Her First Ball" (November 28), "The Voyage" (December 24; omitted from the list of stories first printed in *The Sphere*, *Critical Bibliography*, p. 103), "Marriage à la Mode" (December 31).

46. *Journal*, p. 189.

47. Published in *The Weekly Westminster Gazette* (February 4, 11, 18, 1922).

48. Published in *The Nation* (February 4, 1922).

49. Published in *The London Mercury* (January, 1922).

50. *Letters*, II, 400 f.

51. *Ibid.*, p. 404.

52. *Ibid.*, p. 427.

53. Published in *The Story-Teller* (May, 1922).

54. Published in *The Sketch* (February 22, 1922).

55. *Letters*, II, 441.

56. *Ibid.*, p. 491.

57. *Ibid.*, p. 434.

58. *Ibid.*, p. 491.

59. *Ibid.*, p. 482.

60. XXXIV (June, 1922), 602.

61. "Miss Mansfield's New Stories," *The Queen*, CLI (March 25, 1922), 360.

62. *Letters*, II, 450.

63. *Journal*, p. 198.

64. Murry, *God*, p. 24.

65. Published, respectively, in *The Nation* on March 18 and April 29, 1922.

66. Published in *The Nation* (April 21, 1923).

67. *Journal*, p. 246.

68. With Koteliansky at this time she engaged in the translation from

the Russian of Maxim Gorki's *Reminiscences of Leonid Andreyev,* which was not published until 1928.

69. Letter to Sir Harold Beauchamp, of September 27, 1922, in the possession of Mrs. Bell.

70. Accounts of Gurdjieff and the Gurdjieff Institute are given by C. E. Bechhofer, "The Forest Philosophers," *The Century Magazine,* N.S., LXXXVI (May, 1924), 66–78; Denis Saurat, "Visite à Gourdjieff," *La Nouvelle Revue française,* XLI (1 novembre, 1933), 686–698 (trans. *The Living Age,* CCCXLV [January, 1934], 427–433); James Carruthers Young, "An Experiment at Fontainebleau," *The New Adelphi,* N.S., I (September, 1927), 26–40; Rom Landau, *God is My Adventure* (London, 1935), pp. 233–264; William Seabrook, *Witchcraft* (New York, 1940), pp. 205–213 f.

In January, 1924, sponsored by A. R. Orage and several well-known Americans (among them Zona Gale, Muriel Draper, Claude Bragdon, and Ernest Poole), Gurdjieff brought a dance group made up of forty of his disciples to New York, where his demonstrations attracted considerable attention. Shortly after his return to Fontainebleau he suffered serious injuries in a motor accident and was forced to give up his regular activities at Le Prieuré. Meanwhile, largely through the efforts of Orage, his influence in America was spreading; and after 1930 Gurdjieff established his headquarters in New York. His last years were devoted to philosophical writing. He died in Paris on October 28, 1949.

71. Murry, *God,* pp. 24 f. The *Journal* entry (p. 246), "My first conversation with O. took place on August 30, 1922," undoubtedly refers to this meeting.

72. *Letters,* II, 509.

73. *Journal,* p. 254.

74. *Letters,* II, 503 f.

75. *Ibid.,* p. 509.

76. Saurat, "A Visit to Gourdyev," *The Living Age,* CCCXLV, 429; Olgivanna (Mrs. Frank Lloyd Wright), "The Last Days of Katherine Mansfield," *The Bookman* (New York), LXXIII (March, 1931), 8.

77. *Letters,* II, 511.

78. *Ibid.,* p. 512.

79. A. R. Orage, "Talks with Katherine Mansfield," *The Century Magazine,* N.S., LXXXVII (November, 1924), 37.

80. *Letters,* II, 509.

CHAPTER V. KATHERINE MANSFIELD

1. *Journal,* p. 201.

2. *Letters,* I, 106.

3. *Magiciens et logiciens* (Paris, 1935), p. 266.

4. *Journal,* p. xiv n.

5. *Anton Tchekhov: Literary and Theatrical Reminiscences,* trans. and ed. S. S. Koteliansky (New York, 1927). p. 86.

6. "A Dill Pickle," *Bliss,* p. 228.

7. "The Garden Party," *The Garden Party and Other Stories* (New York, 1922), p. 59.

8. "The Daughters of the Late Colonel," *ibid.,* p. 83.

9. *Letters on the Short Story, the Drama and Other Literary Topics,* ed. Louis S. Friedland (New York, 1924), p. 86.

10. "A Nervous Breakdown," *The Schoolmistress and Other Stories* (*The Tales of Chekhov,* Vol. IX, New York, 1921), p. 20.

11. "The Man Without a Temperament," *Bliss,* p. 177.

12. "The Kiss," *The Party and Other Stories* (*The Tales of Chekhov,* Vol. IV, New York, 1917), p. 178.

13. "The Grasshopper," *The Wife and Other Stories* (*The Tales of Chekhov,* Vol. V, New York, 1920), p. 108.

14. *Letters on the Short Story,* p. 8.

15. *After Strange Gods* (New York, 1934), pp. 38, 40 f.

16. *New Literary Values* (Edinburgh and London, 1936), p. 89.

17. *The Garden Party,* p. 227.

18. Virginia Woolf, *Mrs. Dalloway* (New York, 1925), p. 5, and *passim.*

19. *Letters,* II, 359.

20. CXXXI (May 7, 1921), 385.

21. *Letters,* II, 389.

22. *Bliss,* p. 231.

23. *Letters,* II, 354.

24. *Bliss,* p. 237.

25. *The Garden Party,* p. 114.

26. *Ibid.,* p. 189.

27. H. E. Bates, *The Modern Short Story* (London, 1941), p. 129.

28. *Ibid.,* p. 130.

29. *The Doves' Nest and Other Stories* (New York, 1923), p. 50.

30. *Ibid.,* p. 52.

31. *Bliss,* p. 135.

32. *Ibid.,* pp. 82 f.

33. *The Doves' Nest,* p. 88.

34. *The Garden Party,* p. 148.

35. *Letters,* I, 204.

36. *The Garden Party,* p. 91.

37. *Ibid.*

38. *Letters,* II, 370.

39. *The Doves' Nest,* p. 43.

40. *Ibid.,* p. 44.

41. *Ibid.*
42. *Ibid.*, pp. 112 f.
43. *Bliss*, p. 24.
44. *Ibid.*, p. 99.
45. *Ibid.*
46. *Ibid.*, pp. 124 f.
47. *The Garden Party*, p. 153.
48. *Ibid.*, p. 201.
49. "Prelude," *Bliss*, p. 63.
50. *Ibid.*, pp. 16 f.
51. "The Voyage," *The Garden Party*, p. 180.
52. "The Man Without a Temperament," *Bliss*, p. 190.
53. "*Je ne parle pas français*," *ibid.*, p. 111.
54. *The Garden Party*, p. 111.
55. *Ibid.*, p. 112.
56. *Bliss*, p. 40.
57. *The Doves' Nest*, p. 53.
58. *Bliss*, p. 263.
59. *The Garden Party*, pp. 142 f.
60. *Bliss*, p. 53.
61. *Ibid.*, p. 3.
62. *The Garden Party*, p. 123.
63. *Ibid.*, pp. 23 f.
64. *Bliss*, p. 61.
65. *Ibid.*, p. 279.
66. *Ibid.*, p. 34.
67. *Ibid.*
68. *Ibid.*, p. 61.
69. *Scrapbook*, p. 47.
70. *Journal*, p. 50.
71. *The Garden Party*, p. 48.
72. *Journal*, p. 103.
73. *Bliss*, p. 123.
74. *Letters*, II, 360.
75. "The Art of Katherine Mansfield," *The Nation* (New York), CXLV (October 23, 1937), 436.
76. David Daiches, *The Novel and the Modern World* (Chicago, 1939), p. 73.
77. "The Little Girl," "The Garden Party," "The Voyage," "Her First Ball," "The Stranger," the unfinished "Six Years After."
78. *Not Under Forty*, p. 137.
79. *Letters*, II, 347.

RHYTHM AND THE BLUE REVIEW

As AN undergraduate quarterly founded in the spring of 1911 by John Middleton Murry and Michael Sadleir, *Rhythm* formulated its purpose, in an introductory editorial, "Aims and Ideals," presumably written by Murry, as follows:

"To treat what is being done to-day as something vital in the progress of art, which cannot fix its eyes on yesterday and live; to see that the present is pregnant for the future, rather than a revolt against the past; in creation to give expression to an art that seeks out the strong things of life; in criticism to seek out the strong things of that art—such is the aim of RHYTHM.

" 'Before art can be human it must learn to be brutal.' "

As often happens with the little magazines, the policy stated is vigorous, the execution of the policy uncertain. The first volume of *Rhythm*, comprising the four issues from Spring, 1911, to Spring, 1912, is of decidedly uneven merit. Until the appearance of Katherine Mansfield's "The Woman at the Store" (Spring, 1912) no story possesses the slightest distinction. Art has not even learned to be brutal; it is merely stylistically mannered and technically crude. Of the drawings the reproductions of work by Picasso are exceptionally interesting. In large part the other sketches consist of post-Impressionistic or Fauvistic drawings by such artists as Anne Estelle Rice, Jessie Dismorr, and S. J. Peploe. The articles, most often dealing with current literary or aesthetic problems as is natural, are not arresting. The poetry, except for that by Wilfrid Wilson Gibson, is negligible.

With the issue of June, 1912, the opening number of Volume II, when Stephen Swift and Company took over publication of the magazine, *Rhythm* became a monthly periodical. Its staff consisted of John Middleton Murry as editor, assisted by Katherine Mansfield and, for a short time, Michael Sadleir (Sadleir's name is not listed after the June issue). J. D. Fergusson, an early and regular contributor of drawings, acted as art editor. With the issue of August, 1912, Anne Estelle Rice and Georges Banks, both of whom also had contributed drawings regularly from the initial appearance of *Rhythm*, were added to the staff as French correspondents on the theater; and in the same number Francis Carco, Murry's Parisian friend, is listed as correspondent for French literature. Carco had also been a contributor from the earliest number of *Rhythm*. Except for the assumption of co-editorship by Katherine Mansfield in February, 1913, this staff, with a little variation in the way of Russian, Polish, and American correspondents, remained stable until *Rhythm* was superseded by *The Blue Review*. In November, 1912, after the bankruptcy of Stephen Swift and Company, the first issue under Martin Secker's imprint appeared. The last issue of *Rhythm* was that of March, 1913. *The Blue Review* appeared for three months only: May, June, and July, 1913.

Upon its wider publication under Stephen Swift and Company, *Rhythm* attained some distinction. The quality as a whole is still uneven. Such pieces as the editorial essays by Murry and Miss Mansfield, "The Meaning of Rhythm" (June, 1912) and "Seriousness in Art" (July, 1912), are astonish-

ingly puerile in their conception of the relation of the artist
to the ordinary world, even when taken as part of an editorial
wrangle with *The New Age*. For the most part the stories are
still mediocre, although the technical handling is more
finished and the names of the authors—Frank Harris, Gilbert
Cannan, Lord Dunsany, and Lascelles Abercrombie, among
others—become more generally known. Among the poets,
James Stephens, John Drinkwater, Walter de la Mare, and
Rupert Brooke appear, along with the earlier contributors,
Wilfrid Wilson Gibson and W. H. Davies.

With the introduction of a Literary Supplement, in the
issue of December, 1912, such established writers as H. G.
Wells and Ford Madox Hueffer bring to the magazine the
prestige of reputation. Last of all, D. H. Lawrence joins the
ranks, with an essay, "The Georgian Renaissance," in the
Literary Supplement of March, 1913.

The Blue Review carried on briefly all that was best in
Rhythm. Its list of contributors includes Max Beerbohm,
Walter de la Mare, Wilfrid Wilson Gibson, Oliver Gogarty,
D. H. Lawrence, W. H. Davies, W. L. George, Katherine
Mansfield, James Elroy Flecker, John Drinkwater, J. D.
Beresford, Lascelles Abercrombie, Rupert Brooke, Yone
Noguchi, John Middleton Murry, Frank Swinnerton, Gilbert
Cannan, Hugh Walpole. The whole publication has attained
a greater balance, unity, maturity, and firmness. To a large
extent *The Blue Review* foreshadows the later *London Mer-
cury* under the editorship of J. C. Squire.

SELECTED BIBLIOGRAPHY

I. WORKS BY KATHERINE MANSFIELD

Bliss and Other Stories. New York, 1921.

The Garden Party and Other Stories. New York, 1922.

The Doves' Nest and Other Stories. New York, 1923.

The Little Girl and Other Stories. New York, 1924.

Poems. New York, 1924.

In a German Pension. New York, 1926.

Journal of Katherine Mansfield, ed. J. Middleton Murry. New York, 1927.

Maxim Gorki. Reminiscences of Leonid Andreyev Authorized translation from the Russian by Katherine Mansfield and S. S. Koteliansky. London [1928].

The Letters of Katherine Mansfield, ed. J. Middleton Murry. New York, 1929. 2 vols.

The Aloe. London, 1930.

Novels and Novelists, ed. J. Middleton Murry. New York, 1930.

The Scrapbook of Katherine Mansfield, ed. J. Middleton Murry. New York, 1940.

II. REFERENCE WORKS

Aiken, Conrad. *Costumes by Eros.* New York, 1928 ("Your Obituary, Well Written").

Bashkirtseff, Marie. *The Journal of a Young Artist, 1860–1884,* trans. Mary J. Serrano. New York [1889].

Bates, H. E. *The Modern Short Story*. London, 1941.

Beauchamp, Sir Harold. *Reminiscences and Recollections*. New Plymouth, N. Z., 1937.

Blanche, Jacques-Emile. *More Portraits of a Lifetime*. London [1939].

Brett, Dorothy. *Lawrence and Brett*. Philadelphia [1933].

Brodzky, Horace. *Henri Gaudier Brzeska, 1891–1915*. London [1933].

Carco, Francis. *Bohème d'artiste*. Paris [1940].

———. *Les Innocents*. Paris, 1916.

———. *Montmartre à vingt ans*. Paris [1938].

———. *Souvenirs sur Katherine Mansfield*. Paris, 1934.

Carswell, Catherine. *The Savage Pilgrimage*. London, 1932.

Cather, Willa. *Not Under Forty*. New York, 1936.

[Chekhov, Anton]. *Letters . . .* , trans. Constance Garnett. London, 1920.

———. *Letters on the Short Story, the Drama and Other Literary Topics*, ed. Louis S. Friedland. New York, 1924.

[———]. *The Life and Letters of Anton Tchekhov*, trans. and ed. S. S. Koteliansky and Philip Tomlinson. New York, n.d.

[———]. *Literary and Theatrical Reminiscences*, trans. and ed. S. S. Koteliansky. New York, 1927.

[———]. *The Note-books of Anton Tchekhov, Together with Reminiscences of Tchekhov by Maxim Gorky*, trans. S. S. Koteliansky and Leonard Woolf. Richmond, 1921.

[———]. *The Personal Papers . . .* New York [1948].

[———]. *The Tales of Chekhov*, trans. Constance Garnett. New York, 1917–23. 13 vols.

Clarke, Isabel C. *Six Portraits*. London [1935].

Daiches, David. *New Literary Values*. Edinburgh and London, 1936.

———. *The Novel and the Modern World*. Chicago [1939].

Ede, H. S. *Savage Messiah*. New York, 1931.

Eliot, T. S. *After Strange Gods*. New York [1934].

Harper, George McLean. *Literary Appreciations*. Indianapolis and New York [1937].

Hastings, Beatrice. *The Old "New Age": Orage—and Others* [London, 1936].

Henriot, Emile. *De Marie de France à Katherine Mansfield*. Paris [1937].

Hoare, Dorothy M. *Some Studies in the Modern Novel*. London, 1938.

Jerrold, Douglas. *Georgian Adventure*. New York, 1938.

Joyce, James. *Dubliners*. New York, n.d. (Modern Library edition).

Kingsmill, Hugh. *Frank Harris*. London, 1932.

———. *The Life of D. H. Lawrence*. New York [1938].

Landau, Rom. *God is My Adventure*. London, 1935.

Lawlor, P. A. *The Mystery of Maata*. Wellington, N. Z., 1946.

[Lawrence, D. H.] *Letters* . . . , ed. Aldous Huxley. New York, 1932.

———. *The Rainbow*. London [1915].

———. *Reflections on the Death of a Porcupine*. Philadelphia, 1925.

———. *Women in Love*. London [1921].

Lawrence, Frieda. *"Not I, But the Wind . . ."* New York, 1934.

Lenoël, Odette. *La Vocation de Katherine Mansfield*. Paris [1946].

Leslie, Charles Robert. *Autobiographical Recollections*, ed. Tom Taylor. London, 1860. 2 vols.

———. *The Letters of John Constable, R.A. to C. R. Leslie, R.A. 1826–1837*, ed. Peter Leslie. London, 1931.

Mantz, Ruth Elvish. *The Critical Bibliography of Katherine Mansfield*. London, 1931.

———, and J. Middleton Murry. *The Life of Katherine Mansfield*. London, 1933.

Maurois, André. *Magiciens et logiciens*. Paris [1935]. Trans. Hamish Miles as *Poets and Prophets*. New York and London, 1935.

Merlin, Roland. *Le Drame secret de Katherine Mansfield*. Paris [1950].

Murry, John Middleton. *Between Two Worlds An Autobiography*. New York [1936].

———. *God, Being an Introduction to the Science of Metabiology*. London [1929].

———. *Katherine Mansfield and other Literary Portraits*. London [1949].

———. *Reminiscences of D. H. Lawrence*. London [1933].

———. *Son of Woman*. London and Toronto [1931].

Orage, A. R. *Selected Essays and Critical Writings*, ed. Herbert Read and Denis Saurat. London [1935].

Orton, William. *The Last Romantic*. New York and Toronto [1937].

[Pepys, Samuel]. *Diary* . . . , ed. Henry B. Wheatley. London, 1924. Vols. I, III.

Pound, Ezra. *Gaudier-Brzeska A Memoir*. London and New York, 1916.

Seabrook, William. *Witchcraft*. New York [1940].

Swinnerton, Frank. *The Georgian Scene*. New York [1934].

Woolf, Virginia. *Mrs. Dalloway*. New York, 1925.

———. *A Haunted House and Other Stories*. New York [1944].

The Adelphi, Vol. I (June, 1923–May, 1924); Vol. II (June, 1924–May, 1925).

The Athenaeum, April 4, 1919–February 11, 1921.

The Blue Review, Vol. I (May–July, 1913).

The *New Age*, N.S., Vol. VI (November, 1909–April, 1910); N.S., Vol. VII (May–October, 1910); N.S., Vol. IX (May–October, 1911); N.S., Vol. X (November, 1911–April, 1912); N.S., Vol. XVIII (November, 1915–April, 1916); N.S., Vol. XXI (May–October, 1917).

Rhythm, Vols. I–II (Summer, 1911–March, 1913).

The Signature, Vol. I (October 4–November 1, 1915).

III. ARTICLES AND REVIEWS

Aiken, Conrad. "The Short Story as Poetry," *The Freeman*, III (May 11, 1921), 210 f. (review of *Bliss*).

Armstrong, Martin. "The Art of Katherine Mansfield," *The Fortnightly Review*, N.S., CXIII (March, 1923), 484–490.

Beauchamp, Sir Harold. "Katherine Mansfield's Career," *The Saturday Review of Literature*, X (September 30, 1933), 144.

Bechhofer, C. E. "The Forest Philosophers," *The Century Magazine*, N.S., LXXXVI (May, 1924), 66–78.

Bertrand, G. P. "L'Attitude spirituelle de Katherine Mansfield," *Cahiers du sud*, XVIII (décembre 1931), 646–665.

Blanchet, André. "Le Secret de Katherine Mansfield," *Etudes: Revue catholique d'intérêt général*, CCXLI (20 novembre 1939), 410–427, (5 décembre 1939), 510–529.

Bompard, Jacques. "Sur une jeune femme morte: Katherine Mansfield," *La Grande Revue*, CXL (février 1933), 540–556.

Bordeaux, Henry. "Le Souvenir de Katherine Mansfield," *La Revue hebdomadaire*, 1939-Pt. 6 (17 juin 1939), pp. 265–279.

Cazamian, Louis. "D. H. Lawrence and Katherine Mansfield as Letter-Writers," *The University of Toronto Quarterly*, III (April, 1934), 286–307.

"Chimes, Omana," "Katherine Mansfield at School," *New Zealand Exporter Annual*, October 10, 1929 (item from Mrs. Bell's scrapbook, where it appears without page number).

The English Review, XXXIV (June, 1922), 602 (review of *The Garden Party*).

"A Fashion in the Forest of Fontainebleau," *The Graphic*, CVII (March 10, 1923), 335.

The Free Lance (New Zealand), December 27, 1933, p. 23 (notice of memorial services at Karori).

Freeman, Kathleen. "The Art of Katherine Mansfield," *The Canadian Forum*, VII (July, 1927), 302–307 f.

Gillet, Louis. "Katherine Mansfield," *Revue des deux mondes*, XXIV, 7e période (15 décembre 1924), 929–942.

——. "Les Lettres de Katherine Mansfield," *Revue des deux mondes*, LI, 7ᵉ période (1 mai 1929), 213–227 (joint review of *Letters* and *Journal*).

Henriot, Emile. "Le Souvenir de Katherine Mansfield," *Le Temps*, 12 mars 1935, p. 3.

Hubbell, George Shelton. "Katherine Mansfield and Kezia," *The Sewanee Review*, XXXV (July–September, 1927), 325–335.

Kafian, Adele, "The Last Days of Katherine Mansfield," *The Adelphi*, XXIII (October–December, 1946), 36–38 f.

"Katherine Mansfield's Stories," London *Times Literary Supplement*, March 2, 1946, p. 102 (review of *Collected Stories*).

London *Times*, March 23, 1939, p. 15 (notice of memorial services at Mentone).

Lynd, Sylvia. "Katherine Mansfield," *The Weekly Westminster Gazette*, I (January 20, 1923), 12 f.

Marcel, Gabriel. "Lectures," *La Nouvelle Revue française*, XXXII (1 février 1929), 268–273.

Mills, Tom L. "Katherine Mansfield," *New Zealand Railways Magazine*, VIII (September 1, 1933), 6–7.

Moult, Thomas. "Katherine Mansfield," *The Bookman* (London), LXIII (February, 1923), 227–228.

[Murry, John Middleton]. *The Adelphi*, I (July, 1923), 137 f. (note to "Extracts from a Journal").

[——]. "In Memory of Katherine Mansfield," *The Adelphi*, I (January, 1924), 663–665.

——. "Katherine Mansfield," *New York Evening Post Literary Review*, February 17, 1923, pp. 461 f.

——. "A Month After," *The Adelphi*, I (July, 1923), 94–95 f.

——. "Tchehov Revisited," *The Adelphi*, N.S., XIV (October, 1937), 19–23.

——. "The Weariness of Ivan Bunin," *The Dial*, LXXVI (February, 1924), 194–197.

"The New Cult of Gurdjieff," *Current Opinion*, LXXVI (April, 1924), 467–468.

Olgivanna (Mrs. Frank Lloyd Wright). "The Last Days of Katherine Mansfield," *The Bookman* (New York), LXXIII (March, 1931), 6–13.

Orage, A. R. "Talks with Katherine Mansfield," *The Century Magazine*, N.S., LXXXVII (November, 1924), 36–40.

The same, *The New English Weekly*, I (May 19, 1932), 109–111.

Porter, Katherine Anne. "The Art of Katherine Mansfield," *The Nation* (New York), CXLV (October 23, 1937), 435–436 (review of *The Short Stories of Katherine Mansfield*).

Pritchett, V. S. *New Statesman and Nation*, N.S., XXXI (February 2, 1946), 87 (review of *Collected Stories*).

Randall, Alfred E. "The Open Window: A Review," *The New Age, Literary Supplement*, N.S., IX (May 4, 1911), 1 f.

Ruddick, Marion. "Incidents in the Childhood of Katherine Mansfield" (typescript in the possession of Mrs. Bell).

The Saturday Review, CXXXI (May 7, 1921), 385 (note on "The Daughters of the Late Colonel").

Saurat, Denis. "Visite à Gourdjieff," *La Nouvelle Revue française*, XLI (1 novembre 1933), 686–698.

The same, trans. as "A Visit to Gourdyev," *The Living Age*, CCCXLV (January, 1934), 427–433.

Schneider, Elisabeth. "Katherine Mansfield and Chekhov," *Modern Language Notes*, L (June, 1935), 394–396 f.

Shanks, Edward. "Katherine Mansfield," *The London Mercury*, XVII (January, 1928), 286–293.

———. "Miss Mansfield's New Stories," *The Queen*, CLI (March 25, 1922), 360 (review of *The Garden Party*).

Sitwell, Edith. "Three Women Writers," *Vogue* (London), October, 1924, pp. 81 ff.

Stanley, C. W. "The Art of Katherine Mansfield," *The Dalhousie Review*, X (April, 1930), 26–41.

S[ullivan]., J. W. N. "The Story-Writing Genius," *The Athenaeum*, April 2, 1920, p. 447 (review of "*Je ne parle pas français*").

Thiébaut, Marcel. "Katherine Mansfield," *La Revue de Paris*, 1933–Pt. 6 (15 novembre 1933), pp. 462–480.

T[omlinson]., H. M. "Katherine Mansfield," *The Nation and The Athenaeum*, XXXII (January 20, 1923), 609.

"Tributes to Katherine Mansfield," London *Times*, June 12, 1939, p. 11 (notice of memorial services at Fontainebleau).

Van Kranendonk, A. G. "Katherine Mansfield," *English Studies*, XII (April, 1930), 49–57.

Wagenknecht, Edward. "Katherine Mansfield," *The English Journal*, XVII (April, 1928), 272–283 f.

Whitridge, Arnold. "Katherine Mansfield," *The Sewanee Review*, XLVIII (April–June, 1940), 256–272.

Young, James Carruthers. "An Experiment at Fontainebleau—A Personal Reminiscence," *The New Adelphi*, N.S., I (September, 1927), 26–40.

INDEX

*Unless otherwise indicated, all literary works
are those of Katherine Mansfield.*

Abercrombie, Lascelles, 229
Adelphi, 2
"After the Theatre" (Chekhov),
151
Aiken, Conrad, 3
Alexander Turnbull Library,
Wellington, New Zealand, 6
"Aloe, The," autobiographical in-
fluences upon, 18; inspiration
for writing of, 71, 74; publication of, 75; distinguishing qualities of, 83–86; compared with
revised version, "Prelude," 87–
102; *see also* "Prelude"
Ambrose, Isobel Creelman, 210,
n. 20
Anderson, Sherwood, 197
"Apple-Tree, The," 67, 79
Art and Letters, 75, 122
Artist, the, K. M.'s concept of, 58–
59, 76, 124, 126
"At Lehmann's," 43; naturalism in,
44, 45
"At the Bay," 93, 132, 137, 156, 188,
191, 193, 201, 202; autobiographical elements in, 19; closing of,
156; handling of time element
in, 168–169; symbolism in, 193–
194, 195
"At the Club," 47
Athenaeum, 123, 129, 135; K. M.'s
work appearing in, 113–116, 121,
221, n. 32
"Autumns: I, II"; *see* "Apple
Tree" *and* "Wind Blows"

Baker, Ida Constance, 22, 34, 106,
108, 111, 122, 129, 133, 138, 142,
211, n. 30
Bandol, France, K. M.'s sojourns
in, 69, 70–71, 104–108
Banks, Georges, 228
Bashkirtseff, Marie, similarities between K. M. and, 29–30
Bates, H. E., 182, 184; critical estimate of K. M., 177–178
Beauchamp, Annie (mother of
K. M.), 209, n. 9; character of,
16–17; as model for Linda

Beauchamp, Annie (*continued*) Burnell in New Zealand stories, 17, 89; death of, 111

Beauchamp, Arthur, career of, 14–15, 207–208, n. 5

Beauchamp, Charlotte (Mrs. Cecil Pickthall), 117, 141

Beauchamp, Miss Connie, 118, 119, 120, 122

Beauchamp, Harold (father of K. M.), 117, 208, n. 6; establishes memorials in honor of K. M., 6; character and career of, 15–16; as model for Stanley Burnell in New Zealand stories, 16; K. M.'s sympathy for, 16, 209, n. 7; visits K. M. in Italy, 118

Beauchamp, Henry Herron, 14

Beauchamp, Jeanne, 117, 141

Beauchamp, John, 14

Beauchamp, Leslie (brother of K. M.), 62, 211, n. 30; K. M.'s love for, 20, 67–68, 69, 71, 105–106; death of, 67; as inspiration for writings of K. M., 69–70, 71, 105–106

Beauchamp, Marie Annette. See Russell, Countess

Beauchamp, Vera (Mrs. Mackintosh Bell), 8, 213, n. 10

Beerbohm, Max, 123, 229

Beresford, J. D., 229

"Bet, The" (Chekhov), 151

"Birthday, A," 43, 216, n. 26; naturalism in, 44, 45; emphasis upon inner experience in, 45; lacks subtlety of later stories, 46

"Black Cap, The," 81–82

"Blaze, A," 46

Bliss (book of stories), 1, 2, 123, 150, 164; stories in, 82–83

"Bliss" (story), 47, 51, 114, 178, 198; writing of, 107; ending of, 156; focus of, 164; misapplication of tone in, 180; fanciful

description in, 186–187; symbolism in, 192, 195

Blue Review, 48, 53, 54, 55, 71, 228, 229; *see also Rhythm*

Bowden, George, K. M.'s first husband, 34, 109, 211, nn. 2 and 5

Bowen, Elizabeth, 197

Brett, Dorothy, 73, 76, 83, 109, 132, 141

Brooke, Rupert, 52, 229

Browning, Robert, 82

Brzeska, Sophie, 53–54

Bunin, Ivan, 138, 156

Burnell, Kezia (in New Zealand stories), childhood fears of, 94–95, 196; as focal point in "Prelude," 96–97; in "The Doll's House," 201

Burnell, Linda (in New Zealand stories), based on Annie Beauchamp, K. M.'s mother, 17, 89; character portrayal of, 85, 86, 88, 94, 186, 193, 200; K. M.'s alterations in character of, 89–91, 93, 98

Burnell, Stanley (in New Zealand stories), based on Harold Beauchamp, K. M.'s father, 16; character portrayal of, 79, 85, 86, 88, 94, 200

Campbell, Gordon, 54, 61

"Canary, The," 141, 199; tone of, 182

Cannan, Gilbert, 54, 229

Cannan, Mary, 54

Carco, Francis, 217, n. 57, 228; and K. M., 56–57, 62–64; as model for Raoul Duquette in "*Je ne parle pas français*," 63, 217, n. 54

"Carnation," 111, 221, n. 11

Cather, Willa, on K. M., 202

Chekhov, Anton, 81, 114, 129, 138, 160, 161, 173, 194; influence upon K. M., 43, 76; K. M.'s admiration for, 115, 125; his writings compared and contrasted with K. M.'s, 150–159, 176, 177

"Child-Who-Was-Tired, The-," 35; similarity between Chekhov's "Sleepyhead" and, 43; evaluated, 45

Children, K. M.'s portrayal of, 40–41, 86, 94–95, 201

"Clay" (Joyce), narrative technique of, 161–162; compared with K. M.'s "Miss Brill," 162–163

"Common Round, The," 75, 82–83; *see also* "Pictures"

Conrad, Joseph, 114

Constable, publishers, 123, 136

Coppard, A. E., 197

Cosmic Anatomy (M. B. Oxon), 140

"Counterparts" (Joyce), 170, 173

"Cup of Tea, A," 133; focus of, 164; tone of, 179–180

Daiches, David, 5, 165

"Daughters of the Late Colonel," 123, 130, 137, 199; method used in, 169–170, 174; fanciful perception in, 184–185; natural imagery in, 189

Davies, W. H., 229

"Dead, The" (Joyce), 169; theme and structure of, 164–165; similarities to K. M.'s "The Stranger," 165, 167

"Death of a Rose, The," 26, 27

de la Mare, Walter, 229

Dialogue, K. M.'s handling of, 46, 47–48, 81–82

"Dill Pickle, A," 75; method of, 170–171, 174

Dismorr, Jessie, 228

"Doll's House, The," 132, 195, 199; autobiographical elements in, 19, 89; ending of, 156; presentation of a child's world in, 201

Dorian Gray (Oscar Wilde), 22

Dostoevski, 115, 133; K. M.'s response to, 125

Doves' Nest (book of stories), 1, 2

"Doves' Nest" (story), 133, 141; tone of, 183

Drinkwater, John, 229

Dubliners (Joyce), 177, 197; Joyce's technique in, compared with that of K. M., 159–167, 170–171; skilled portraiture in, 173

Dunsany, Lord, 53, 229

Duquette, Raoul (in "*Je ne parle pas français*"), based on character of Francis Carco, 63, 217, n. 54; character portrayal of, 154, 167–168, 181, 186, 191–192

Dyer, Belle (aunt of K. M.), 17

Dyer, Joseph, 16

Dyer, Margaret Mansfield (grandmother of K. M.), 210, n. 26; depicted in New Zealand stories, 17; role of, in K. M.'s childhood, 17–18; K. M.'s affection for, 34

"Einsame, Die," 12, 28

"Elephant, the," Hampstead, 109, 111

Eliot, T. S., 135, 150, 165, 177, 196

Elizabeth and Her German Garden ("Elizabeth"), 14

"Enemies" (Chekhov), 154

English Review, 114, 136

Epiphany, as structural unit of James Joyce, 160, 167

"Escape, The," 121, 180; symbolism in, 192

Fairfield, Beryl (in New Zealand stories), character portrayal of, 17, 86, 91–93, 94

Fairfield, Grandmother (in New Zealand stories), based on K. M.'s own grandmother, 17; character portrayal of, 85, 86, 94

"Fairy Story, A," 39

"Father and the Girls," 140

Faulkner, William, 48

Fell, Rosemary (in "A Cup of Tea"), 164, 179-180

Fergusson, J. D., 109

"Festival of the Coronation, The," 81

Flecker, James Elroy, 229

"Fly, The," 140, 196; expression of despair in, 137-138; symbolism in, 194, 195

Ford, Ford Madox, 53, 229

France, cult of K. M. in, 7-8

Fraser, Lovat, 51

"Frau Brechenmacher Attends a Wedding," naturalism in, 43-44

Fullerton, Miss Jinnie, 118, 119, 120, 122

Galsworthy, John, 114, 137

Garden Party, The (book of stories), 1, 2, 132, 136, 137

"Garden Party, The" (story), 132; autobiographical elements in, 20; purpose of, 154-155

Garsington Manor, 73, 75

Gaudier-Brzeska, Henri, 53, 54

"Gentleman Friend, A" (Chekhov), 154

George, W. L., 50, 229

German character, K. M.'s presentation of, 41-42, 43-44

German Pension. See In a German Pension

Gibson, Wilfrid Wilson, 229

Gillet, Louis, 7

Gogarty, Oliver, 229

Goodyear, Frederick, 52, 74

Grandmother (in New Zealand stories). See Fairfield, Grandmother

Gurdjieff, in America, 223, n. 70

Gurdjieff Institute, program of, 142-143

Hardy, Thomas, 137

Harmon, Dick (in "Je ne parle pas français"), 167, 168, 188

Harris, Frank, 51, 229

Hastings, Beatrice, 211-212, n. 6

Hogarth Press, 75, 114

Honey, Mrs., 109

"Honeymoon," 140; fanciful perception in, 185

"House, The," 39

"How Pearl Button was Kidnapped," 39

Hudson, Stephen, 121

Hueffer, Ford Madox, 53, 229

Huxley, Aldous, 3

"Ideal Family, An," 183

Idler, 39

Imagery, K. M.'s use of, 28, 46-47, 77, 156, 187-190, 191-192

"In a Café," 26, 27

In a German Pension, 2, 35, 50, 53, 123; reception of, 38-39; stories in, characterized and evaluated, 43-47, 101

"In Confidence," 82

"Indiscreet Journey, An," 98; based on K. M.'s trip to join with Francis Carco, 63; as elaboration of Journal material, 63, 78-79

Innocents, Les (Francis Carco), portrait of K. M. in, 63-64

Interior monologue, K. M.'s use of, 45-47, 78, 80-81, 82, 155, 179-180; Browning's use of, 82; Joyce's use of, 178-179

Jackson, Holbrook, 51

"Je ne parle pas français," 63, 137, 149; writing of, 106; purpose of, 154; technique of, 167-168, 174; tone of, 181; fanciful description in, 186; see also Duquette, Raoul

Jeunesse de Katherine Mansfield, La (Mantz and Murry), 5

Journal, 43; contributes to growth of K. M. legend, 2, 3; "An Indis-

creet Journey" as expansion of material in, 63, 78–79; quoted, 23, 71, 88, 107, 116, 119, 132, 140, 194, and *passim*
"Journey to Bruges, The," as forerunner of later stories, 42–43
Joyce, James, 150, 197; his expatriation compared to that of K. M., 11; K. M.'s response to writings of, 135; his work compared and contrasted with K. M.'s, 45, 159–167, 169, 170, 176–177; skill at portraiture, 173; use of interior monologue, 178–179
Juliet, juvenile novel of K. M., 22–23, 25, 89

Kafka, Franz, 126, 150
Karori, New Zealand, 18
Karori Primary School, 6, 19
Keats, 125, 128, 129
Kelveys, the (in "The Doll's House"), 19, 89, 201
Kezia (in New Zealand stories). *See* Burnell, Kezia
Kingsmill, Hugh, 51
"Kiss, The" (Chekhov), 153, 165
Knopf, publishers, 123, 136
Koteliansky, S. S., 61, 64, 65, 66, 72, 114, 143

"Lady's Maid, The," 182
"Late at Night," 81
Lawrence, D. H., 129, 150, 229; relationship with K. M. and J. M. Murry, 55–56, 59–60, 61–62, 66, 72–73; plans Utopian society, 61–62, 66, 72; encourages K. M. after her brother's death, 69–70; his view of life contrasted with that of K. M., 112–113; K. M.'s estimate of, as a writer and thinker, 135–136
Lawrence, Frieda, 55, 56, 60, 61, 73, 112
Lear (Shakespeare), 194

Lenoël, Odette, 5
Leslie, Charles Robert, 206–207, n. 4
Letters, 43; contributes to growth of K. M. legend, 2, 3; quoted, 17, 69, 72, 75, 76, 83–84, 107, 109–110, 113, 117, 118, 124, 126, 132–135 *passim*, 143–146 *passim*, 169, 170, 171–172, 184, 202, and *passim*
Life of Katherine Mansfield (Mantz and Murry), 5, 6
"Life of Ma Parker," 130; tone of, 182–183
Linda (in New Zealand stories). *See* Burnell, Linda
"Little Girl, The," 2, 40, 41, 46, 229; *see also* "Something Childish"
"Little Governess, The," 65, 67; technique of, 80
London, K. M.'s early love for, 24, 29; and her later reaction against, 74, 141–142
London Mercury, 169, 229; stories of K. M. in, 130, 137

Macfall, Haldane, 51
MacKelveys, the, 19, 89
Manoukhin, tuberculosis specialist, 133, 134, 137, 138, 141–144 *passim*
Mansfield, Katherine
    I. *Life:* legend and cult of, 1–4, 7; revolt against her life in New Zealand, 11, 24–25, 29, 31; ancestry of, 14–15, 206, n. 2; childhood, 18–22; relationship to her brother, Leslie Beauchamp, 20, 67–68, 69, 71, 105–106; education in New Zealand, 20–21; at Queen's College, 22–24, 210, n. 20; life in New Zealand after return from Queen's College, 24–31; leaves New Zealand and goes to London, 31, 33; first marriage and subsequent separation, 34, 211, nn. 2 and 5; seclusion at Bavarian village of

Mansfield, Katherine (*continued*)
Woerishofen, 34–35; returns to
London and embarks upon consciously exotic mode of life, 35–
37; her literary and artistic associates, 48, 52, 53–55, 56, 121;
meets and forms alliance with
John Middleton Murry, 50–52;
financial difficulties of, 52–53, 57,
60; goes to Paris with Murry,
56–57; unhappiness after return
to London, 57–58, 59; relationship with D. H. Lawrence, 55,
56, 59–60, 61–62, 66, 69–70, 135–
136; joins Francis Carco in
France, 62–64; suffers ill health,
64, 103–104, 107, 108, 112, 116,
129, 130, 132, 133, 137, 142; seeks
literary inspiration in Paris, 65,
66; rejoins Murry in England,
66; spends several happy months
in Bandol, France, with Murry,
69–71; in Cornwall with Murry
and the Lawrences, 72–73; in
London—temporary separation
from Murry, 74–75; goes to
Bandol, France, to recover
health, 104–108; desperate efforts
to return to England, 104, 107–
108; marriage to Murry, 109; sojourn in Cornwall, 109–111; in
her home at Portland Villas,
Hampstead, 111–112, 116, 120–
121; in Italy, 117–119; in Mentone, France, 119–120, 122–123;
in Switzerland, 129–132, 138–
139; in Paris for treatment at
Manoukhin's clinic, 133–134,
137–138, 142; brief return to
England, 141–142; joins Gurdjieff Institute, Fontainebleau,
142–146; death and burial, 146–
147

II. *Mind and Character:* feelings for New Zealand, 11, 24–
25, 35, 58, 83–84, 142; spiritual
loneliness, 12–14, 16, 37, 38, 118;

childlike qualities, 13, 127, 128,
191; character as a child, 19, 20,
21–22; literary tastes and judg-
ments, 22, 111, 114–115, 124–125,
130, 131, 134–136, 151–152; ambition to become a writer, 22, 24,
25–26, 29–30, 210, n. 29; interest
in music, 22, 25; qualities of
mind, 23, 150; hunger for experience, 24, 33; restlessness and
dissatisfaction with environment, 24–25, 28–29, 36, 65, 72,
109, 120; response to natural
world, 30, 37, 107, 113, 127–128,
129, 132; strength and will to
dominate, 44; desire for human
sympathy, 50; ambivalent emotional relationship to Murry, 50,
51, 61, 72, 73, 74, 107, 119, 121–
122; periods of depression and
despair, 58, 61, 109–111, 118–120;
effect of physical surroundings
on her creative ability, 58, 65,
70, 71, 75; her concept of the
artist, 58–59, 76, 124, 126; emotional reaction to the war, 60,
74, 105, 113; affection for humble people and servants, 105,
109, 122, 128; Keatsian reaction
to impending death, 107, 123,
128, 144–145; her vision of life,
112–113, 124, 125–127, 139,
144–145, 146, 159, 195–196,
199; disgust with ugliness and
corruption in human life, 109–
110, 113, 118, 133–134; ethical
concept of art, 126, 132, 137,
139–140, 146, 149; desire for self-
purification and spiritual rebirth, 126–127, 131–132, 138–140,
143–145, 146

III. *Writings:* posthumous
publications, 1–2, 3–4; growth of
her literary reputation, 1–8, 113–
114, 122–123, 130, 136–137; excel-
lence of New Zealand stories, 11,
199–202; juvenile writings, 11–

12, 21, 22–23, 25, 89; recurring themes in her stories, 13, 28, 49, 85, 86, 107, 154–155, 167, 177, 196–197; autobiographical elements in stories, 16, 17, 18, 19, 40–41, 51, 63, 71, 88–89, 106, 132–133, 184; poetry, 25, 35, 37–38, 213–214, n. 10; Symbolist tradition in early pieces, 26–27; creation of mood, 27, 97–98, 188–190; development of literary technique and achievement of greater subtlety of style, 39–49, 76–102, 167–177 *passim*, 197–198; her writings compared and contrasted with: Joyce's, 45, 159–167, 169, 170, 176–177, Chekhov's, 150–159, 176, 177, Virginia Woolf's, 168–169, 175–176, 179; use of imagery, 28, 46–47, 77, 156, 187–190, 191–192; portrayal of children, 40–41, 86, 94–95, 201; satiric quality, 41–42, 47–48, 198; focus and point of view, 41, 42, 47, 49, 77, 96–97, 163–164, 167, 168, 169, 177; character portrayal, 42, 84–86, 88–94 *passim*, 173–174, 200; treatment of sex, 43–44, 46; naturalism, 43–45; portrayal of women, 44, 121, 180; portrayal of men, 44, 181; treatment of time, 45, 168–169; use of interior monologue, 45–47, 78, 80–81, 82, 155, 179–180; handling of dialogue and speech, 46, 47–48, 81–82, 93–95; treatment of murder and insanity, 48–49; self-criticism and comments on her writings, 64, 83, 88, 92, 96, 100, 132, 132–133, 169–170, 171–172, 202; effect upon her writings of death of her brother, 69–70, 71, 105–106; original and revised versions of work compared, 78–79, 82–83, 87–102; Dickensian quality, 87, 97, 184; use of adjectives, 99–

100; her literary criticism, 114–116; conciseness in openings and endings of stories, 156, 169, 171; descriptive technique, 156–158, 173; settings of stories, 157, 201; device of associating emotion with a concrete object, 174–175, 176; tone of stories, 178–180, 181–183; fanciful perception and whimsical quality, 184–187; concentration on the miniature, 190–191; symbolism, 174–175, 176, 192–195; writings evaluated, 197–203; *see also individual works, particularly* "At the Bay," "The Daughters of the Late Colonel," "The Doll's House," "The Garden Party," "*Je ne parle pas français,*" *and* "Prelude"

"Man Without a Temperament, The," 122, 191; writing of, 119; technique used in, 174

Mantz, Ruth Elvish, 5, 6

March, Edward, 52

"Marriage à la Mode," 47, 51, 180, 183, 187, 188, 198

"Marriage of Passion, A," satire in, 47–48

"Married Man's Story, A," tone of, 183; fanciful perception in, 185–186

"Mary," 39–40

Maupassant, 160, 197

Maurois, André, 150, 177

Men, K. M.'s portrayal of, 44, 181

Mentone, France, 118, 119, 120, 122

"Millie," technique of, 48–49

Mills, Tom L., 210, n. 29

"Miss Brill," compared with Joyce's "Clay," 162–163; technique used in, 175

Moore, George, *The Untilled Field*, 159–160

Morrell, Lady Ottoline, 73, 74–75, 103, 110, 113, 129

Morris, G. N., 6

Moss, Ada (in "Pictures"), 83, 182, 202

Mouse (in "*Je ne parle pas français*"), 154, 167, 168, 174, 186, 188, 192

"Mr. and Mrs. Dove," 181, 190; symbolism in, 192, 195

"Mr. Reginald Peacock's Day," 75, 181

Mrs. Dalloway (Virginia Woolf), handling of time element in, 168–169

Murry, John Middleton, 5, 105, 110, 111, 113, 117, 118, 120, 129, 134, 147, 151; issues posthumous works of K. M., 1–2, 3; meets and forms alliance with K. M., 50–52; emotional relationship to K. M., 50, 51, 61, 72, 73, 74, 107, 119, 121–122; and *Rhythm*, 52–53, 227, 228; and D. H. Lawrence, 55, 59–60, 61, 66, 72–73; goes to Paris with K. M., 56–57; unhappiness after return to London, 57–58; joins K. M. in Bandol, France, 70–71; reaction to the war, 60, 74; marriage to K. M., 109; in Switzerland with K. M., 130–131

Murry, Richard, 120, 169; friendship between K. M. and, 111–112

Nation (London), 1, 129, 130, 137

Naturalism, in stories of K. M., 43–45

New Age, K. M.'s contributions to, 35, 42, 43, 47, 75, 81–82, 212, 218–219, n. 12

"New Dress, The" (Virginia Woolf), 179

"New Dresses," 89; as forerunner of later stories, 40–41, 45

New Literary Values (Daiches), 5

New Zealand, growth of K. M.'s literary reputation in, 5–6; K. M.'s feelings for, 11, 24–25, 35, 58, 83–84, 142; beauty of scene, captured in stories of K. M., 83–84

New Zealand stories, as K. M.'s highest accomplishment, 11, 199–202

Noguchi, Yone, 229

Novel and the Modern World, The (Daiches), 5

Novels and Novelists, 2

"November," 213, n. 10

O'Connor, Frank, 197

O'Faolain, Sean, 197

"Old Age" (Chekhov), 154

"Ole Underwood," treatment of murder in, 48

Open Window, 39

Orage, A. R., 146, 211, n. 6; encourages K. M., 35–36

Ouspenski, P. D., as publicizer of Gurdjieff Institute, 142–143

Parker, Dorothy, 42

Pater, Walter, 22, 27

Peploe, S. J., 228

Picasso, 228

"Pic-nic, A," 82

"Pictures," 75, 122, 182, 191; as revised version of "The Common Round," 82–83

Poetry, of K. M., 25, 35, 37–38, 213–214, n. 10

Point Counter Point (Aldous Huxley), 3

"Poison," technique of, 171–172

Porter, Katherine Anne, 177; on K. M., 198

"Prelude," 75, 114, 167, 195, 202; autobiographical influences upon, 18; compared with original version, "The Aloe," 87–102; focus of, 96–97; duck-decapitation scene, 101–102, 201; inspiration for, 106; imagery in, 190; symbolism in, 192–193; publication of, 221, n. 14; *see also* "Aloe, The"

Proust, 150; K. M.'s reaction to writings of, 135

"Psychology," 164, 190, 191

Queen's College, K. M.'s life at, 22–24, 210, n. 20

Queen's College Magazine, K. M.'s stories appear in, 11–12

Rananim, Utopian retreat of D. H. Lawrence, 61–62, 66, 72

"Revelation," 121

Rhythm, 55, 56, 67, 71; K. M.'s writings appearing in, 38, 39, 48, 50, 213–214, n. 10, 214–215, n. 11; history of, 52–53; evaluated, 227–229

Rice, Anne, 109, 110, 228

Rider, Dan, 51

Romantic poets, K. M.'s affinity for, 124–125

Ruddick, Marion, 209, n. 18

Russell, Countess, 14, 130

Russian authors, K. M.'s affinity for, 124, 125; *see also* Chekhov

Sadleir, Michael, 227, 228

Satire, in works of K. M., 41–42, 47–48, 198

Saturday Review, 169

Schiff, Sidney, 121, 135

Schiff, Violet, 121, 133

Schneider, Elisabeth, 43

Scrapbook, 206, n. 1, 215, n. 11, 217, n. 49, 219, n. 32, 220, n. 50, 221, n. 26, 225, n. 69

Secker, Martin, 53, 228

Sewell, Arthur, 6

Shakespeare, 194; K. M.'s love of, 124–125

Shanks, Edward, 136

Shaw, G. B., 27, 39, 134

Shelley, 125

Signature, launching and failure of, 66–67; stories of K. M. in, 67, 79–80

"Silhouettes," 26

"Singing Lesson, The," 175, 178, 187

Sitwell, Edith, evaluates K. M.'s stories, 4

"Sixpence," 183

Sketch, 137

"Slater's Pins Have No Points" (Virginia Woolf), symbolism in, 175–176

"Sleepyhead" (Chekhov), 43

"Small Fry" (Chekhov), 194

"Something Childish But Very Natural," 2; technique used in, 77–78; *see also* "Little Girl"

Sons and Lovers (D. H. Lawrence), 60

Sorapure, Dr. Victor, 116–117, 141

Sphere, stories of K. M. appearing in, 132, 183, 222, n. 45

"Spring in a Dream," 39

Squire, J. C., 229

Stanley (in New Zealand stories). *See* Burnell, Stanley

"Stay-laces," 81

Stephen Hero (Joyce), 160

Stephens, James, 229

"Stranger, The," 123, 130, 136, 188, 199, 202; method of presentation and theme of, 165–167; similarities to Joyce's "The Dead," 165, 167

Stream of consciousness device, 81; *see also* Interior monologue

Sullivan, J. W. N., 120

"Sun and Moon," 106

"Sunday Lunch," 48

Swift, Stephen & Co., 52, 53, 228

"Swing of the Pendulum, The," use of interior monologue in, 46–47

Swinnerton, Frank, 53, 229

Symbolism, K. M.'s use of, 174–175, 176, 192–195; Virginia Woolf's use of, 175–176

Symbolist tradition, K. M.'s early works influenced by, 26–27

Symons, Arthur, 22, 27

"Taking the Veil," 133, 183
"Tales of a Courtyard," 39
Tchehov, Anton. *See* Chekhov
"Three Years" (Chekhov), 151
Time, K. M.'s treatment of, 45, 168–169; Virginia Woolf's treatment of, 168–169
Times (London) *Literary Supplement*, Murry's work for, 56, 57, 73
"Tiredness of Rosabel, The," 45, 174
Tolstoi, 81, 115; K. M.'s response to, 125
Tomlinson, H. M., 123
Trout, Jonathan (in New Zealand stories), 19, 193–194, 195, 200
Trowell, Arnold, romantic friendship between K. M. and, 25, 27, 33
Trowell, Garnet, 33–34
"Truthful Adventure, A," as forerunner of later stories, 42–43
Turgenev, possible literary relationship to James Joyce and K. M., 159–160
"Two Gallants" (Joyce), 173
"Two Tuppenny Ones, Please," 81

Ulysses (Joyce), 45; K. M.'s response to, 135
Untilled Field, The (George Moore), 159–160

Verlaine, Paul, 22, 27
"Vignettes," 26
Villa Isola Bella, Mentone, France, 7, 122, 129
Villa Pauline, Bandol, France, 70–71, 104, 105

Vocation de Katherine Mansfield, La (Lenoël), 5
"Voyage, The," 194

Walpole, Hugh, 229
Waters family (relatives of K. M. in New Zealand), 18–19
Wellington, New Zealand, 11, 20, 28
Wellington Girls' High School, K. M. attends, 20–21
Wells, H. G., 53, 229
Welty, Eudora, 197
Westminster Gazette, 54, 56, 57
Wharton, Edith, 114
Wilde, Oscar, 22, 23, 27, 39
"Wind Blows, The," 67, 79
Winnie (in *Les Innocents* by Francis Carco), character based on K. M., 63–64
"Woman at the Store," 50; treatment of murder in, 48
Women, K. M.'s portrayal of, 44, 121, 180
Women in Love (D. H. Lawrence), 218, n. 10
Woolf, Leonard, 75
Woolf, Virginia, 75, 112, 114, 123; K. M. feels an artistic bond with, 76; her literary technique compared with that of K. M., 168–169, 175–176, 179
Wordsworth, Dorothy, 111; her response to nature compared with K. M.'s, 127–128
Wordsworth, William, 125
World War I, K. M.'s reaction to, 60, 74, 105, 113

Yale Review, 2
Young, Bertha (in "Bliss"), 156, 164, 180, 186–187, 192, 195
"Your Obituary, Well Written" (Conrad Aiken), 3